By

PANEL OF AUTHORS

EDITION : 2022

ISBN : 978-93-92563-13-3

PRICE : ₹ 240.00

PUBLISHED BY

OSWAL PUBLISHERS

Head Office : 1/12, Sahitya Kunj, M.G. Road, Agra - 282 002

Phone : (0562) 2527771-4

Whatsapp : +91 74550 77222

E-mail : info@oswalpublishers.in

Website : www.oswalpublishers.com

The cover of this book has been designed using resources from Freepik.com

PREFACE

Board exams are a crucial milestone for every student. For students to perform well in this exam, we have introduced CBSE Chapterwise Objective and Subjective book for the TERM II Examinations for class XII. We have designed this book, keeping in mind all the changing scenarios and exam patterns. The content of the book is strictly based on the latest circular (Acad- 51 and 53) issued by the board in July, 2021 for TERM II examinations. This book will help the learners achieve the learning objectives in an easy to grasp manner.

This book contains matter compiled by highly proficient teachers and subject matter experts from across the country. Questions are segregated as per their respective chapters to facilitate easy navigation between them. Every attempt has been made to keep the language of the book crisp and accessible.

We hope you will find this book helpful in your preparations for Std. XII board examinations. We would advise you to stay calm and manage your time wisely. Don't be overwhelmed with the amount of resources and study guides available, be selective and efficient in your preparation.

—**Publisher**

Note : Questions marked with :
* are board exam questions from previous years.

CONTENTS

SYLLABUS

English Core (Code No. 301)

<table>
<tr><th>SECTION</th><th>Term – II</th><th>WEIGHTAGE (IN MARKS)</th></tr>
<tr><td>A</td><td>Reading Comprehension:
(Two Passages)
• Unseen passage (factual, descriptive or literary/discursive or persuasive)
• Case Based Unseen (Factual) Passage</td><td>14 (8 + 6 Marks)</td></tr>
<tr><td>B</td><td>Creative Writing Skills:
<u>Short Writing Tasks</u>
• Formal & Informal Invitation Cards or the Replies to Invitation/s
<u>Long Writing Tasks (One)</u>
• Letter of Application for a Job
• Report Writing</td><td>3 + 5 Marks
Total = 08</td></tr>
<tr><td>C</td><td>Literature:
Questions based on extracts/texts to assess comprehension and appreciation, analysis, inference, extrapolation
<u>Book-Flamingo (Prose)</u>
• The Rattrap
• Indigo
<u>Book-Flamingo (Poetry)</u>
• A Thing of Beauty
• Aunt Jennifer's Tigers
<u>Book-Vistas (Prose)</u>
• Should Wizard Hit Mommy?
• On the Face of It
• Evans Tries an O Level</td><td>11 Marks for Flamingo
+ 7 Marks for Vistas = 18 Marks</td></tr>
<tr><td colspan="2">TOTAL</td><td>40</td></tr>
<tr><td colspan="2">ASL</td><td>10</td></tr>
<tr><td colspan="2">Grand Total</td><td>40 + 10 = 50</td></tr>
</table>

Prescribed Books:

1. **Flamingo:** English Reader published by National Council of Education Research and Training, New Delhi.
2. **Vistas:** Supplementary Reader published by National Council of Education Research and Training, New Delhi

SECTION - A

READING COMPREHENSION

Discursive Passage

1

Passages

1. Read the passage given below.

1. A bookshop is not something you find in every street or area these days. Books, which were once a permanent accompaniment for youngsters in their formative years, are fading out of their list of engagements.
2. Ask any youngster which is the latest book he has read and he will be baffled. Apart from a few consistent readers, others just befool themselves with a bookseller's name or lament the curriculum load for justifying themselves, like this seventeen-year-old school-goer who says, 'I just read my Physics book.'
3. Television has been blamed for this calamitous situation, which is producing square-faced people and a bookless society. Furthermore, today's children are under pressure to be smart and popular and to succeed on a social level. Parties, dancing and hanging out at different places begin early. Moreover, computers, video games, the Internet, swimming lessons, cricket and a youngster's passion for an hour-long tete-a-tete on the telephone with friends eat up all their leisure time.
4. A child who is constantly under pressure to live up to his parents' expectations, which are at times unreasonable, does not like to throw himself into another set of books after the laborious school work, unless he comes from a family of readers where the engrossing work of Shakespeare and Dickens are just a matter of pulling them out from the shelves.
5. Many parents also believe that today's children have become more aware and demand logical reasoning for everything. They can no longer be fooled by fairy tales or animal stories, as they have not seen any fairies or animals except for those old and tired ones in the city zoo. This has made them more interested in movies or TV serials than a turtle talking to a rabbit or a frog changing into a prince.
6. But a visit to the capital's leading bookstores presents a contrasting picture of youngsters' reading habits. These bookshops claim they are doing healthy business and have many regular buyers from this age group.
7. Though the works of Shakespeare, Charles Dickens, Jane Austen and Mark Twain no longer interest teenagers, best-sellers from Daniel Steele, Sidney Sheldon and Jeffery Archer are on the list of all reading teens. Self-help books, such as those on personality development or relationship management, are also picked up by many of them.
8. Mystery books like Nancy Drew and Hardy Boys are popular with kids and Mills and Boons and other romance novels with their fairly predictable formula with teenage girls. For parents of children below ten, volumes of Panchatantra Stories, Amar Chitra Katha and other bedtime stories are worthy purchases as these teach the child what is wrong in their own special way. What seems to be the case is that parents have surrendered to others, what was their most precious right—that of making their children what they should become. With the old techniques of child rearing losing ground, modern parents must consciously spend time with their children. Taste and enthusiasm for literature can be communicated artfully to children by reading bedtime stories to them, encouraging them to play historical characters and giving books as birthday gifts.
9. The family reading which was once popular in the West could well be adopted here. Reading aloud the works of great men by parents to their children not only forms a warm bond between them but also attracts young minds to the world of books which gives them a chance to explore the sea of life.

1.1 Based on your understanding of the passage, answer <u>any eight</u> out of the ten questions by choosing the correct option.

(a) Choose the CORRECT option that takes away the teenagers from reading good books.

(i) Cinema

(ii) Television

(iii) Dance shows

(iv) Music programs

(b) Select the option that would suitably complete the given dialogue between the parents and the child as per the context in paragraph 5.

Parents: Why don't read the books that we bought you? All you do is to look at the television the entire day!

Child: I don't (1) ....

Parents: And does the television provide you any logic to what you see?

Child: Yes! (2) .... I enjoy it.

(i) (1) want to read the books (2) they do.

(ii) (1) understand the logics behind those fairy tales (2) the stories are realistic and well described through animations.

(iii) (1) want to exhaust my mind thinking about the logic in them (2) totally.

(iv) (1) like to read (2) it makes my imagination vivid.

(c) The passage uses a French word *'tete-a-tete'*. This refers to:

(i) Making group calls.

(ii) Bad-mouthing people behind them.

(iii) Having an argument.

(iv) Having a private conversation between two people.

(d) Select the CORRECT image of the activity that was once popular in the West.

(1)

(2)

(3)

(4)

(i) Option 1 (ii) Option 2 (iii) Option 3 (iv) Option 4

(e) Select the correct hobby that youngsters use to posses before and the one they posses today.

Before	Today
Watching television	Reading books

(i)

Before	Today
Reading poetry	Reading novels

(ii)

Before	Today
Reading books	Watching television

(iii)

Before	Today
Watching movies on television	Watching movies online

(iv)

(f) What is the relationship between (1) and (2).

(1) Children have become more logic-demanding.

(2) Children prefer watching television to reading fairy tales.

(i) (1) is the cause of (2).

(ii) (2) elaborates the affirmation of (1).

(iii) (2) is the reason behind (1).

(iv) (1) is the advice for (2).

(g) Based on information given in the passage, select the option that describes the cause of children ignoring books.

(i) They find them uninteresting.

(ii) They are more addicted to online entertainment.

(iii) They lament the curriculum load.

(iv) They don't have patience to read books.

(h) Select the option that lists the importance of reading for writer.

(i) It warms the bond between parents and children, attracts young minds to the world of books, a chance to explore the sea of life.

(ii) It bring harmony among people, create calm, keep people busy.

(iii) It makes people look trendy, learn something new, a chance to revive self.

(iv) It creates a huge burden on young minds, makes them anxious, an intense mind activity.

(i) Which quote summarizes the importance of the books as given in the last paragraph of the passage?

(i) "You can swim all day in the Sea of Knowledge and still come out completely dry. Most people do." *–Norton Juster*

(ii) Sleep is good, he said, and books are better. *– George R.R. Martin*

(iii) If you don't like to read, you haven't found the right book. *– J.K. Rowling*

(iv) Books should go where they will be most appreciated, and not sit unread, gathering dust on a forgotten shelf, don't you agree? *– Christopher Paolini*

(j) Select the option that can be concluded from the text.

(1) Youngsters are no longer interested in reading books.

(2) The number of Bookshops is increasing due to the increase in demand of the books.

(3) Shakespeare is the most beloved writer among the youngsters.

(4) Children desire logical content.

(i) (1), (2) and (3) are true (4) is false.

(ii) (1) and (3) are true (2) and (4) are false.

(iii) (1) and (4) are true, (2) and (3) are false.

(iv) All are false.

ANSWERS

1.1. (a) (ii) Television

(b) (ii) (1) understand the logics behind those fairy tales (2) the stories are realistic and well described through animations.

(c) (iv) Having a private conversation between two people.

(d) (iii) Option 3

(e)

	Before	Today
(iii)	Reading books	Watching television

(f) (i) (1) is the cause of (2).

(g) (i) They find them uninteresting.

(h) (i) It warms the bond between parents and children, attracts young minds to the world of books, a chance to explore the sea of life.

(i) (iv) Books should go where they will be most appreciated, and not sit unread, gathering dust on a forgotten shelf, don't you agree? *— Christopher Paolini*

(j) (iii) (1) and (4) are true, (2) and (3) are false.

2. Read the passage given below:

1. The Titanic, in its watery grave, is a great museum of human history and is at risk of being lost forever because of curious voyagers and treasure hunters, fears Bob Ballard, who first discovered the remains of the iconic ship in 1985. Famous for discovering the great ship, Ballard is a former US Navy Officer and a professor of oceanography.

2. "Titanic is a museum of human history without door and guard. I am deeply concerned about not only the Titanic but all the ancient history that is now at risk. If we cannot save this iconic ship, then there is a very little hope we can save ancient ships. The world should realize that you don't have to go down and take everything and you do not have to do a treasure hunt. This is a common heritage of all of us and if we really want to take steps to preserve human history in the ocean, we need to start with Titanic," Ballard said in a telephonic interview from London.

3. Ballard, as part of a tie-up, is presenting a documentary called "Save the Titanic" on the 100th anniversary of the sinking of the great ship – April 15, 1912. The ship and her fate continue to fascinate, largely because of the horror that took place that night, with 1,522 passengers and crew losing their lives.

4. Ballard says that despite being on the ocean floor for 100 years, the ship is full of human footprints. "You will find pairs of shoes everywhere. The sea and the life below has claimed everything but they do not know what to do with shoes so you will find a pair of mother's shoes next to her little daughter's shoes and that's their grave-stone. At her wreckage, we almost felt that we were surrounded by the lifeboats of all the people that were in the water at that spot".

5. Ballard says that the fate of Titanic continues to fascinate so many years after it sank because it is "irony personified in history". "The story has all the ingredients to make it timelessly fascinating. You have this revolutionary ship that's unsinkable and carrying a cross-section of people in society. And then, it goes and hits an iceberg and sinks on its maiden journey. It's an irony personified in history".
6. Talking about this discovery, which came after great research and 75 years later, Ballard, says it was a somber moment when they first spotted the boiler of the Titanic. "In the 90s, advanced technology gave us double diving capabilities in the Atlantic Ocean. I knew that the Titanic was sitting at almost 12,000 feet. What led me to her discovery was a simple technique that I followed. We decided to look for the debris trail instead of the ship".
7. Ballard says the ship, if preserved well and not subjected to constant submarine journeys, will last for a long time on the Atlantic floor. "The deep sea, because of its darkness, its cold temperatures and its great pressure, creates a high state of preservation. With a little caution, we can protect the Titanic for future generations to visit."
8. Ballard has also connected to the people of Belfast, who refused to talk about the tragedy. "The ship's construction took place at Belfast. After the tragedy, families of the workers refused to talk about it because of the shame and sadness in the loss of life involved".

(**Source:** archive.indianexpress.com)

2.1 Based on your understanding of the passage, answer <u>any eight</u> out of the ten questions by choosing the correct option.

(a) The vandalism on the remains of the Titanic ship by divers makes the writer feel:

(i) Shocked (ii) Concerned (iii) Awestruck (iv) Annoyed

(b) Euphemism is a word or phrase used to avoid saying an unpleasant or offensive word.

The writer says that the titanic is in its <u>watery grave</u>.

Select the word from the options that correctly translates to the euphemism presented here.

(i) Sunk (ii) Saved (iii) Stopped (iv) Shifted

(c) Select the option that suitably completes the given dialogue as per the context in paragraph 8.

Writer: Are you related to the workers who made the Titanic?

Man from Belfast: Yes, but (1)..................

Writer: I just wanted to know about the incident.

Man from Belfast: I am sorry but (2)............

(i) (1) it wasn't me who made it (2) I am willing to tell you only if you pay me.

(ii) (1) I cannot recognize you (2) we don't disclose such confidential affairs.

(iii) (1) only distantly (2) you don't look like you care enough.

(iv) (1) why do you ask? (2) I would rather not talk about that unfortunate tragedy.

(d) What could've been the news headline when the writer first discovered the remains of the Titanic ship in 1985?

1. Titanic the unsinkable now in ruins.	2. Headed to the port, now in the ocean.	3. Titanic found preserved in its watery grave.	4. Positive news for voyagers, Titanic found.

(i) Option 1 (ii) Option 2 (iii) Option 3 (iv) Option 4

(e) Select the option that clearly indicates the situation before and after Titanic was discovered in 1985.

	Before 1985	**After 1985**
(i)	Ruins preserved in cold dark ocean.	Hunters and voyagers exploiting the ruins.
(ii)	Ruins sinking deeper into the ocean.	Hunters and voyagers bringing the entire ship out.
(iii)	Ruins remaining intact.	Ruins preserved untouched.
(iv)	Ship getting lost to sea creatures.	Conservationists saving the remains.

(f) What is the relationship between (1) and (2)?

(1) .... In the 90s, advanced technology gave us double diving capabilities in the Atlantic Ocean.

(2) ....We decided to look for the debris trail instead of the ship.

(i) (2) is the cause of (1).
(ii) (1) and (2) were independent of each other.
(iii) (2) did not cause (1).
(iv) (1) is the cause of (2).

(g) The writer mentions the Titanic as a great museum of human history. He says so because he realises that:

(i) no matter what may come, we should protect the Titanic as it is the only reminder of the greatest ship that sunk into the ocean.
(ii) Titanic contains hidden treasures from the century old rich passengers that boarded the ship.
(iii) the deep dark and cold conditions of the ocean has well preserved a century old specimen of human endeavour and failure which is an irony personified in history.
(iv) Titanic has been claimed by the sea life below so there's no point now in trying to salvage it from further disintegration.

(h) Select the option that lists the eulogy for the Titanic's passengers by the ship-makers from Belfast.

(i) We are all grieving today for the greatest loss to mankind in recent history. We have failed all those on board by not building them a strong enough Titanic.
(ii) Loss to human life is the most miserable one can imagine, but remember it was the fury of nature that took it down, and nothing more.
(iii) Grieve we must yes ! But life goes on for us unfortunates who are still alive and have to live with the horrors of this tragedy.
(iv) Titanic and its human companions are resting in the depths of the ocean. The tragedy has immortalized them all forever.

(i) Which quote summarises the writer's feelings about the conservation of Titanic as a cultural icon for human history?

(i) The object of war is victory; that of victory is conquest; and that of conquest preservation.– *Montesquieu*
(ii) The people without the knowledge of their past history, origin and culture is like a tree without roots. – *Marcus Garvey*
(iii) Until the moment she actually sinks, the Titanic is unsinkable. – *Julia Hughes*
(iv) Government has no other end, but the preservation of property. – *John Locke*

(j) Select the option that lists what we can conclude from the text.

(1) The writer has unrealistic expectations of protecting Titanic from degradation.
(2) The writer is addressing all of us to be responsible in preserving our heritage.
(3) The technologies haven't advanced much since the 90s to help save the ruins of the ship.
(4) Before going for deep sea treasure hunting, one must understand the cultural impact of their actions.

(i) (2) and (3) are true.
(ii) (2), (3) and (4) are true.
(iii) (1) and (4) are true.
(iv) (2) and (4) are true.

ANSWERS

2.1. (a) (ii) Concerned
(b) (i) Sunk
(c) (iv) (1) why do you ask? (2) I would rather not talk about that unfortunate tragedy.
(d) (iii) Option 3
(e)

	Before 1985	After 1985
(i)	Ruins preserved in cold dark ocean.	Hunters and voyagers exploiting the ruins.

(f) (iv) (1) is the cause of (2).
(g) (iii) the deep dark and cold conditions of the ocean has well preserved a century old specimen of human endeavour and failure which is an irony personified in history.
(h) (i) We are all grieving today for the greatest loss to mankind in recent history. We have failed all those on board by not building them a strong enough Titanic.
(i) (ii) The people without the knowledge of their past history, origin and culture is like a tree without roots. —*Marcus Garvey*
(j) (iv) (2) and (4) are true.

3. Read the passage given below.

1. No student of a foreign language needs to be told that grammar is complex. By changing word sequences and by adding a range of auxiliary verbs and suffixes, we are able to communicate tiny variations in meaning. We can turn a statement into a question, state whether an action has taken place or is soon to take place, and perform many other word tricks to convey subtle differences in meaning. Nor is this complexity inherent to the English language. All languages, even those of so-called 'primitive' tribes have clever grammatical components. The Cherokee pronoun system, for example, can distinguish between 'you and I', 'several other people and I' and 'you, another person and I'. In English, all these meanings are summed up in the one, crude pronoun 'We'. Grammar is universal and plays a part in every language, no matter how widespread it is. So, the question which has baffled many linguists is—who created grammar?

2. At first, it would appear that this question is impossible to answer. To find out how grammar is created, someone needs to be present at the time of a language's creation, documenting its emergence. Many historical linguists are able to trace modern complex languages back to earlier languages, but in order to answer the question of how complex languages are actually formed, the researcher needs to observe how languages started from scratch. Amazingly, however, this is possible.

3. Some of the most recent languages evolved due to the Atlantic slave trade. At that time, slaves from a number of different ethnicities were forced to work together under colonial rule. Since, they had no opportunity to learn each other's languages, they developed a make-shift language called a pidgin. Pidgins are strings of words copied from the language of the landowner. They have little in the way of grammar, and in many cases it is difficult for a listener to deduce when an event happened, and who did what to whom. Speakers need to use circumlocution in order to make their meaning understood. Interestingly, however, all it takes for a pidgin to become a complex language is for a group of children to be exposed to it at the time when they learn their mother tongue. Slave children did not simply copy the strings of words uttered by their elders, they adapted their words to create a new, expressive language. Complex grammar systems which emerge from pidgins are termed creoles and they are invented by children.

4. Further evidence of this can be seen in studying sign languages for the deaf. Sign languages are not simply a series of gestures; they utilise the same grammatical machinery that is found in spoken languages. Moreover, there are many different languages used worldwide. The creation of one such language was documented quite recently in Nicaragua. Previously, all deaf people were isolated from each other, but in 1979 a new government introduced schools for the deaf. Although children were taught speech and lip reading in the classroom, in the playgrounds they began to invent their own sign system, using the gestures that they used at home. It was basically a pidgin. Each child used the signs differently, and there was no consistent grammar. However, children who joined the school later, when this inventive sign system was already around, developed a quite different sign languages. Although it was based on the signs of the older children, the younger children's language was more fluid and compact, and it utilised a large range of grammatical devices to clarify meaning. What is more, all the children used the signs in the same way? A new creole was born.

5. Some linguists believe that many of the world's most established languages were creoles at first. The English past tense –ed ending may have evolved from the verb 'do'. 'It ended' may once have been 'It end-did'. Therefore, it would appear that even the most widespread languages were partly created by children. Children appear to have innate grammatical machinery in their brains, which springs to life when they are first trying to make sense of the world around them. Their minds can serve to create logical, complex structures, even when there is no grammar present for them to copy.

3.1 Based on your understanding of the passage, answer <u>any eight</u> out of the ten questions by choosing the correct option.

(a) The linguists are .... at the complexity of grammar.

(i) annoyed (ii) bewildered (iii) indifferent (iv) confident

(b) Circumlocution is the use of a large number of words to express an idea or thing.
The writer says that sign languages are not simply a series of gestures.
Select from the options that is correctly circumlocutory for the word *gestures*.

(i) Systematic form of expressions by leg movements.
(ii) Random actions performed to deliver messages.
(iii) Expressing through different emojis.
(iv) Systematic form of expressions by hand movements.

(c) Select the option that suitably completes the given dialogue as per the context in paragraph 5.

Student: It is sometimes hardtop make sense how children can learn something as complex as grammar when even adults have a hard time getting it.

Professor: You mustn't underestimate a (1)…...… .

Student: How come a child sensibly understands grammar then?

Professor: (2)………………… in their brains !

(i) (1) child's capability to learn new things (2) The whole magic lies
(ii) (1) human being like that even if it's a child (2) They have complex neurological connections
(iii) (1) child who wants to learn new things (2) They can have unlimited power
(iv) (1) child's ability to make sense of this world (2) They have an innate grammatical machinery

(d) Which signboard can be chosen for the government school for deaf in Nicaragua?

1. Government school for deaf, Nicaragua	2. Public school for Nicaraguan studies.	3. Government school for sign language, Nicaragua	4. Sign language school for deaf and dumb, Nicaragua

(i) Option 1 (ii) Option 2 (iii) Option 3 (iv) Option 4

(e) Select the option that clearly indicates the situation before and after slave children were exposed to pidgin.

	Before exposure to pidgin	After exposure to pidgin
(i)	Little complexity to the grammar.	Adapting new words to create a fresh expressive language.
(ii)	Grammar existent and full of big words.	Grammar became less expressive.
(iii)	Difficulty in understanding the language.	Language becomes more difficult and complex.
(iv)	Lack of words and inconvenience for landowners.	New words added for the sake of landowners.

(f) What is the relationship between (1) and (2)?

(1) …….. the researcher needs to observe how languages started from scratch.
(2) …….. complex grammar systems which emerge from pidgins are termed creoles.

(i) (2) explains the question described in (1).
(ii) (1) repeats the question in (2).
(iii) (1) is not the cause for (2).
(iv) (1) and (2) are unrelated.

(g) The writer mentions looking at Atlantic slave trade for a better understanding of languages because he realises that:

(i) Atlantic slave trade was filled with teachers who were well versed in linguistics.
(ii) It is the most effective way to check the linguistic development which requires no books.
(iii) It is the most recent and well documented form of linguistic study in how grammar is created.
(iv) Atlantic slave trade was a blotch in human history and should not be forgotten.

(h) Select the option that lists a linguist's review for the Nicaraguan sign language.

(i) Children are not that silly when it comes to bringing up names or new words after all.
(ii) Interesting how something like the sign language made by children can be so inventive and fluid.
(iii) Needless to say that the children have done what their teachers couldn't have expected.
(iv) Each child was using the signs differently, and there was no consistent grammar.

(i) Which quote summarises the unmatched ingenuity of children?

(i) "If a cluttered desk is a sign of a cluttered mind, of what, then, is an empty desk a sign?" *–Albert Einstein*
(ii) "It is easier to build strong children than to repair broken adults." *– F. Douglas*
(iii) "Children have real understanding only of that which they invent themselves." *– Jean Piaget*
(iv) "By education I mean an all-round drawing out of the best in the child and man; body, mind and spirit." *– Mahatma Gandhi*

(j) Select the option that lists what we can conclude from the text.

(1) Grammar develops over a generation gradually.

(2) Children are credited with new inventive forms of transforming languages.

(3) English grammar derives a lot from French and Germanic languages.

(4) Creole is a mix of different language forms.

(i) (1), (2) and (3) are true.
(iii) (1) and (2) are true.
(ii) (1), (2) and (4) are true.
(iv) (3) and (4) are true.

ANSWERS

3.1. (a) (ii) bewildered

(b) (iv) Systematic form of expressions by hand movements.

(c) (iv) (1) child's ability to make sense of this world

(2) They have an innate grammatical machinery

(d) (iii) Option 3

(e)

	Before exposure to pidgin	After exposure to pidgin
(i)	Little complexity to the grammar.	Adapting new words to create a fresh expressive language.

(f) (i) (2) explains the question described in (1).

(g) (iii) It is the most recent and well documented form of linguistic study in how grammar is created.

(h) (ii) Interesting how something like the sign language made by children can be so inventive and fluid.

(i) (iii) "Children have real understanding only of that which they invent themselves." — *Jean Piaget*

(j) (ii) (1), (2) and (4) are true.

4. Read the passage given below.

1. I got posted in Srinagar in the 1980s. Its rugged mountains, gushing rivers and vast meadows reminded me of the landscapes of my native place – the Jibhi Valley in Himachal Pradesh. Unlike Srinagar that saw numerous tourists, Jibhi Valley remained clouded in anonymity. That's when the seed of starting tourism in Jibhi was planted. I decided to leave my service in the Indian Army and follow the urge to return home.

2. We had two houses – a family house and a traditional house, which we often rented out. I pleaded with my father to ask the tenant to vacate the house so that I could convert it into a guest house. When my family finally relented, I renovated the house keeping its originality intact, just adding windows for sunlight.

3. I still remember the summer of 1992 when I put a signboard outside my first guest house in Jibhi Valley! The village residents, however, were sceptical about my success. My business kept growing but it took years for tourism to take off in Jibhi Valley. Things changed significantly after 2008 when the government launched a homestay scheme. People built homestays and with rapid tourism growth, the region changed rapidly. Villages turned into towns with many concrete buildings. Local businesses and tourists continued putting a burden on nature.

4. Then, with the 2020-21 pandemic and lockdown, tourism came to a complete standstill in Jibhi Valley. Local people, who were employed at over a hundred homestays and guesthouses, returned to their villages. Some went back to farming; some took up pottery and some got involved in government work schemes. Now, all ardently hope that normalcy and tourism will return to the valley soon. In a way, the pandemic has given us an opportunity to introspect, go back to our roots and look for sustainable solutions.

5. For me, tourism has been my greatest teacher. It brought people from many countries and all states of India to my guest house. It gave me exposure to different cultures and countless opportunities to learn new things. Most people who stayed at my guest house became my repeat clients and good friends. When I look back, I feel proud, yet humbled at the thought that I was not only able to fulfil my dream despite all the challenges, but also play a role in establishing tourism in the beautiful valley that I call home. (394 words)

Source: *https://www.outlookindia.com/outlooktraveller/explore/story/71458/how-one-mansconviction-put-jibhi-valley-on-the-world-tourism-map*

4.1 Based on your understanding of the passage, answer any eight out of the ten questions by choosing the correct option.

(a) The scenic beauty of Srinagar makes the writer feel.

(i) Awestruck (ii) Nostalgic (iii) Cheerful (iv) Confused

(b) A collocation is a group of words that often occur together.

The writer says that Jibhi valley remained <u>clouded in anonymity</u>.

Select the word from the options that correctly collocates with *clouded in.*

(i) Disgust (ii) Anger (iii) Doubt (iv) Terror

(c) Select the option that suitably completes the given dialogue as per the context in paragraph 2.

Father: Are you sure that your plan would work?

Writer: I can't say (1) ....

Father: That's a lot of uncertainty, isn't it?

Writer: (2) .... , father Please let's do this.

(i) (1) that I would be able to deal with the funding (2) Well begun is half done

(ii) (1) anything along those lines, as the competition is tough (2) Think before you leap

(iii) (1) that, because it's a question of profit and loss (2) All's well that ends well

(iv) (1) I'm sure, but I can say that I believe in myself (2) Nothing venture nothing win

(d) Which signboard would the writer have chosen for his 1992 undertaking, in Jibhi Valley?

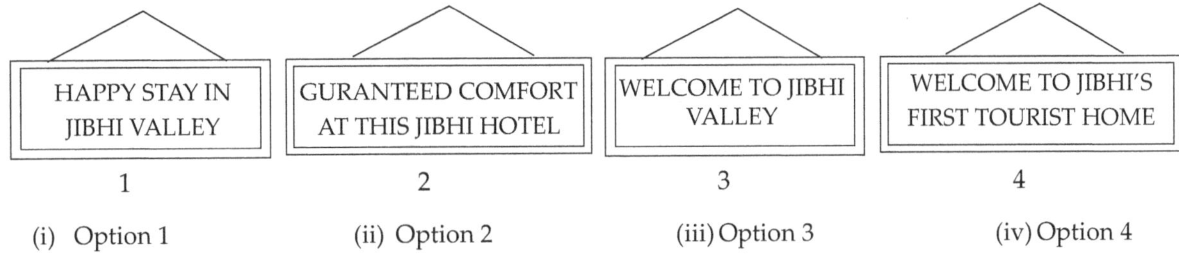

(i) Option 1 (ii) Option 2 (iii) Option 3 (iv) Option 4

(e) Select the option that clearly indicates the situation before and after 2008, in Jibhi Valley.

	Before 2008	**After 2008**
(i)	picturesque landscapes	construction sites and commerce
(ii)	zero tourism in the valley	sceptical villagers
(iii)	buildings and hotels	profitable ventures
(iv)	scenic surroundings	zero tourism in the valley

(f) What is the relationship between (1) and (2)?

(1) ...tourism came to a complete standstill in Jibhi Valley.

(2) ... tourism has been my greatest teacher.

(i) (2) is the cause for (1).

(ii) (1) repeats the situation described in (2).

(iii) (2) elaborates the problem described in (1).

(iv) (1) sets the stage for (2).

(g) The writer mentions looking for sustainable solutions. He refers to the need for sustainable solutions because he realises that:

(i) even though all natural ecosystems are essential pillars of resilience, we need to focus on using their resources to address the economic needs of mankind, as a priority.

(ii) the exposures to pandemics are a reality and a big threat to the countries across the world.

(iii) for an economic recovery to be durable and resilient, a return to 'business as usual' and environmentally destructive investment patterns and activities must be avoided.

(iv) there is an increasing urgency in the climate movement and the need for collaborative action for the future.

(h) Select the option that lists the customer review for the writer's project.

(i) Beautiful accommodation in the lap of nature. Luxurious cottage with indoor pool and garden.

(ii) Comfortable and peaceful. Neat room with ample sunlight. Pleasant and warm host.

(iii) Enjoyed the sprawling suite on the fifth floor. Great view. Professional service.

(iv) Remote locale, good food and clean room. Would have loved more natural light, though.

(i) Which quote summarises the writer's feelings about the pace of growth of tourism in Jibhi Valley?

(i) We kill all the caterpillars, then complain there are no butterflies. *– John Marsden*

(ii) Nature will give you the best example of life lessons, just open your eyes and see. *– Kate Smith*

(iii) We do not see nature with our eyes, but with our understanding and our hearts. *– William Hazlett*

(iv) I'd rather be in the mountains thinking of God than in church thinking of the mountains. *– John Muir*

(j) Select the option that lists what we can conclude from the text.

(1) The people of Jibhi Valley practiced sustainable tourism.

(2) The people of Jibhi Valley gradually embraced tourism.

(3) Tourists never revisited Jibhi Valley.

(4) The writer was an enterprising person.

(i) (1) and (2) are true.

(ii) (2), (3) and (4) are true.

(iii) (2) and (4) are true.

(iv) (1), (3) and (4) are true.

ANSWERS

4.1. (a) (ii) Nostalgic

(b) (iii) Doubt

(c) (iv) (1) I'm sure, but I can say that I believe in myself (2) Nothing venture nothing win

(d) (iv) Option 4

(e)

	Before 2008	After 2008
(i)	picturesque landscapes	construction sites and commerce

(f) (iv) (1) sets the stage for (2).

(g) (iii) for an economic recovery to be durable and resilient, a return to 'business as usual' and environmentally destructive investment patterns and activities must be avoided.

(h) (ii) Comfortable and peaceful. Neat room with ample sunlight. Pleasant and warm host.

(i) (i) We kill all the caterpillars, then complain there are no butterflies. *– John Marsden*

(j) (iii) (2) and (4) are true.

5. Read the passage given below.

1. Education is crucial for shaping the life of every individual in our modern society. A well-educated person is esteemed worthy in both their private and public lives as an ethical human being. We learn to appreciate and distinguish things of value, which consequently creates room for self-improvement.

2. Education facilitates the character development of every individual. It is primarily through education that a person imbibes the integral aspects of being human. Qualities like respect, compassion, kindness, helpfulness and so on are predominantly acquired through education that not only makes us morally upright but also aid us in our journey. Education does not merely signify the learning of facts and the accumulation of irrelevant information. True education is achieved only when people can successfully apply the knowledge and values they have acquired and become assets to society.

3. It is no secret that being educated and having the proper qualifications are necessary for securing job prospects. Each step towards educational progress acts as the foundation stone of one's career. Only proper education can provide the necessary knowledge and skills required for the respective opportunities in one's career ahead. Education allows the evolvement of one's personality through the adaptation of skills like problem-solving, critical thinking, effective communication, creativity, leadership, and so on.

4. The economic and general development of a country is also dependent on the proper education of its youth. The literacy rate of a country is one of the deciding factors to evaluate the country as an advanced nation. In India, the constitution recognises education as a fundamental right of every child. The Right of Children to Free and Compulsory Education (RTE) Act (2009), among other constitutional measures and efforts made by the government, ensures elementary education of children between the age of 6 and 14 years.

5. Education not only promotes individual development but also enriches the overall community. However, it is also important to acknowledge that the degree of positive impact being perpetuated effectively depends on the quality of education. The motive behind education should never be strictly career-driven or delimit one's outlook in life. Education should expand one's mind and equip one with everything necessary for a healthy experience of life.

5.1 Based on your understanding of the passage, answer <u>any eight</u> out of the ten questions by choosing the correct option.

(a) Select the correct inference with reference to the following:

We learn to appreciate and distinguish things of value, which consequently creates room for self-improvement.

(i) As we learn to appreciate costly things, we improve the rooms created for them.

(ii) We distinguish ourselves from others by the costly things we own, which improves us and makes us valuable.

(iii) When we appreciate valuable things and contrast them with baser things, we take a step towards improving ourselves.

(iv) Self-improvement is not possible if we fail to distinguish things of value from those that have none.

(b) Select the central theme of the passage.

(i) Career selection through education.

(ii) Progress of education in India.

(iii) Role of education.

(iv) Skills attained through education.

(c) What is the relation between (1) and (2)?

(1) ...economic and general development of a country...

(2) ...elementary education of children...

(i) (1) is accelerated by (2)

(ii) (2) cannot occur without (1)

(iii) (1) remains unaffected by (2)

(iv) (1) is accelerated in the absence of (2)

(d) Which option is most appropriately suited:

(1) Education helps us improve our personality.

(2) We learn skills to be used practically in life.

(3) Education should be career-centric only.

(4) Education helps us to be economically stable.

(i) (1) and (2) are true.

(ii) (1) and (3) are true.

(iii) (1), (2) and (4) are true.

(iv) (1), (3) and (4) are true.

(e) Select the option that suitably completes the given dialogue as per the context in paragraph 5.

Student: I have finally secured a job and my education is complete at last.

Teacher: Great news! And how do you plan on fulfilling your duties, now that you are established?

Student: Oh, that's simple. My duties are limited to the work I am responsible for at my job.

Teacher: Ah!...

(i) But then your education is not yet complete, for your sense of duty is inadequate. You must realise the duty you have to others and your community.

(ii) Your job will make your education complete. You have indeed learned everything.

(iii) You will perform excellently in your job, and that is all that matters. I wish you the best!

(iv) You must strive to complete your duties at work. Your job is enough to aid your community.

(f) Which of the following qualities would you include in your resume to show that you are an asset to society and a well-educated person?

1. Can memorise a vast amount of information.	2. Plays football on weekends.	3. Respectful, interactive and works as a team-player.	4. Knows the work and needs to further guidance.

(i) Option 1

(ii) Option 2

(iii) Option 3

(iv) Option 4

(g) The phrase 'foundation stone' refers to:

(i) finding something concrete or stone–like, that will remain strong.

(ii) getting hints about the future of something.

(iii) the essential element needed for the creation of something.

(iv) the founder of something unique.

(h) Read the two statements given below and select the option that suitably explains them:

(1) Education facilitates the character development of every individual.

(2) It is primarily through education that a person imbibes the integral aspects of being human.

(i) Development of character provides facilities of education and these facilities teach us how to be human.

(ii) The development of character becomes easy mainly through education, as a person learns the important elements of being human.

(iii) Character development is a result of being human and this is aided by education.

(iv) Primary education is important for the character development of human beings.

(i) Select the option that displays the correct cause-effect relationship.

	Cause	Effect
(i)	Learning necessary skills and being knowledgeable in a field of education.	Securing a job in the respective field.
(ii)	Knowing facts about a broad spectrum of topics without having and interpersonal skills.	Securing multiple jobs from various fields.
(iii)	Securing a job in any particular field.	Learning skills like problem-solving and critical thinking.
(iv)	Educating about necessary life skills with no expertise of a field of study.	Securing a job based on the skills possessed.

(j) Which quote is best suited to summarize passage 2?

(i) "An investment in knowledge pays the best interest." *– Benjamin Franklin*

(ii) "Education is not the learning of facts, but the training of minds to think." *– Albert Einstein*

(iii) "The highest result of education is tolerance." *– Hellen Keller*

(iv) "The roots of education are bitter, but the fruit is sweet." *– Aristotle*

ANSWERS

5.1. (a) (iv) Self-improvement is not possible if we fail to distinguish things of value from those that have none.

(b) (iii) Role of education.

(c) (i) (1) is accelerated by (2).

(d) (iv) (1), (3) and (4) are true.

(e) (i) But then your education is not yet complete, for your sense of duty is inadequate. You must realise the duty you have to others and your community.

(f) (iii) Option 3

(g) (iii) the essential element needed for the creation of something.

(h) (ii) The development of character becomes easy mainly through education, as a person learns the important elements of being human.

(i) (i)

Cause	Effect
Learning necessary skills and being knowledgeable in a field of education.	Securing a job in the respective field.

(j) (ii) "Education is not the learning of facts, but the training of minds to think." *– Albert Einstein*

6. Read the passage below and answer the questions that follow :

1. "Who doesn't know how to cook rice? Cooking rice hardly takes time." said my father. So I challenged myself. I switched from news to YouTube and typed, "How to cook rice?" I took one and a half cups of rice. Since I didn't have access to a rice cooker, I put the rice in a big pot. Firstly, the rice has to be washed to get rid of dust and starch. I thought I won't be able to drain the rice and that it will fall out of the pot. I observed the chef as I swirled the rice around and used my dexterous hands to drain it, not once, not twice, but three times. I looked down at the sink and saw less than 50 grains that made their way out of the pot. Suffice to say, I was up to the mark.

2. The video stated that the key to perfect rice is equal amount of rice and water. I have heard that professionals don't need to measure everything; they just know what the right amount is. But as this was my first time in the kitchen. I decided to experiment by not measuring the water needed for boiling the rice. I wanted the rice to be firm when bitten, just like pasta. I don't enjoy the texture of mushy rice. It has to have that chutzpah; it has to resist my biting power just for a bit before disintegrating.

3. After what seemed like 10 minutes, all the water disappeared. I went in to give it a good stir. To my surprise, some of the rice got stuck to the pot. I tried to scrape it off but to no avail. At the same time, there was a burning smell coming from it. I quickly turned the stove off. "What have you done to the kitchen?" shouted Mother, while coming towards the kitchen. I managed to ward her off.

4. Finally, when the time came to taste my creation, I was surprised! It wasn't bad at all. The rice had the desired consistency. Sure, a little more salt would've been better, but I just added that while eating. The experience was fairly rewarding and memorable. It taught me a new sense of respect for those who cook food on a regular basis at home or engage in gourmet creations professionally.

6.1. On the basis of your understanding of the above passage, answer any ten of the following questions by choosing the most appropriate option:

(a) Father's question to the narrator, about knowing how to cook rice, was intended to:

(i) criticize the narrator's lack of abilities.
(ii) make the process sound simple.
(iii) encourage the narrator to take up cooking.
(iv) showcase his own expertise in cooking rice.

(b) "I switched from news to YouTube...." Pick the option in which the meaning of 'switch(ed)' is NOT the same as it is in the passage.

(i) He switched on the radio to listen to the news while having dinner.
(ii) "Forget these diet supplements and switch to yoga, if you want a true sense of well-being."
(iii) Mom switched to reading fiction recently because she was bored with cook-books.
(iv) The company will switch the trucks to other routes to bring down city pollution.

(c) Based on your understanding of the passage, choose the option that lists the correct sequence of the process.

1. Use water to wash the rice.
2. Repeat the process three times.
3. Drain the water off.
4. Put rice in a utensil.
5. Swirl the water in and around the rice.

(i) 4, 2, 1, 3, 5 (ii) 1, 3, 2, 5, 4 (iii) 4, 1, 5, 3, 2 (iv) 5, 1, 2, 4, 3

(d) The narrator says that he has dexterous hands. He would have had a problem had it been the opposite. NOT BEING dexterous means, being:

(i) uncomfortable
(ii) clumsy
(iii) unclear
(iv) clueless

(e) Which option represents the correct ratio of water to rice for cooking 'perfect rice'?

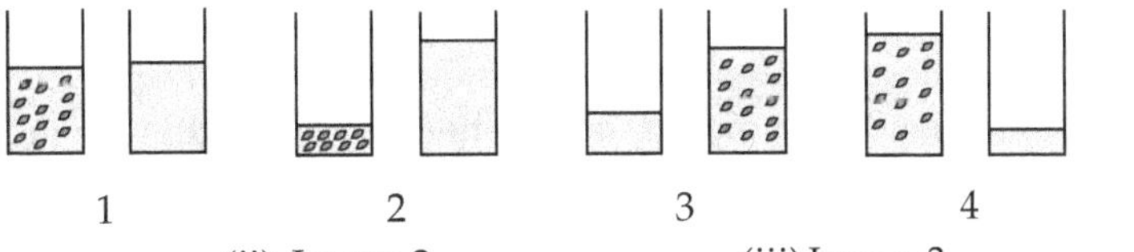

(i) Image 1 (ii) Image 2 (iii) Image 3 (iv) Image 4

(f) How did mother react to the burning smell?

(i) She commented on it.
(ii) She brushed it aside.
(iii) She enquired about it.
(iv) She handled it.

(g) According to the passage, the fact that the narrator risked experimentation, on his maiden attempt in the kitchen, shows that he was:

(i) conscientious
(ii) nervous
(iii) presumptuous
(iv) courteous

(h) Pick the option showing the CORRECT use of the word 'chutzpah'.

(i) It is the court's duty to dispense chutzpah to everyone irrespective of caste or creed.
(ii) The speaker may not have much of a stage presence, but you've got to admit she's got chutzpah.
(iii) I could crack the code easily which proved me to be a chutzpah and I was the only one who could do so.
(iv) After his father's demise, the daughter took over the family's chutzpah to save it from disaster.

(i) Pick the option that correctly states what DID NOT happen after the writer checked on the rice.

(i) Turning the stove off
(ii) Being taken aback at the condition of rice
(iii) Forgetting to scrape the stuck rice
(iv) Smelling the delicious aroma of cooked rice

(j) The narrator's creation was:

(i) almost perfect to taste.
(ii) way off from what he wanted.
(iii) overly seasoned.
(iv) quite distasteful.

(k) Pick the option that correctly lists the final feelings of the writer with reference to the cooking experience.

1. frustrating
2. amusing
3. satisfying
4. disillusioning
5. exacting
6. enlightening

(i) 1 and 4 (ii) 2 and 5 (iii) 3 and 6 (iv) 1 and 3

ANSWERS

(a) (ii) make the process sound simple.
(b) (i) He switched on the radio to listen to the news while having dinner.
(c) (iii) 4, 1, 5, 3, 2
(d) (ii) clumsy
(e) (i) Image 1
(f) (iii) She enquired about it
(g) (iii) presumptuous.
(h) (ii) The speaker may not have much of a stage presence, but you've got to admit she's got chutzpah.
(i) (iv) Smelling the delicious aroma of cooked rice.
(j) (i) almost perfect to taste.
(k) (iii) 3 and 6

7. Read the passage given below.

1. We sit in the last row, bumped about but free of stares. The bus rolls out of the dull crossroads of the city, and we are soon in open countryside, with fields of sunflowers as far as the eye can see, their heads all facing us. Where there is no water, the land reverts to desert. While still on level ground, we see in the distance the tall range of the Mount Bogda, abrupt like a shining prism laid horizontally on the desert surface. It is over 5,000 metres high, and the peaks are under permanent snow, in powerful contrast to the flat desert all around. Heaven Lake lies part of the way up this range about 2,000 metres above sea-level, at the foot of one of the higher snow-peaks.

2. As the bus climbs, the sky, brilliant before, grows overcast. I have brought nothing warm to wear: it is all down at the hotel in Urumqi. Rain begins to fall. The man behind me is eating overpoweringly smelly goat's cheese. The bus window leaks inhospitably but reveals a beautiful view. We have passed quickly from desert through arable land to pasture, and the ground is now green with grass, the slopes dark with pine. A few cattle drink at a clear stream flowing past moss-covered stones; it is a Constable landscape. The stream changes into a white torrent, and as we climb higher, I wish more and more that I had brought with me something warmer than the pair of shorts that have served me so well in the desert. The stream which, we are told, rises in Heaven Lake, disappears, and we continue our slow ascent. About noon, we arrive at Heaven Lake, and look for a place to stay at the foot, which is the resort area. We get a room in a small cottage, and I am happy to note that there are thick quilts on the beds.

3. Standing outside the cottage, we survey our surroundings. Heaven Lake is long, sardine-shaped and fed by snowmelt from a stream at its head. The lake is an intense blue, surrounded on all sides by green mountain walls, dotted with distant sheep. At the head of the lake, beyond the delta of the flowing stream, is a massive snow-capped peak which dominates the vista; it is part of a series of peaks that culminate, a little out of view, in Mount Bogda itself.

4. For those who live in the resort, there is a small mess-hall by the shore. We eat here sometimes, and sometimes buy food from the vendors outside, who sell Kabab and naan until the last buses leave. The kababs, cooked on skewers over charcoal braziers, are particularly good; highly spiced and well-done. Horse's milk is available too from the local Kazakh herdsmen, but I decline this. I am so affected by the cold that Mr. Cao, the relaxed young man who runs the mess, lends me a spare pair of trousers, several sizes too large but more than comfortable. Once I am warm again, I feel a pre-dinner spurt of energy— dinner will be long in coming—and I ask him whether the lake is good for swimming in. "Swimming?" Mr. Cao says, "You aren't thinking of swimming, are you?"

5. "I thought I might," I confess. "What's the water like?" He doesn't answer me immediately, turning instead to examine some receipts with exaggerated interest. Mr. Cao, with great off-handedness, addresses the air. "People are often drowned here", he says. After a pause, he continues. "When was the last one?" This question is directed at the cook, who is preparing a tray of "mantou" (squat, white steamed bread rolls), and who now appears, wiping his doughy hand across his forehead. "Was it the Beijing athlete?" asks Mr. Cao.

7.1. On the basis of your understanding of the passage, answer any ten of the following questions by choosing the most appropriate option:

(a) One benefit of sitting in the last row of the bus was that....... .

(i) the narrator enjoyed the bumps
(ii) no one stared at him
(iii) he could see the sunflowers
(iv) he avoided the dullness of the city

(b) The narrator was travelling to....... .

(i) Mount Bogda
(ii) Heaven Lake
(iii) a 2,000-metre high snow-peak
(iv) Urumqi

(c) Based on your understanding of the passage, choose the option that lists the correct sequence of the process.

1. As the bus climbs, the sky, brilliant before, grows overcast.
2. The kababs, cooked on skewers over charcoal braziers, are particularly good; highly spiced and well-done.
3. The bus rolls out of the dull crossroads of the city, and we are soon in open countryside.
4. We get a room in a small cottage, and I am happy to note that there are thick quilts on the beds.

(i) 1, 3, 4, 2 (ii) 2,3,4,1 (iii) 3, 1, 4, 2 (iv) 4,3,1,2

(d) Mount Bogda is compared to....... .

(i) a horizontal desert surface
(ii) a shining prism
(iii) a constable landscape
(iv) the overcast sky

(e) Which option represents the shape of the 'Heaven Lake'?

(1)

(2)

(3)

(4)

(i) Image 1 (ii) Image 2 (iii) Image 3 (iv) Image 4

(f) The man behind the narrator was eating overpoweringly....... .

(i) smelly goat's cheese
(ii) smelly pickles
(iii) fragrant fruits
(iv) none of these

(g) What did the narrator see at distance from the bus when they were still on ground?

(i) The tall range of the Mount Bogda.
(ii) The wide range of forests.
(iii) Snow-covered hills.
(iv) Sheep and goats mounting the hills.

(h) Where has the narrator left his warm clothes?

(i) At home
(ii) In the bus
(iii) In the hotel
(iv) At his friend's house

(i) What is 'Mantou'?

(i) A thick hamburger.
(ii) A squat, garlic bread.
(iii) A squat, white steamed bread roll.
(iv) A Squat, hotdog.

(j) Which word in the passage means same as 'terminate'? (para 3)

(i) Culminate (ii) Intense (iii) Dominate (iv) Distant

(k) As the bus climbs up while heading towards Mount Bogda, how did the weather begin to change?

1. It was becoming warmer.
2. It was becoming cooler.
3. It began raining.
4. The snow started falling down.

(i) 1 and 2 (ii) 2 and 3 (iii) 1 and 3 (iv) 3 and 4

ANSWERS

(a) (ii) no one stared at him
(b) (ii) Heaven Lake
(c) (iii) 3, 1, 4 ,2
(d) (ii) a shining prism
(e) (ii) Image 2
(f) (i) smelly goat's cheese
(g) (i) The tall range of Mount Bogda.
(h) (iii) In the hotel
(i) (iii) A squat, white steamed bread roll.
(j) (i) Culminate
(k) (ii) 2 and 3

8. Read the passage given below.

1. A fisherman, enfeebled with age, could no longer go out to sea so he began fishing in the river. Every morning he would go down to the river and sit there fishing the whole day long. In the evening he would sell whatever he had caught, buy food for himself and go home. It was a hard life for an old man. One hot afternoon while he was trying to keep awake and bemoaning his fate, a large bird with silvery feathers alighted on a rock near him. It was Kaha, the heavenly bird. "You have no one to care for you, grandpa?" asked the bird. "Not a soul." "You should not be doing such work at your age, " said the bird. "From now on I will bring you a big fish every evening. You can sell it and live in comfort." True to her word, the bird began to drop a large fish at his doorstep every evening. All that the fisherman had to do was take it to the market and sell it. As big fish were in great demand, he was soon rolling in money. He bought a cottage near the sea, with a garden around it and engaged a servant to cook for him. His wife had died some years earlier. He had decided to marry again and began to look for a suitable woman.
2. One day he heard the royal courtier make an announcement. "Our king has news of a great bird called Kaha," said the courtier. "Whoever can give information about this bird and help catch it, will be rewarded with half the gold in the royal treasury and half the kingdom!" The fisherman was sorely tempted by the reward. Half the kingdom would make him a prince!
3. "Why does the king want the bird?" he asked. "He has lost his sight," explained the courtier. "A wise man has advised him to bathe his eyes with the blood of Kaha. Do you know where she can be found?" "No…I mean …no, no…" Torn between greed and his sense of gratitude to the bird, the fisherman could not give a coherent reply. The courtier, sensing that he knew something about the bird, informed the king. The king had him brought to the palace.
4. "If you have information about the bird, tell me," urged the king. "I will reward you handsomely and if you help catch her, I will personally crown you king of half my domain." "I will get the bird for you," cried the fisherman, suddenly making up his mind. "But Kaha is strong. I will need help." The king sent a dozen soldiers with him. That evening when the bird came with the fish, the fisherman called out to her to wait. "You drop the fish and go and I never get a chance to thank you for all that you've done for me," he said. "Today I have laid out a feast for you inside. Please alight and come in." Kaha was reluctant to accept the invitation but the fisherman pleaded so earnestly that she finally gave in, and alighted. The moment she was on the ground, the fisherman grabbed one of her legs and shouted to the soldiers hiding in his house to come out. They rushed to his aid but their combined effort could not keep Kaha down.
5. She rose into the air with the fisherman still clinging onto her leg. By the time he realised he was being carried away, the fisherman was too high in the air to let go. He hung on grimly and neither he nor Kaha was ever seen again.

8.1. On the basis of your understanding of the passage, answer any ten of the following questions by choosing the most appropriate option:

(a) Why could the fisherman no longer go to the sea?

(i) He had grown weak.
(ii) He had grown too old.
(iii) He had lost his wife.
(iv) He had lost his eyesight.

(b) Why did the King want Kaha bird?

(i) The bird was supposed to bring good luck.
(ii) Kaha was the biggest bird in the kingdom.
(iii) Kaha had the silvery feathers.
(iv) King wanted Kaha's blood for his lost eyesight.

(c) Based on your understanding of the passage, choose the option that lists the CORRECT sequence of the given sentences.

1. Kaha rose into the air with the fisherman still clinging onto her leg.
2. The fisherman said to the king 'Kaha is strong, I will need help'.
3. The fisherman was torn between greed and his sense of gratitude to Kaha.
4. Kaha began dropping large fish at the fisherman's doorstep every evening.

(i) 1, 2, 3, 4 (ii) 4, 3, 2, 1 (iii) 3, 4, 1, 2 (iv) 2, 1, 4, 3

(d) How did the courtier sense that the fisherman might know something about Kaha?

(i) The courtier had seen the fisherman talking to Kaha.

(ii) The fisherman fumbled when asked about Kaha.

(iii) The courtier had observed Kaha alight at the fisherman's house every evening.

(iv) Word went around that the fisherman was in contact with Kaha.

(e) Which option represents INCORRECT data relating to the passage given?

(i) At dawn, the fisherman would sell whatever he had caught, buy food for himself and go home.

(ii) Kaha, the heavenly bird, with silvery feathers alighted on a rock near him.

(iii) Kaha, the bird, began to drop a large fish at the fisherman's doorstep every evening.

(iv) As big fish were in great demand, the fisherman was soon rolling in money.

(f) At last, neither the fisherman nor Kaha ....

(i) were ever seen again

(ii) were sad

(iii) died

(iv) none of these

(g) How did old fisherman carry out his livelihood?

(i) He began fishing in the sea.

(ii) He began hunting animals.

(iii) He began catching birds.

(iv) He began fishing in the river.

(h) What does the phrase 'rolling in money' in the passage refer to?

(i) Playing with money.

(ii) To become wealthy.

(iii) Rolling the coins on the floor.

(iv) Having lot of coins.

(i) What do you understand by the character trait of the fisherman from the story?

(i) Greedy and selfish.

(ii) Caring and selfless.

(iii) Feeble and humble.

(iv) Generous and selfless.

(j) Which word in the passage means opposite to 'willing'? (para 4)

(i) Reluctant (ii) Accept (iii) Pleaded (iv) Earnestly

(k) Pick the option that correctly lists the qualities of Kaha in the passage.

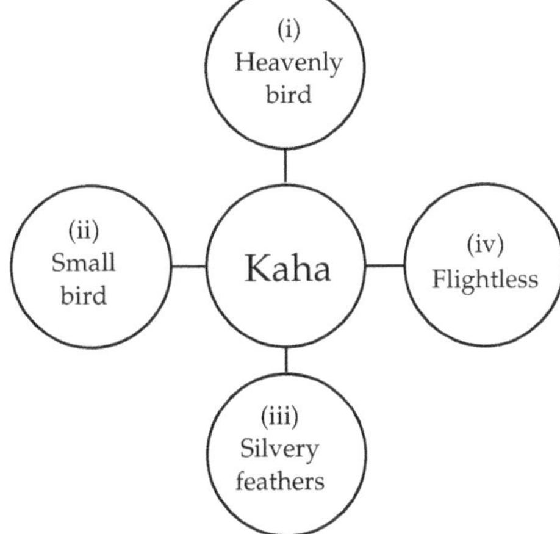

(i) 1 and 3

(ii) 1 and 4

(iii) 1, 2 and 4

(iv) all of the options

ANSWERS

(a) (ii) He had grown too old.

(b) (iv) King wanted Kaha's blood for his lost eyesight.

(c) (ii) 4, 3, 2, 1

(d) (ii) The fisherman fumbled when asked about Kaha.

(e) (i) At dawn, the fisherman would sell whatever he had caught, buy food for himself and go home.

(f) (i) were ever seen again.

(g) (iv) He began fishing in the river.

(h) (ii) To become wealthy.

(i) (i) Greedy and selfish

(j) (i) Reluctant

(k) (i) 1 and 3

9. Read the passage given below.

1. Marie Curie was one of the most accomplished scientists in history. Together with her husband, Pierre, she discovered radium, an element widely used for treating cancer and studied uranium and other radioactive substances. Pierre and Marie's amicable collaboration later helped to unlock the secrets of the atom.

2. Marie was born in 1867 in Warsaw, Poland, where her father was a professor of physics. Curie was the youngest of five children, following siblings Zosia, Józef, Bronya and Hela. Both of Curie's parents were teachers. Her father, Wladyslaw, was a math and physics instructor. When she was only 10, Curie lost her mother, Bronislawa, to tuberculosis. As a child, Curie took after her father. She had a bright and curious mind and excelled at school. But despite being a top student in her secondary school, Curie could not attend the men's—only University of Warsaw. At an early age, she displayed a brilliant mind and a blithe personality. Her great exuberance for learning prompted her to continue with her studies after high school. She became disgruntled, however, when she learned that the university in Warsaw was closed to women. She instead continued her education in Warsaw's "floating university," a set of underground, informal classes held in secret. Determined to receive a higher education, she defiantly left Poland and in 1891 entered the Sorbonne, a French university, where she earned her master's degree and doctorate in physics.

3. Both Curie and her sister Bronya dreamed of going abroad to earn an official degree, but they lacked the financial resources to pay for more schooling. Undeterred, Curie worked out a deal with her sister: She would work to support Bronya while she was in school, and Bronya would return the favour after she completed her studies. For roughly five years, Curie worked as a tutor and a governess. She used her spare time to study, reading about physics, chemistry and math. In 1891, Curie finally made her way to Paris and enrolled at the Sorbonne. She threw herself into her studies, but this dedication had a personal cost: with little money, Curie survived on buttered bread and tea and her health sometimes suffered because of her poor diet. Curie completed her master's degree in physics in 1893 and earned another degree in mathematics the following year.

4. Marie was fortunate to have studied at the Sorbonne with some of the greatest scientists of her day, one of whom was Pierre Curie. Marie and Pierre were married in 1895 and spent many productive years working together in the physics laboratory. A short time after they discovered radium, Pierre was killed by a horse-drawn wagon in 1906. Marie was stunned by this horrible misfortune and endured heart breaking anguish. Despondently she recalled their close relationship and the joy that they had shared in scientific research. The fact that she had two young daughters to raise by herself greatly increased her distress.

5. Curie's feeling of desolation finally began to fade when she was asked to succeed her husband as a physics professor at the Sorbonne. She was the first woman to be given a professorship at the world famous university. In 1911 she received the Nobel Prize in chemistry for isolating radium. Although Marie Curie eventually suffered a fatal illness from her long exposure to radium, she never became disillusioned about her work. Regardless of the consequences, she had dedicated herself to science and to revealing the mysteries of the physical world.

6. Marie Curie became the first woman to win a Nobel Prize and the first person — man or woman — to win the award twice. With her husband Pierre Curie, Marie's efforts led to the discovery of polonium and radium and, after Pierre's death, the further development of X-rays. The famed scientist died in 1934 of aplastic anaemia likely caused by exposure to radiation.

9.1 On the basis of your understanding of the passage, answer any ten of the following questions by choosing the most appropriate option:

(a) The Curies' .... collaboration helped to unlock the secrets of the atom.

(i) friendly (ii) competitive (iii) courteous (iv) industrious

(b) Marie had a bright mind and a .... personality.

(i) strong (ii) light hearted (iii) strange (iv) humorous

(c) Based on your understanding of the passage, choose the option that lists the CORRECT sequence of the events in Marie's life.

1. She used her spare time to study, reading about physics, chemistry and maths.
2. Curie completed her master's degree in physics in 1893 and earned another degree in mathematics the following year.
3. Marie and Pierre were married in 1895 and spent many productive years working together in the physics laboratory.
4. At an early age, Marie displayed a brilliant mind and a blithe personality.

(i) 2, 1, 4, 3 (ii) 3, 2, 4, 1 (iii) 4, 1, 2, 3 (iv) 2, 3, 4, 1

(d) Marie .... by leaving Poland and travelling to France to enter the Sorbonne.

(i) challenged authority
(ii) short intelligence
(iii) was distressed
(iv) was happy

(e) Which image correctly shows the subject in which Marie received the Nobel Prize?

1 2 3 4

(i) Image 1 (ii) Image 2 (iii) Image 3 (iv) Image 4

(f) Who was Marie Curie's husband ?

(i) Peter Curie (ii) Pierre Curie (iii) Perrie Curie (iv) Pirre Curie

(g) How many siblings did Curie have ?

(i) Five (ii) Two (iii) Three (iv) Four

(h) How did Curie's mother die ?

(i) Pneumonia (ii) Cancer (iii) Tuberculosis (iv) Anaemia

(i) From where did Curie receive her higher education ?

(i) University of Poland
(ii) University of Warsaw
(iii) University of Zurich
(iv) University of Sorbonne

(j) Which word in the passage means opposite to 'gloomy'? (para 2)

(i) Exuberance (ii) Blithe (iii) Excelled (iv) Bright

(k) Pick the option that CORRECTLY shows the feelings of Marie when she learned that the university in Warsaw was closed to women.

1. Angry 2. Dissatisfied 3. Melancholy 4. Joy

(i) 1 and 2
(ii) 2 and 3
(iii) 3 and 4
(iv) 1 and 4

ANSWERS

(a) (i) friendly
(b) (ii) light-hearted
(c) (iii) 4, 1, 2, 3
(d) (iii) was distressed
(e) (iv) Image 4
(f) (ii) Pierre Curie
(g) (iv) Four
(h) (iii) Tuberculosis
(i) (iv) University of Sorbonne
(j) (i) Exuberance
(k) (i) 1 and 2

❑❑

Factual (Case Based Unseen) Passage

2

Passages

1. Read the passage given below.

1. The passenger pigeon (Ectopistes Migratorius) was once found in huge numbers in North America. Records tell of passing flocks that darkened the skies for several days at a time. The species may have peaked at five billion individuals. A more conservative estimate is three billion.

2. Within a short time, the species disappeared completely.

   "Given the huge size of the population, it's simply amazing that the species disappeared so quickly," says Tom Gilbert. Gilbert is a professor at the University of Copenhagen's Centre for Geogenetics, but he also has a part-time position as an adjunct professor at the Norwegian University of Science and Technology (NTNU).

3. The history of the passenger pigeon is interesting, partly because it can tell us something about how and why species become extinct. Native Americans also relied on passenger pigeons for food. But at least in parts of the passenger pigeons' range, people had learned to harvest the species at a sustainable level that didn't threaten to eradicate it. It was common in some parts of North America to only eat young pigeons that were hunted at night, since this did not seem to scare away the adult birds or prevent them from re-nesting.

4. But starting around 1500, a more aggressive variant of humans came to the continent with the arrival of Europeans. The hunt for passenger pigeons grew and culminated in a massive hunt for the species throughout the 1800s, before the species finally collapsed and disappeared. In 2014, a study in published in the scientific journal PNAS strongly suggested that humans were simply the final straw in destroying a species that was already vulnerable and headed to oblivion.

   The cladogram below follows the 2012 DNA study showing the position of the passenger pigeon among its closest relatives:

```
┌──┬──┬──┬── Macropygia (cuckoo-doves)
│  │  │  └── Reinwardtoena
│  │  └───── Turacoena
│  ├──────── Columba (Old World pigeons)
│  └──────── Streptopelia (turtle doves and collared doves)
├─────────── Patagioenas (New World pigeons)
└─────────── Ectopistes (passenger pigeon)
```

5. The researchers asserted that despite their enormous numbers, the passenger pigeons were already in trouble. The population of the species varied greatly, similar to lemmings, but over a longer period of time. When the Europeans arrived, the species was already in a strong decline. The population was plummeting long before Europeans arrived, and perhaps Europeans even contributed to a short-term increase in numbers.

6. Studies of the genetic variation of the species using an investigative method called PSMC formed the background for these assertions. And now we have to concentrate a bit. The PSMC method can use the information in the genes of a single individual of a species to map the history of the species.

7. You should therefore be able to see how the species developed over many generations, and estimate how many individuals there were at any given time, all based on a single genome. Using this method, researchers found that the number of passenger pigeons was in free fall even before the arrival of the Europeans.

   Although the species might not have become extinct, it would have shrunk significantly in any case, maybe to only a few hundred thousand individuals.

1.1. Based on your understanding of the passage, answer <u>any six</u> out of the eight questions by choosing the correct option.

(a) Select the correct inference with reference to the following:

"Records tell of passing flocks that darkened the skies for several days at a time.

(i) The innumerable individual passenger pigeons flocked the skies of North America.

(ii) The black pigeons together turned the blue sky dark.

(iii) When the pigeons passed through the skies of North America, the sky was covered with black clouds.

(iv) The pigeons carried bad omens with them which were visible through the sky getting dark.

(b) According to cladogram 2012 DNA study in figure 1, the species that was famous among Old World pigeons were:

(i) Reinwardtoena (ii) Columba (iii) Patagioenas (iv) Turacoena

(c) Choose the correct cause and effect relationship from the given options.

	Cause	Effect
(i)	The hunt for passenger pigeons grew and culminated in a massive hunt for the species throughout the 1800s.	The species finally collapsed and disappeared.
(ii)	The history of the passenger pigeon is interesting.	It can tell us something about how and why species become extinct.
(iii)	The PSMC method can use the information in the genes of a single individual of a species.	Mapping the history of the species.
(iv)	Studies of the genetic variation of the species is using an investigative method called PSMC.	It formed the background for these assertions.

(d) Select the central message in paragraph 2 according to Tom Gilbert's study about Passenger pigeon. It conclude that:

(i) It's simply astonishing that the species found in large number, disappeared so quickly.

(ii) It's pathetic that passenger pigeons were disliked by Europeans.

(iii) It's incredible that the species flourished quickly.

(iv) It's unbelievable that the species suddenly migrated.

(e) Based on your reading of paragraph 3, select the appropriate counter-argument to the given argument.

Argument : The North Americans ate young pigeons that were hunted at night, since this did not seem to scare away the adult birds or prevent them from re-nesting.

(i) I think the North Americans could have eaten the birds at day too as it won't make any difference.

(ii) I don't think that eating young birds at night wouldn't scare the adult birds. After all, they can sense fear and it is just an assumption of the North Americans.

(iii) I feel that hunting adult birds could have been better because the young birds wouldn't have been able to judge the scene.

(iv) I don't feel that what North Americans did was right.

(f) The phrase "The population was plummeting long before Europeans arrived" refers to:

(i) The number of migrating passenger pigeons was decreasing slowly.

(ii) There was a rapid decrease in the population of passenger pigeons.

(iii) The species of passenger pigeons were extinct.

(iv) There was a rapid increase in the population of passenger pigeons.

(g) Based on the reading of the passage, choose the fact that the researchers find about the number of passenger pigeons.

(i) It's number started deteriorating with the arrival of Europeans.

(ii) It was in free fall even before the arrival of the Europeans.

(iii) It became extinct after the arrival of Europeans.

(iv) It's species began to multiply with the arrival of Europeans.

(h) Read the two statements given below and select the option that explains them.

(1) PSMC method uses the information in the genes of a single individual of a species.

(2) It is important to map the history of the species to know more.

(i) (1) is the result of (2).

(ii) (2) is the requirement for (1).

(iii) (1) is true, but (2) is false.

(iv) (2) is the research through (1).

ANSWERS

1.1. (a) (i) The innumerable individual passenger pigeons flocked the skies of North America.

(b) (ii) Columba

(c)

	Cause	Effect
(i)	The hunt for passenger pigeons grew and culminated in a massive hunt for the species throughout the 1800s.	The species finally collapsed and disappeared.

(d) (i) It's simply astonishing that the species found in large number, disappeared so quickly.

(e) (ii) I don't think that eating young birds at night wouldn't scare the adult birds. After all, they can sense fear and it is just an assumption of the North Americans.

(f) (ii) There was a rapid decrease in the population of passenger pigeons.

(g) (ii) It was in free fall even before the arrival of the Europeans.

(h) (iv) (2) is the research through (1).

2. Read the passage given below.

1. If NSYNC singer Lance Bass can't afford the $20 million price tag for a ride into space now, he should try again, in say, a decade. But within a decade or so, even some of Bass's fans could afford a quick and safe trip to the suborbital edge of space, roughly 50-60 miles above earth, says Frank Seitzen, President of the Space Transport Association.

2. "I think you're may be 10 or 12 years away from having companies that are reliable and that can go through that process for $5,000 or $10,000," Seitzen said. There's a hungry demand from would be space tourists and a $10 million prize is inspiring designers. The Prize, created in 1994 to spur the development of new space travel technologies, has attracted at least 21 space vehicle designs from people in five countries. The non-profit X Prize Foundation, founded by a group of donors inspired by the $25,000 Orteig Prize that Charles Lindbergh won in 1927, will give the prize.

3. Each design team is hoping to develop the first reusable rocket capable of blasting a pilot and two to five passengers to a height of 62 miles. NASA awards astronaut status for flights above 50 miles. Some design contestants boast that such trips will be available by 2005, although the first few travellers will face $100,000 bills until the market matures.

4. Despite steep prices and lagging technology, Seitzen and others are convinced that a lucrative travel business awaits. Space Adventures, a travel agency that helped coordinate the first tourist trip to the International Space Station last year by US businessman Dennis Tito, claims it has collected $2 million in deposits from more than 120 would-be suborbital tourists. For client Wally Funk, who has paid her deposit, suborbital travel is a disappointing, yet feasible, alternative to decades of trying to reach space. Funk, a retired aviation safety investigator says, "I would do (a space station trip) in a heartbeat, but I can't because I'm not a millionaire."

5. Compared to Tito's groundbreaking effort last year, future suborbital flights look easy. Tito was subjected to rigid medical requirements and a gruelling six-month training course in Russia. But suborbital travellers will need only a few days of training and pending FAA approval, would have to pass a much lower bar for medical standards."We always say that if you can safely ride a roller coaster, then you are fit for a suborbital flight," says Space Adventures spokeswoman Tereza Predescu.

6. Four commercial spaceports, which launch rockets into space like airports launch planes, are already licensed to operate by the FAA in Virginia, California, Alaska and Florida, and they are eager to welcome extra business from space tourists, negating the need to catch a ride to Russia. For those reasons, suborbital travel may represent a $1 billion in a year market, according to Space Adventures President and CEO Eric Anderson, that's 10,000 travellers paying $100,000 each during the first few years of adventure space travel.

(*Source*: auto.economictimes.indiatimes.com)

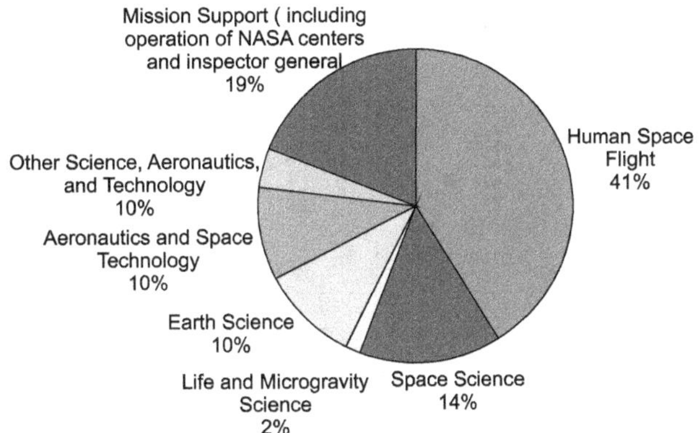

NASA budget for science-related programs and activities, FY 1997 (constant FY 1995 dollars)

2.1. Based on your understanding of the passage, answer any six out of the eight questions by choosing the correct option.

(a) Select the correct inference with reference to the following:

There's a hungry demand from would be space tourists and a $10 million prize is inspiring designers……

(i) Space tourists have collectively bet a $10 million prize to anyone who can take them for a space trip.

(ii) Space tourists are demanding for restaurants in space to satiate a hungry stomach.

(iii) There's a potential for space tourism market but unfortunately no one is tapping into it.

(iv) Spacecraft designers are competing to bring the quickest and most affordable options for space tourism.

(b) Select the central idea of the paragraph 1.

(i) Space tourism may not be feasible as of now but next decade may prove more promising.

(ii) Space tourism is only for the super-rich, be it at present or in the next decade.

(iii) Space tourism is a wasteful venture of resources and fuels.

(iv) Space tourism is going to be accessible only through NASA.

(c) Select the option that displays the true statement with reference to the figure given.

(i) NASA's budget lays more emphasis on the study of Life and Microgravity science.

(ii) NASA's budget for Human Space Flight and Mission Support are in the priority.

(iii) It is not possible to correctly tell NASA's preferences as everything is for science at the end.

(iv) Space Science and Earth Science are the highest funded NASA programs.

(d) Based on your reading of paragraphs 4-5, select the appropriate counter-argument to the given argument.

Argument: Space trips are an egotistical way to flaunt your wealth to the poor and middle class, because at the end of the day you're contributing nothing to science and advancement.

(i) The wealthy have collected about $ 2 million for space travel, so they all are working together setting their egos aside.

(ii) It is not for us to judge what others are doing as long as they are aware of the carbon footprints they are going to leave behind.

(iii) History holds testimony that the rich has always had unrealistic tastes, earlier it was precious stones and ivory, now it is space travel.

(iv) The wealthiest are willing to fund for research and development in space science, so even if it is for their ego, it will still be a way for advancement in faster and cheaper technologies.

(e) Select the option that displays the correct cause-effect relationship.

	Cause	Effect
(i)	$10 million prize for spacecraft designers.	Faster development of cost-effective space trips.
(ii)	Rising interest in space tourism.	Decrease in space science studies.
(iii)	Lower budget constraints for researchers.	Lesser productivity and slow advancements.
(iv)	Faster development of cost-effective space trips.	$10 million prize for spacecraft designers.

(f) The survey statistics mention the speculated average space flight budget, indicating that:

(i) The ticket price can be either of $100,000 or $5,000.

(ii) The demand and development lack the potential to lower ticket price from $100,000 to $5,000.

(iii) The demand for a space flight is now saturating.

(iv) The demand and development have the potential to lower ticket price from $10,000 to $5,000

(g) The phrase 'blasting a pilot' refers to the:

(i) bombing the pilot into shreds.

(ii) launching a pilot into space.

(iii) shooting a pilot into space.

(iv) hurling a pilot into space.

(h) Read the two statements given below and select the option that suitably explains them.

(1) Each design team is hoping to develop the first reusable rocket.

(2) Suborbital travel may represent a $1 billion in a year market.

(i) (2) is false but (1) is true.

(ii) (1) is true and (2) is the reason of (1).

(iii) (1) and (2) are false.

(iv) (2) and (1) are true but independent of each other.

ANSWERS

2.1. (a) (iv) Spacecraft designers are competing to bring the quickest and most affordable options for space tourism.

(b) (i) Space tourism may not be feasible as of now but next decade may prove more promising.

(c) (ii) NASA's budget for Human Space Flight and Mission Support are in the priority.

(d) (iv) The wealthiest are willing to fund for research and development in space science, so even if it is for their ego, it will still be a way for advancement in faster and cheaper technologies.

(e)

	Cause	Effect
(i)	$10 million prize for spacecraft designers.	Faster development of cost-effective space trips.

(f) (iv) The demand and development have the potential to lower ticket price from $10,000 to $5,000.

(g) (ii) launching a pilot into space.

(h) (ii) (1) is true and (2) is the reason of (1).

3. Read the passage given below.

1. When plastic waste is burnt, a complex weave of toxic chemicals is released. Breaking down Poly Vinyl Chloride (PVC) used for packaging, toys and coating electrical wires. It produces dioxin, an organochlorine which belongs to the family of Persistent Organic Pollutants (POPs). A recent Dioxin Assessment Report brought out by the United States Environment Protection Agency (USEPA) says the risk of getting cancer from dioxin is ten times higher than reported by the agency in 1994.

2. Yet the Delhi government is giving the green signal to a gasification project which will convert garbage into energy without removing plastic waste. Former transport minister Rajendra Gupta, the promoter of this project, says this is not necessary.

He claims no air pollution will be caused and that the ash produced can be used as manure. An earlier waste-to-energy project set-up in Timarpur failed. The new one, built with Australian assistance, will cost ₹ 200 crore. It will generate 25 megawatts of power and gobble 1,000 tonnes of garbage everyday.

3. "Technologies like gasification are a form of incineration," says Madhumita Dutta, central coordinator with Toxics Link, New Delhi. Incineration merely transfers hazardous waste from a solid form to air, water and ash, she points out. Toxins produced during incineration include acidic gases, heavy metals as well as dioxins and furans. "The 'manure' will be hazardous and a problem to dispose," says Dutta.

4. Municipal solid waste contains a mix of plastics. Breaking down this waste emits hydrochloric acid which attacks the respiratory system, skin and eyes, resulting in coughing, vomiting and nausea.

Polyethylene generates volatile compounds like formaldehyde and acetaldehyde, both suspected carcinogenic. Breathing styrene from polystyrene can cause leukaemia. Polyurethane is associated with asthma. Dioxin released by PVC is a powerful hormone disrupter and causes birth defects and reproductive problems. There is no threshold dose to prevent it and our bodies have no defence against it.

5. "Even the best run incinerators in the world have to deal with stringent norms, apart from contaminated filters and ash, making them hugely expensive to operate," says Dutta. In Germany, air pollution devices accounted for two-thirds the cost of incineration. Despite such efforts, the European Dioxin Inventory noted that the input of dioxin into the atmosphere was the highest from incineration.

6. How has global plastic waste disposal method changed over time? In the chart, we see the share of global plastic waste that is discarded, recycled or incinerated from 1980 through to 2015. Prior to 1980, recycling and incineration of plastic was negligible; 100 per cent was therefore discarded. From 1980 for incineration and 1990 for recycling, rates increased on average by about 0.7 per cent per year. In 2015, an estimated 55 per cent of global plastic waste was discarded, 25 per cent was incinerated and 20 per cent recycled.

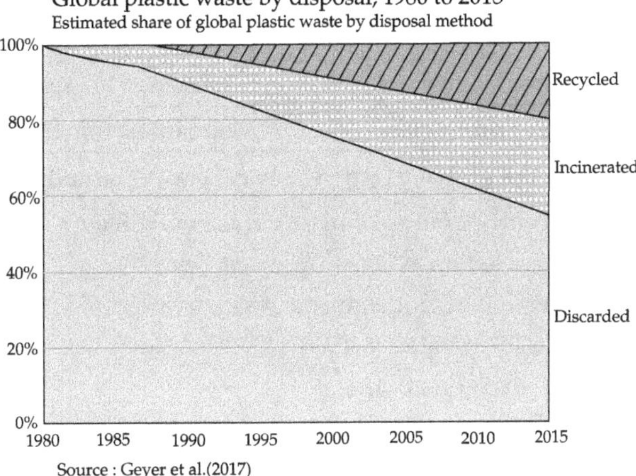

7. "India does not have the facility to test dioxin and the cost of setting one up is prohibitively expensive," says Dutta. Besides, Indian garbage has a low calorific content of about 800 cal/kg, since it has high moisture and requires additional fuel to burn. Toxics link calculates that the electricity generated from such technology will cost between ₹5-7 per unit, which is six times higher than conventional energy. India has chosen a dioxin preventive route and burning of chlorinated plastics is prohibited under Municipal Solid Waste and Biomedical Rules.

   Nearly 80 per cent of Indian garbage is recyclable or compostable. Resident associations, the informal sector and the municipal corporation can make Delhi's garbage disappear in a sustainable manner. "Instead, the government promotes end of pipeline solutions," says Dutta.

3.1. Based on your understanding of the passage, answer any six out of the eight questions by choosing the correct option.

(a) Select the correct inference with reference to the following:

Instead, the government promotes end of pipeline solutions.

(i) Government is promoting solutions which can end the supply of garbage.
(ii) Government is planning to promote effective measures for waste disposal.
(iii) Government is planning to connect garbage disposal pipelines.
(iv) Government is promoting last stage actions instead of tackling the problem in initial steps.

(b) Select the central idea of the paragraph 3.

(i) Incineration is only going to bring more pollutants in the air.
(ii) Incineration will control the air quality index of Delhi.
(iii) Delhi air quality isn't improving anyway, so incineration will have little to no effect.
(iv) The benefits of incineration outweigh the risks in Delhi.

(c) Select the option that displays the true statement with reference to the given figure.

(i) Incineration of plastic waste has stabilized since 1995.
(ii) Awareness towards recycling of plastic is reflected in recent years.
(iii) The trend of discarding garbage hasn't changed much since 1980.
(iv) Incineration of waste now is almost double that of discarded garbage.

(d) Based on your reading of paragraphs 4-5, select the appropriate counter- argument to the given argument.

Argument: Incineration is the quickest way of waste disposal, and even if it generates harmful toxins, proper measures can ensure that they don't escape in the environment.

(i) Recycling and reducing waste consumption are better options.

(ii) Regulations are not enough to contain the toxic carcinogens it will generate along with a huge cost of operating it.

(iii) Incinerators are a form of infrastructure development that is going to generate jobs.

(iv) They are expensive to operate and do not generate enough electrical output.

(e) Select the option that displays the correct cause-effect relationship.

	Cause	Effect
(i)	Burning of polyurethane.	Leukaemia.
(ii)	Emission of hydrochloric acid from wastes.	Birth defects and reproductive problems.
(iii)	Burning of polyethylene.	Release of formaldehyde and acetaldehyde.
(iv)	Wasteful consumption of products.	Dissatisfaction by the consumers.

(f) The survey statistics mention the global plastic waste disposal methods, indicating that:

(i) Prior to 1980, recycling and incineration of plastic was negligible.

(ii) In 1990, recycling rates increased on average by about 7 per cent.

(iii) In 2015, an estimated 55 percent of global plastic waste was recycled.

(iv) 100 per cent of garbage was incinerated in 1980.

(g) The phrase 'low calorific content' refers to the:

(i) lower calories for a healthy consumption.

(ii) lower content to remove all the moisture.

(iii) lower spectrum of behaving as toxin.

(iv) lower quality to burn as a fuel on its own.

(h) Read the two statements given below and select the option that suitably explains them.

(1) India has chosen a dioxin preventive route.

(2) USEPA says the risk of getting cancer from dioxin is ten times higher than reported by the agency in 1994.

(i) (1) is the problem and (2) is the solution.

(ii) (1) and (2) don't relate.

(iii) (1) is true and (2) correctly explains it.

(iv) (2) is false but (1) is true.

ANSWERS

3.1. (a) (iv) Government is promoting last stage actions instead of tackling the problem in initial steps.

(b) (i) Incineration is only going to bring more pollutants in the air.

(c) (ii) Awareness towards recycling of plastic is reflected in recent years.

(d) (ii) Regulations are not enough to contain the toxic carcinogens it will generate along with a huge cost of operating it.

(e)

	Cause	Effect
(iii)	Burning of polyethylene.	Release of formaldehyde and acetaldehyde.

(f) (i) Prior to 1980, recycling and incineration of plastic was negligible.

(g) (iv) lower quality to burn as a fuel on its own.

(h) (iii) (1) is true and (2) correctly explains it.

4. Read the passage given below.

1. Over the last five years, more companies have been actively looking for intern profiles, according to a 2018-19 survey by an online internship and training platform. This survey reveals that India had 80% more internship applications — with 2.2 million applications received in 2018 compared to 1.27 million in the year before. The trend was partly due to more industries looking to have fresh minds and ideas on existing projects for better productivity. What was originally seen as a western concept, getting an internship before plunging into the job market, is fast gaining momentum at Indian workplaces.

2. According to the survey data, India's National Capital Region has been the top provider of internships, with a total of 35% internship opportunities, followed by Mumbai and Bengaluru at 20% and 15%, respectively. This includes opportunities in startups, MNCs and even government entities. The survey also revealed popular fields to find internships in (Fig. 1). There has been growing awareness among the students about the intern profiles sought by hiring companies that often look for people with real-time experience in management than B- school masters.

Internship Trends 2018
Popular fields to find internships in

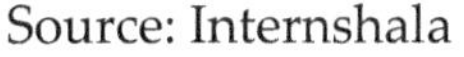

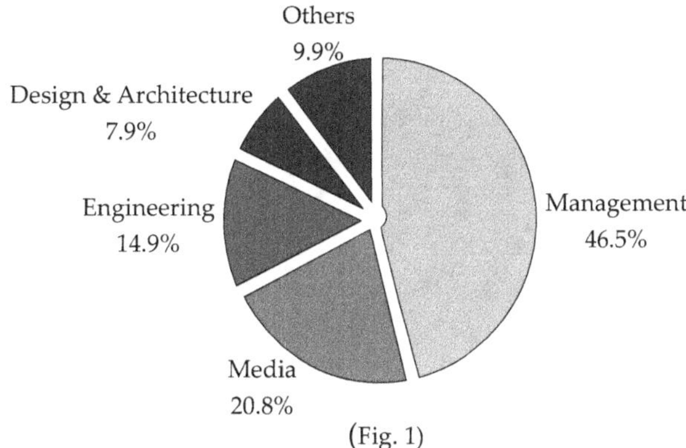

(Fig. 1)

3. The stipend has been an important factor influencing the choice of internships. The survey data reveals that the average stipend offered to interns was recorded as ₹7,000 while the maximum stipend went up to ₹85,000. According to statistics, a greater number of people considered virtual internships than in-office internships. Virtual internships got three times more applications than in-office, since a large chunk of students were the ones already enrolled in various courses, or preferred working from home.

4. Internship portals have sprung up in the last three to four years and many of them already report healthy traffic per month. Reports suggest that on an average, an internship portal company has around 200,000-plus students and some 8,000 companies registered on it. It gets around two lakh visits online every month. The Managing Director of a leading executive search firm says that though these web platforms are working as an effective bridge between the industry and students, most established companies are still reluctant to take too many interns on board for obvious reasons. (355 words)

Source:

(1) *https://www.businessinsider.in/internships-in-india-on-the-rise-with-startups-leading-theway/articleshow/67655265.cms*

(2) *https://www.businesstoday.in/magazine/features/story/online-portals-helping-collegestudents-paid-internships-46215-2014-06-03*

4.1. Based on your understanding of the passage, answer <u>any six</u> out of the eight questions by choosing the correct option.

(a) Select the correct inference with reference to the following:

Over the last five years, more companies have been actively looking for intern profiles...

(i) The past five years have seen active applications by interns to several companies.

(ii) The activity for intern profiling by the companies has reached a gradual downslide over the past five years.

(iii) There were lesser companies searching for intern profiles earlier, as compared to those in the recent five years.

(iv) Several companies have initiated intern profiling five times a year in the recent past.

(b) Select the central idea of the paragraph likely to precede paragraph 1.

(i) Process of registering for internships.

(ii) Knowing more about internships.

(iii) Do's and Don'ts for an internship interview.

(iv) Startups and internships.

(c) Select the option that displays the true statement with reference to Fig. 1.

(i) Internships for Engineering and Management are the top two favourites.

(ii) Design and Architecture internships are significantly more popular than others.

(iii) Internships for Media and others have nearly equal popularity percentage.

(iv) Management internships' popularity is more than twice that for Media.

(d) Based on your reading of paragraphs 2-3, select the appropriate counter-argument to the given argument.

Argument: I don't think you'll be considered for an internship just because you've been the student editor and Head of Student Council.

(i) I think I have a fair chance because I'm applying for a virtual position than an in office one.

(ii) I have real-time experience in managing a team and many companies consider it more meritorious than a degree in management.

(iii) I know that my stipend might be on the lower side but I think that it's a good 'earn while you learn' opportunity.

(iv) Lot of metro-cities have a good percentage of positions open and I think I should definitely take a chance.

(e) Select the option that displays the correct cause-effect relationship.

	Cause	Effect
(i)	Several students had academic courses to complete.	Students applied for online internship.
(ii)	A large chunk of students preferred in-office internships.	Applications were three times more than for virtual internships.
(iii)	A greater number of students wanted to work from home.	Several students had courses to complete.
(iv)	Students applied for online internship.	An equal number of students applied for work-from-home.

(f) The survey statistics mention the average stipend, indicating that:

(i) 50% interns were offered ₹85,000.

(ii) ₹7,000 was the lowest and ₹85,000 was the highest.

(iii) most interns were offered around ₹7,000.

(iv) no intern was offered more than ₹7,000.

(g) The phrase 'healthy traffic' refers to the:

(i) updates from portals about health and road safety.

(ii) statistics about adherence to traffic rules by the portals.

(iii) sizeable number of visitors to the portal per month.

(iv) monthly data about the health of internship applicants.

(h) Read the two statements given below and select the option that suitably explains them.

(1) Established companies are reluctant to take too many interns on board.

(2) Probability of interns leaving the company for a variety of reasons, is high.

(i) (1) is the problem and (2) is the solution for (1).

(ii) (1) is false but (2) correctly explains (1).

(iii) (1) summarises (2).

(iv) (1) is true and (2) is the reason for (1).

ANSWERS

4.1. (a) (iii) There were lesser companies searching for intern profiles earlier, as compared to those in the recent five years.

(b) (ii) Knowing more about internships

(c) (iv) Management internships' popularity is more than twice that for Media.

(d) (ii) I have real time experience in managing a team and many companies consider it more meritorious than a degree in Management.

(e) (i)

Cause	Effect
Several students had academic courses to complete	Students applied for online internship

(f) (iii) most interns were offered around ₹7,000.

(g) (iii) sizeable number of visitors to the portal per month.

(h) (iv) (1) is true and (2) is the reason for (1).

5. Read the passage given below.

1. Over 100 persons have died in the floods in Assam so far while another 147 were killed in lightning strikes in Bihar last month. But with the monsoon season less than half way through, more loss of lives and property are expected if the trend in the past five years is anything to go by.
2. Take for instance human lives lost. In 2015, a little less than 1,000 persons died of flood and rain-related incidents, but in 2019, nearly 2,500 persons had lost their lives, according to government data. The loss of cattle also increased. While in 2015, less than 30,000 cattle died, in 2019, it was nearly 72,000.(See graphic 1)
3. To sum up the flood and its impact in the past five years, over 8,700 people were killed, over 2 lakh cattle died and more than 36 lakh houses were destroyed in floods. The cost of damage to property has also shot up in these five years. While in 2015, the damage suffered totalled ₹33,257 crore, in 2018, the last year for which data is available, it went up to ₹95,736 crore. The cost of damage is likely to be more in 2019 as over a dozen states, including Bihar, Assam, Himachal Pradesh, Kerala and Maharashtra, witnessed large-scale devastation.

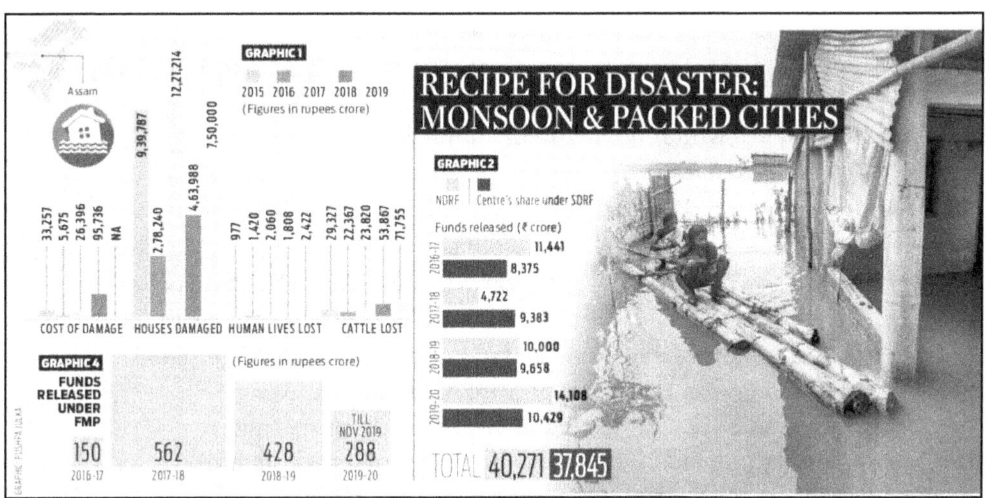

Committees & commissions	Aim	Work
Ganga Flood Control Commission	Flood, erosion in Ganga basin states.	Prepared 23 comprehensive master plans.
Rashtriya Barh Aayog	To evolve coordinated, integrated approach for flood control.	Submitted report in 1980 recommending measures Brahmaputra Board.
Brahmaputra Board	Flood, erosion problems in northeastern states.	Prepared 57 master plans for implementation.
Task Force-2004	Flood management and erosion control.	Submitted report in December 2004, recommending short, long-term measures.
Flood Management Programme	To provide financial assistance for river management, flood control, erosion.	Other than allocating financial aid, it is involved in flood forecasting.

4. Besides the rising damages, the cost to the exchequer towards relief work has also increased. In 2016-17, the Centre released ₹11,441 crore under the National Disaster Relief Fund while its share under the State Disaster Relief Fund was ₹8,375 crore. This increased to ₹14,108 crore and ₹10,429 crore respectively in 2019-20. (See graphic 2)
5. The flood's increasing loss of lives and property appears to make a mockery of all the expert committees, task forces and commissions the government has formed. In 1972, the Ganga Flood Control Commission was set-up in Patna to address the flood problem and erosion in the Ganga basin states. In 1980, the Brahmaputra Board came into existence to address the flood erosion problem in the northeastern states and Sikkim. (See table)

6. The government also launched a Flood Management Programme in the Eleventh Plan (2007-12) for providing financial assistance to state governments to undertake work related to river management, flood control, anti-erosion, drainage development, flood proofing, among others. The FMP was continued for three years under the Twelfth Plan from 2017-18 to 2019-20. It has subsequently been included as a component of the Flood Management and Border Areas Programme in the Ministry of Jal Shakti. But all these appear to have come to a naught as the government's approach is more reactive than proactive, according to experts. Instead of focusing on the real problem, it was only concerned about relief measures, they said.

7. They pointed out that the area affected by floods has doubled since 1950. "The flood-affected area in 1950 was 25 million hectare, now it has doubled to nearly 50 million hectare. But, what is surprising is that nobody looks concerned about the real issues. Earlier, only villages used to be affected but now cities are also getting flooded. Chennai and Patna are just examples. I had written to the government in 2015, highlighting the poor drainage system in cities," said former IIT professor Dinesh Kumar Mishra.

   Himanshu Thakkar, the coordinator of the South Asia Network of Dams, Rivers and People, said effective management of dams could bring down the damage caused by floods. "We have over 5,000 dams. Every dam can help moderate floods in the downstream area but only if it is operated properly," Thakkar said.

5.1. Based on your understanding of the passage, answer any six out of the eight questions by choosing the correct option.

(a) Select the correct inference with reference to the following:

The government's approach is more reactive than proactive, according to experts.

(i) Instead of focusing on the relief measures, the government is only concerned about real problem.
(ii) The government focuses more after damage rather than handling the root cause of the problem.
(iii) The government reacts in a proactive way which is commended by the experts.
(iv) The government focuses on the Ministry of Jal Shakti for such natural disasters.

(b) Select the central idea from the given table on the Committees and commissions:

(i) These committees and commissions are only for North Indian rivers.
(ii) These committees and commissions are involved in flood forecasting.
(iii) These committees and commissions have a severe lack of infrastructure.
(iv) These committees are solely dedicated for flood and erosion relief with their financial aids.

(c) Select the option that displays the true statement with reference to figure given:

(i) The cost of house damages was the highest in 2017.
(ii) Cattle loss was highest in the flood of 2016.
(iii) NDRF released the lowest funds for the year 2019-2020.
(iv) Funds released under FMP were the highest for the year 2016-2017.

(d) Based on your reading of paragraphs 3-4, select the appropriate counter-argument to the given argument:

Argument: The damage relief fund costs are rising because of inflation. However, the overall loss of life and livestock is consistent.

(i) The rising costs are in no way related to inflation because Indian economy does not rely on global market for its currency value.
(ii) Damage to property is greater as compared to loss of lives and livestock.
(iii) Center isn't giving more relief funds for loss of life, so people have stopped reporting the dead.
(iv) It is very clear that the rising damage costs are only because life and livestock damage have increased, because they are the indicator of fund prices.

(e) Select the option that displays the correct cause-effect relationship.

	Cause	Effect
(i)	Cities are also getting flooded.	Poor drainage system in cities.
(ii)	Monsoon season caused flood in Brahmaputra valley.	Over 147 people die in Bihar last month.
(iii)	Flood and erosion in Ganga basin states.	Ganga Flood Control Commission prepared 23 comprehensive master plans.
(iv)	Government task forces are a mockery of all the expert committees.	More than 36 lakh houses were destroyed in floods.

(f) The survey statistics mention the funds released under the NDRF, indicating that:

(i) The center's share under SDRF is always more than NDRF.

(ii) The center's share under SDRF was more than NDRF in 2017-2018.

(iii) The center's share under SDRF is almost similar to NDRF.

(iv) The center's share under SDRF was more than NDRF in 2019-2020.

(g) The phrase 'exchequer' refers to the:

(i) former staff of bank who handles cheques.

(ii) cheques that are given to victims.

(iii) relief funds from NGOs.

(iv) national government treasury.

(h) Read the two statements given below and select the option that suitably explains them.

(1) Every dam can help moderate floods in the downstream area but only if it is operated properly.

(2) Chennai and Patna have poor drainage systems.

(i) (2) is the problem and (1) is the solution for (2).

(ii) (1) and (2) are both false.

(iii) (1) is true but (2) is not the reason for (1).

(iv) (2) is false and (1) explains it.

ANSWERS

5.1. (a) (ii) The government focuses more after damage rather than handling the root cause of the problem.

(b) (iv) These committees are solely dedicated for flood and erosion relief with their financial aids.

(c) (i) The cost of house damages was the highest in 2017.

(d) (iv) It is very clear that the rising damage costs are only because life and livestock damage have increased, because they are the indicator of fund prices.

(e) (iii)

Cause	Effect
Flood and erosion in Ganga basin states.	Ganga Flood Control Commission prepared 23 comprehensive master plans.

(f) (ii) The center's share under SDRF was more than NDRF in 2017-2018.

(g) (iv) national government treasury.

(h) (iii) (1) is true but (2) is not the reason for (1).

6. Read the passage given below.

1. India can easily be considered as one of the most famous religious and cultural hubs in the world. Especially, the southern part of India is home to some of the most famous and historical temples. The temples there are not only religious hubs, but also carry a great historical significance.

2. One such famous temple is the Meenakshi Temple in Madurai, Tamil Nadu. This temple is grand, both in terms of its architecture and in terms of its historical and religious significance. Meenakshi Amman Temple is located in the middle of the city of Madurai in Tamil Nadu. This 2500 years old temple has a glorious past which dates back to 1560. It was designed by Vishwanatha Nayak.

3. The Meenakshi temple is easily the masterpiece of Dravidian architecture. Its complex is huge and is divided into a number of quadrangular enclosures supported by high brick walls. The temple has four entrances facing the four cardinal directions, which is very unusual for a temple in Tamil Nadu. At the core of the temple, there are two temples for Meenakshi (Parvati) and Sundareswarar (Shiva) towards the south and west directions respectively.

4. Meenakshi Temple has the largest temple complex in South India. The temple boasts of a 6-hectare complex which is among the largest temple complexes in the whole of India. Meenakshi Temple is dedicated to the triple-breasted, fish-eyed goddess Meenakshi Amman (or goddess Parvati, as known in the north). 'Fish-eyed' is a phrase often used for a perfect pair of beautiful eyes in Tamil poetry. This temple is special because unlike other temples in South India, which are dedicated to a male deity (mostly, Shiva and Vishnu), this temple is dedicated to a female deity.

5. The Meenakshi temple is one of the most famous temples because of its great architecture and religious value. It attracts approximately 15,000 visitors a day. The number often increases to 25,000 on Fridays. The temple receives an annual revenue of ₹60 million from all the devotees and visitors. (336 words)

Number of Foreigners Visited the Temple during 2012-13 to 2016-17

S. No.	Year	Number of Foreign Visitors	Amount earned as entry fees (in ₹)
1.	2012-13	55,669	27,83,450
2.	2013-14	52,518	26,25,900
3.	2014-15	51,089	25,54,450
4.	2015-16	50,120	25,06,000
5.	2016-17	33,369	16,68,450
6.	Total	2,42,765	2,71,38,250

Source: Joint Commissioner (HRCE) Madurai Meenakshi Amman Temple.

[Source: https://www.newsgram.com.>facts-meenakshi-temple]

6.1. Based on your understanding of the passage, answer any six out of the eight questions by choosing the correct option.

(a) Select the correct inference with reference to the following:

Especially, the southern part of India is home to some of the most famous and historical temples.

(i) The Southern part of India is the only place where temples can be found.

(ii) The most famous and religious temples are not found in the northern part of India.

(iii) The maximum number of famous historical temples of India is exclusively found in the southern part.

(iv) The history of temples begins from the southern part of India.

(b) Select the central idea of the paragraph likely to precede paragraph 1.

(i) Comprehensive study of the temples of India.

(ii) History of the temples of India.

(iii) Glorifying the image of India through its temples.

(iv) Beginning of the religious era in southern India.

(c) Select the option that displays the true statement with reference to the table given above.

(i) The foreign visitors to the temple are gradually increasing.

(ii) Totally, 2,45,765 persons visited the temple during the last five years.

(iii) The visitors paid approximately 2.71 crores as entry fee to the temple during the last five years.

(iv) There is nearly a decline of 60% visitors to the temple since 2012-13 till 2016-17.

(d) Based on your reading of paragraph 5, select the appropriate counter-argument to the given argument.

Argument: The Meenakshi Temple receives a huge amount from all the devotees and visitors.

(i) I think it is the only temple in South India which is dedicated to a female deity.

(ii) I have never seen such a magnificent work of architecture and religious value for which people in large numbers visit here.

(iii) I consider that it attracts more than 15,000 visitors a week who come from all over India.

(iv) The people I consider are bound by a superstition which forces them to visit temple every Friday.

(e) Select the option that displays the correct cause-effect relationship.

	Cause	Effect
(i)	The Meenakshi temple is very special.	The temple is dedicated to a female deity.
(ii)	The Meenakshi Temple is dedicated to a female deity.	This temple is very special.
(iii)	The temple boasts of a 6-hectare complex.	The temple receives an annual revenue of ₹60 million.
(iv)	The Meenakshi Temple is divided into a number of quadrangular enclosures.	It is supported by massive stone walls.

(f) The survey statistics mention in the passage regarding the temple indicates that----

(i) This 2500 years old temple has a glorious past which dates back to late 15th century.

(ii) The number of visitors just increased to double on Fridays.

(iii) The total area in which the temple built is among the largest temple complexes in the whole of India.

(iv) The amount earned as the entry fee in the temple in the year 2016-17 is ₹ 2554450.

(g) The phrase 'religious hubs' refers to the:

(i) place where all religious activities take place.

(ii) center of great religious importance.

(iii) resting place for all the spiritual leaders and saints.

(iv) meetings and decisions related to religious matters take place here.

(h) Read the two statements given below and select the option that suitably explains them.

(1) Meenakshi Temple is special because unlike other temples in South India, which are dedicated to a male deity, this temple is dedicated to a female deity.

(2) This temple is dedicated to goddess Meenakshi Amman (or goddess Parvati, as known in the north).

(i) (1) is the problem and (2) is the solution for (1).

(ii) (1) is false but (2) correctly explains (1).

(iii) (1) summarises (2).

(iv) (1) is true and (2) is the reason for (1).

ANSWERS

6.1. (a) (iii) The maximum number of famous historical temples of India is exclusively found in the southern part.

(b) (ii) History of the temples of India

(c) (iii) The visitors paid approximately 2.71 crores as entry fee to the temple during the last five years.

(d) (ii) I have never seen such a magnificent work of architecture and religious value for which people in large numbers visit here.

(e) (ii)

Cause	Effect
The Meenakshi Temple is dedicated to a female deity.	This temple is very special.

(f) (iii) The total area in which the temple built is among the largest temple complexes in the whole of India.

(g) (ii) center of great religious importance.

(h) (iv) (1) is true and (2) is the reason for (1).

7. Read the passage given below.

1. A new Pew Research Center survey of U.S. adults finds that the social media landscape in early 2018 is defined by a mix of long-standing trends and newly emerging narratives.

2. Facebook and YouTube dominate this landscape, as notable majorities of the US adults use each of these sites. At the same time, younger Americans (especially those ages 18 to 24) stand out for embracing a variety of platforms and using them frequently. Some 78% of 18- to 24-years-old use Snapchat, and a sizeable majority of these users (71%) visit the platform multiple times per day. Similarly, 71% of Americans in this age group now use Instagram and close to half (45%) are Twitter users.

3. As has been the case since the centre began surveying about the use of different social media in 2012, Facebook remains the primary platform for most Americans. Roughly two-thirds of the U.S. adults (68%) now report that they are Facebook users, and roughly three-quarters of those users access Facebook on a daily basis. With the exception of those 65 and older, a majority of Americans across a wide range of demographic groups now use Facebook.

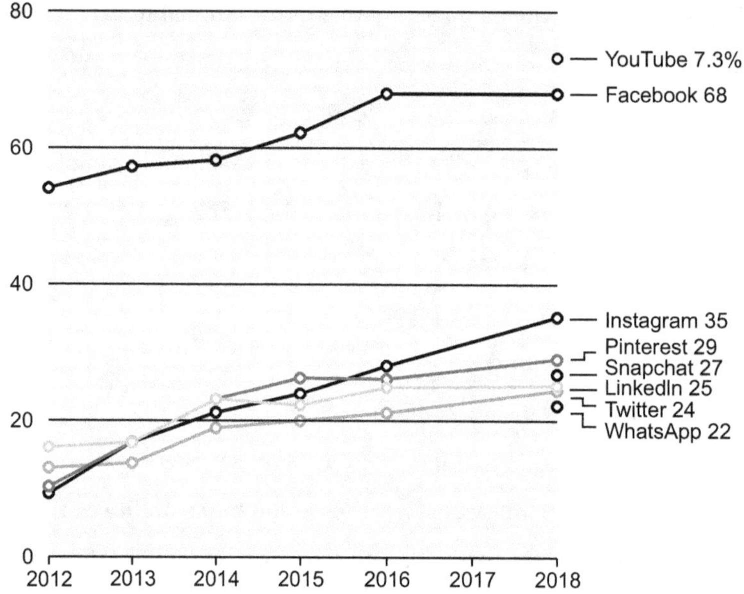

4. But the social media story extends well beyond Facebook. The video-sharing site YouTube – which contains many social elements, even if it is not a traditional social media platform – is now used by nearly three-quarters of the U.S. adults and 94% of 18- to 24-years-old. And the typical (median) American reports that they use three of the eight major platforms that the Centre measured in this survey.
5. These findings also highlight the public's sometimes conflicting attitudes toward social media. For example, the share of social media users who say these platforms would be hard to give up has increased by 12 percentage points compared with a survey conducted in early 2014. But by the same token, a majority of users (59%) say it would not be hard to stop using these sites, including 29% who say it would not be hard at all to give up social media. [SOURCE : https://www.pewresearch.org>]

7.1. Based on your understanding of the passage, answer any six out of the eight questions by choosing the correct option.

(a) Select the correct inference with reference to the following:

Facebook and YouTube dominate this landscape....

(i) Facebook and YouTube have become the most widely held social media sites.
(ii) Facebook and YouTube are the least used social platforms.
(iii) People have regulated using Facebook and YouTube as compared to other sites.
(iv) Majority of Americans prefer Snapchat over Facebook and YouTube.

(b) Select the central idea of the paragraph likely to precede paragraph 1.

(i) Americans addiction to social media.
(ii) Research on social media users.
(iii) Social Media platform and it's abuse.
(iv) Obsession for Facebook and YouTube.

(c) Select the option that displays the true statement with reference to the graph given above.

(i) The least number of users are of Linkedin.
(ii) Pinterest outnumbers Instagram with reference to its users.
(iii) YouTube users are nearly 7% more than the Facebook users.
(iv) Snapchat and Twitter have equal number of users.

(d) Based on your reading of paragraph 2, select the appropriate counter-argument to the given argument.
Argument: 71% of Americans in the age group 18-24 now use Instagram.

(i) The young generation prefers using other platforms as compared to Facebook.
(ii) Facebook has become outdated for the young generation.
(iii) The left out generation, *i.e.*, 29% are old enough to use any social media platform.
(iv) The Americans in the age group 18-24 use multiple platforms along with Facebook.

(e) Select the option that displays the correct cause-effect relationship.

	Cause	Effect
(i)	Younger Americans stand out for embracing a variety of platforms.	They use these platforms recurrently.
(ii)	A majority of generation between 18-24 years visit the Snapchat multiple times per day.	It effects their productive time.
(iii)	Facebook remains the primary platform for most Americans.	It has gained popularity among young users.
(iv)	The YouTube is a video-sharing site which contains many social elements.	It is accepted by majority of the U.S. adults and 94% of 18- to 24-years-old.

(f) The survey statistics mention in the passage regarding Americans indicates that:

(i) people above the age of 45 now use Facebook.
(ii) people below the age of 65 have left using Twitter.
(iii) the video-sharing site YouTube is used by 75% population.
(iv) according to majority of users it would be difficult to stop using these sites.

(g) The phrase 'social media landscape' refers to the:

(i) platform where business relationships are maintained.
(ii) media world and how different platforms are reigning in the digital world.
(iii) landscape which conveys message to social media users and provide them opportunities.
(iv) landscape which help users in finding jobs and securing their future.

(h) Read the two statements given below and select the option that suitably explains them.

(1) The share of social media users who say that it would be hard to give up these platforms has decreased.
(2) Percentage of users who say that it would not be hard to give up these platforms has increased.

(i) (1) is the problem and (2) is the solution for (1).
(ii) (1) is false but (2) correctly explains (1).
(iii) (1) summarises (2).
(iv) (1) is true and (2) is the reason for (1).

ANSWERS

7.1. (a) (i) Facebook and YouTube have become the most widely held social media sites.
(b) (iii) Social Media platforms and it's abuse.
(c) (iii) YouTube users are nearly 7% more than the Facebook users.
(d) (iv) The Americans in the age group 18-24 use multiple platforms along with Facebook.
(e) (iv)

Cause	Effect
The YouTube is a video-sharing site which contains many social elements.	It is accepted by majority of the U.S. adults and 94% of 18- to 24-years-old.

(f) (iii) the video-sharing site YouTube is used by 75% population.
(g) (ii) media world and how different platforms are reigning in the digital world.
(h) (ii) (1) is false but (2) correctly explains (1).

8. Read the passage given below.

1. The cryptocurrency has hit a $2 trillion market cap once again and the big question everyone is asking is how to wade through this crypto universe and they also want to know about the volatility that cryptocurrencies like Bitcoin and Ethereum have seen over the years. Investors might also like to know, which are good ones to buy, which ones one should stay away from.

2. Between July 2020, and January 2021, Bitcoin has seen a meteoric rise all the way to $40,500 -- a rise of 340 percent in just five months, following which had hit a high of $63,500 in April of 2021 and that is where the downfall began. So, between April of 2021, and July, the bitcoin price halved, and now it's back to above $47,000.

3. Not just Bitcoin, massive moves come across a whole host of cryptos -- from Cardano, to Solana to Binance, to Dogecoin. Dogecoin has seen an 8,000 percent performance year-to-date between last year and now. To discuss where the cryptocurrencies would go from here, CNBC-TV18's spoke to Siddharth Menonilind, COO, WazirX; and Sidharth Sogani, founder and CEO, CREBACO.

4. Milind said, "It is a growing market, just last year, probably in August this time, we have much below $400 billion market, and even back then I would have not even thought about, you know, where it can go. But it is good to see a healthy market that's been growing, we reached about some $2.5 trillion and then briefly saw $1.5 trillion, and there has been a good push back now at $2 trillion."

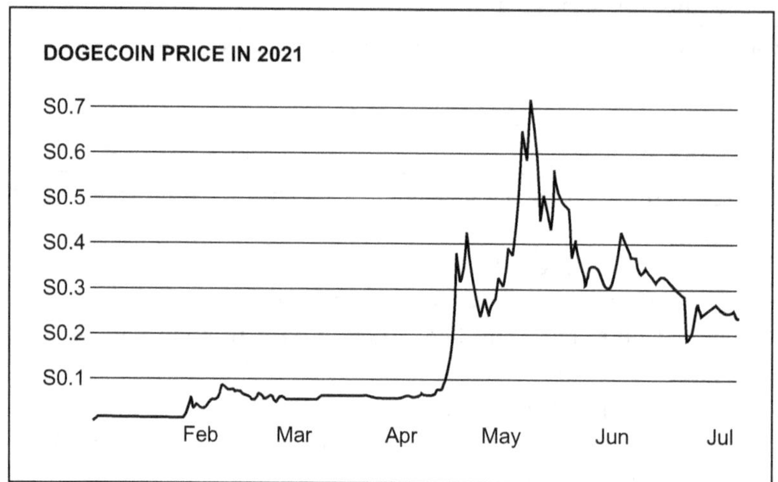

5. "When you think about the whole bull market that we are talking about one thing is very different this time, is that we see a lot more institutional participation, right. And that has changed a lot of things fundamentally, for a lot more people; probably to hedge their risk, in terms of their treasury they want to take a position in terms of hedging against inflation, or this could also be an investment for them," said Menon. (344 words)

[**SOURCE :** https://www.cnbctv18.com › cryptocurrency]

8.1. Based on your understanding of the passage, answer any six out of the eight questions by choosing the correct option.

(a) Select the correct inference with reference to the following:

.......the volatility that cryptocurrencies like Bitcoin and Ethereum have seen over the years.

(i) The graph of cryptocurrency has continuously been risen up in the past few years.

(ii) People are suspicious about the stability of the cryptocurrency so they are unwilling to invest.

(iii) The world of cryptocurrency is persistent and promises good outcomes.

(iv) The value of cryptocurrency has been unstable over the years.

(b) Select the central idea of the paragraph likely to precede paragraph 1.

(i) Youngsters shortcut to succeed.

(ii) An escape from the world of sweats.

(iii) Craze for cryptocurrency.

(iv) Decreasing value of money.

(c) Select the option that displays the true statement with reference to the table given above.

(i) The price of Dogecoin in July was same as it was in the beginning of the year 2021.

(ii) The value of Dogecoin was at peak in the month of May.

(iii) The value of Dogecoin was $0.3 in June.

(iv) After the month of April, there was stability in the price of Dogecoin.

(d) Based on your reading of paragraph II, select the appropriate counter-argument to the given argument.

Argument: Not just Bitcoin, massive moves come across a whole host of cryptos.

(i) The Bitcoin market has seen an enormous downfall.

(ii) There was not only Bitcoin but other cryptocurrencies which also show volatility.

(iii) I think the risk factor can be experienced in any investment.

(iv) We must not put faith in cryptocurrencies but invest in nationalized institutions only.

(e) Select the option that displays the correct cause-effect relationship.

	Cause	Effect
(i)	We see a lot more institutional participation in Bull market.	It has changed a lot of things fundamentally.
(ii)	The cryptocurrency has hit a $2 trillion market cap once again.	The big question everyone is asking is how to stride through this crypto universe.
(iii)	Bitcoin has seen a meteoric rise between July 2020 and January 2021.	More and more people had invested in it
(iv)	Between April of 2021 and July, the price of bitcoin halved.	People have lost their faith in cryptocurrencies.

(f) The survey statistics mention in the passage regarding the cryptocurrency indicates that:

(i) after facing a huge downfall, bitcoin is back to above $47,000.

(ii) there was a rise of 300 percent in the value of bitcoin in just five months.

(iii) there is steadiness in the growth of bitcoin in the year 2021.

(iv) last year during August the market was below $400 million.

(g) The phrase 'healthy market' refers to the:

(i) market which has multiple shops.

(ii) market which is flourishing economy wise.

(iii) market where supply and demand is in proportion.

(iv) market where resources are owned by individuals.

(h) Read the two statements given below and select the option that suitably explains them.

(1) It has evaded public's risk.

(2) There is a lot more institutional participation in the bull market.

(i) (1) is the problem and (2) is the solution for (1).

(ii) (1) is false but (2) correctly explains (1).

(iii) (1) summarises (2).

(iv) (1) is true and (2) is the reason for (1).

ANSWERS

8.1. (a) (iv) The value of cryptocurrency has been unstable over the years.

(b) (iii) Craze for cryptocurrency.

(c) (iii) The value of Dogecoin was $0.3 in June.

(d) (ii) There was not only Bitcoin but other cryptocurrencies which also show volatility.

(e) (ii)

Cause	Effect
The cryptocurrency has hit a $2 trillion market cap once again.	The big question everyone is asking is how to stride through this crypto universe.

(f) (i) after facing a huge downfall, bitcoin is back to above $47,000.

(g) (ii) market which is flourishing economy wise.

(h) (iv) (1) is true (2) is the reason for (1).

9. Read the passage given below.

1. The present generation is well updated in the use of internet and computers. The rapid development in computer technology and increase in accessibility of the internet for academic purposes has changed the face of education for everyone associated with it. Let's look at the data arising out of a recent survey that was done to ascertain the time spent on utilisation of the computer and internet:

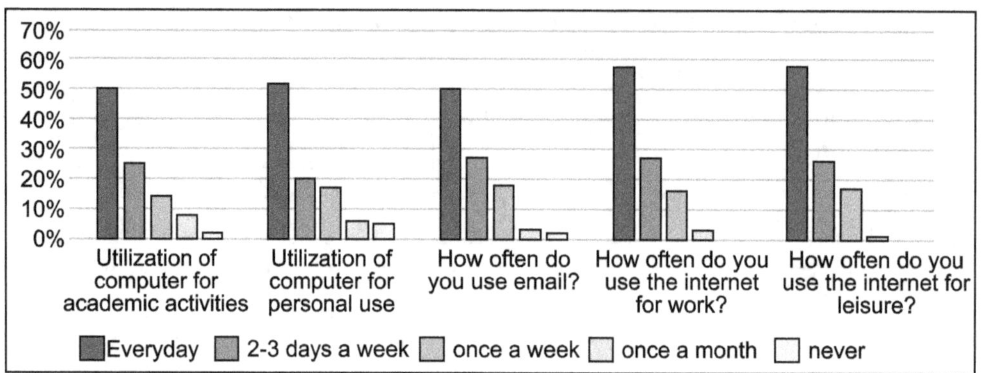

2. At present, many schools and universities have been implementing internet-based learning, as it supplements the conventional teaching methods. The internet provides a wide variety of references and information to academics as well as scientific researchers. Students often turn to it to do their academic assignments and projects.

3. However, research on the Net is very different from traditional library, and the differences can cause problems. The Net is a tremendous resources, but it must be used carefully and critically.

4. According to a 2018 Academic Student e-book Experience Survey, conducted by LJ's research department and sponsored by EBSCO, when reading for pleasure, almost 74% of respondents said they preferred print books for leisure whereas, 45% of respondents chose e-books rather than the printed versions, for research or assignments.

5. When asked what e-book features make them a favourite for research, the respondents were clear. Having page numbers to use in citations, topped the list (75%); followed by the ability to resize text to fit a device's screen (67%); the ability to bookmark pages, highlight text, or take notes for later reference (60%); downloading the entire e-book (57%); and allowing content to be transferred between devices (43%) were the varied responses.

9.1 On the basis of your understanding of the passage, answer any ten of the following questions by choosing the most appropriate option:

(a) According to the passage, one of the reason for the recent transformation of education is the:

(i) techno-efficiency of the present generation.

(ii) expanse of courses on technology.

(iii) simplification of the teaching and learning method.

(iv) easy availability of the internet.

(b) Pick the option that lists statements that are NOT TRUE according to the passage.

1. Internet-based education can only complement familiar methods of education.
2. Net-based learning will replace face-to-face education.
3. The resources that the net provides are a danger to the education system.
4. The current times has seen a rise in the convenience of using the internet for academic purposes.

(i) 1 and 2 (ii) 3 and 4 (iii) 2 and 3 (iv) 1 and 4

(c) The word 'tremendous', as used in paragraph 3, means the same as:

(i) 'expensive' (ii) 'renowned' (iii) 'innovative' (iv) 'incredible'

(d) Based on the graphical chart in the passage, choose the option that correctly states the depiction of internet usage for work and for leisure, for once a month.

1

2

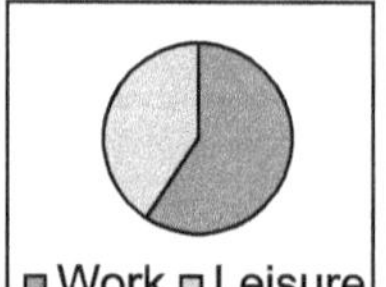

3

4

(i) Option 1 (ii) Option 2 (iii) Option 3 (iv) Option 4

(e) "... but it must be used carefully and critically." The idea of being careful and critical while using the internet, is mainly a reference to:

(i) hardware malfunction.
(ii) plagiarism.
(iii) troubleshooting.
(iv) virus threats.

(f) Based on the given graphical representation of data in the passage, choose the option that lists the statements that are TRUE with respect to the usage of email.

1. The everyday usage of email is more than the everyday usage of computer for personal use.
2. About 18% people use email once a week.
3. There are a smaller number of email users using it 2-3 times a week than the ones using it once a month.
4. Less than 5% of people never use the email.

(i) 1 and 3 (ii) 2 and 4 (iii) 1 and 2 (iv) 3 and 4

(g) Based on the given graphical chart, pick the option that lists the area of zero response from respondents:

(i) never using the internet for work and leisure.
(ii) daily use of the computer for academic activities.
(iii) writing and receiving emails once a week.
(iv) using the internet for personal tasks once a month.

(h) In the cartoon, the student's reaction reveals that he is.......................... .

(i) indignant (ii) apologetic (iii) obedient (iv) inquisitive

(i) Which of the following statements is NOT substantiated by information in paragraph 4?

(i) About three-quarters of the respondents preferred print books for recreational reading.
(ii) A little less than a 50% of the respondents voted for e-books for research or assignments.
(iii) More than 50% respondents stated enjoying both versions of books for leisure reading.
(iv) The survey was intended for understanding the e-book experience among students.

(j) According to the 2018 survey, which is the option that correctly displays the features of:

(A) page numbers for use in citation and (B) content transfer between devices respectively.

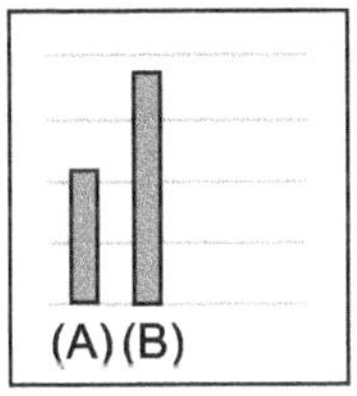

(A) (B) (A) (B) (A) (B) (A) (B)

1 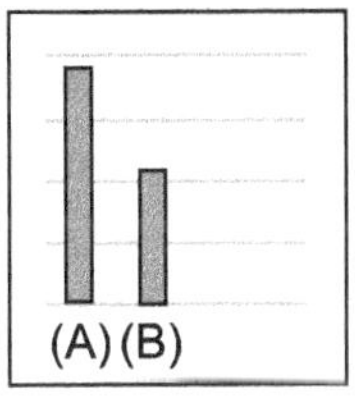 2 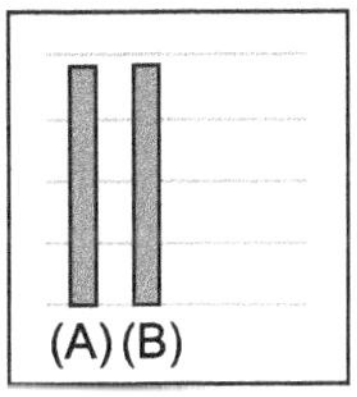 3 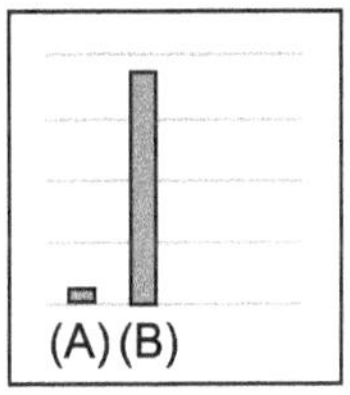 4

(i) Option 1 (ii) Option 2 (iii) Option 3 (iv) Option 4

(k) Arrange the given e-book features preferred for research from the least favourite to the most favourite, from the following:

1. downloading the entire e-book.
2. choosing page numbers in critations.
3. highlighting text.
4. resizing text to fit screen.

(i) 1, 3, 4, 2 (ii) 3, 2, 1, 4 (iii) 2, 4, 3, 1 (iv) 4, 1, 2, 3

ANSWERS

(a) (iv) easy availability of the internet.
(b) (iii) 2 and 3
(c) (iv) 'incredible'.
(d) (iii) Option 3
(e) (ii) plagiarism.
(f) (ii) 2 and 4
(g) (i) never using the internet for work and leisure.
(h) (i) indignant
(i) (iii) More than 50% respondents stated enjoying both versions of books for leisure reading.
(j) (ii) Option 2
(k) (i) 1, 3, 4, 2

10. Read the passage given below.

1. Call it a blessing or a curse of Mother Nature, we have to breathe in over 10,000 litres of air in a day (more than four million litres in a year) to remain alive. By making it essential for life, God has wished that we try to keep the air we breathe clean. Everyone can see the food that is not clean and perhaps refrain from eating it, but one cannot stop breathing even if one can feel the air to be polluted.

2. Several harmful and noxious substances can contaminate the air we breathe. Generally, much is said and written about outdoor air pollution, most of which is due to vehicular and industrial exhausts.

3. Given the fact that most of us spend over 90% of our time indoors, it is most important to recognise that the air we breathe in at home or in offices can be polluted. It can be a cause of ill-health. Air pollutants that are generally present in very low concentrations can assume significance in closed ill-ventilated places.

4. The indoor air pollution can lead to allergic reactions and cause irritation to the skin, the eyes and the nose. But as is logical to assume, the brunt of insult by pollutants is borne by the lungs. It can lead to the development of fresh breathing problems, especially in those who have allergic tendencies, or it can worsen the existing respiratory illnesses like asthma and bronchitis.

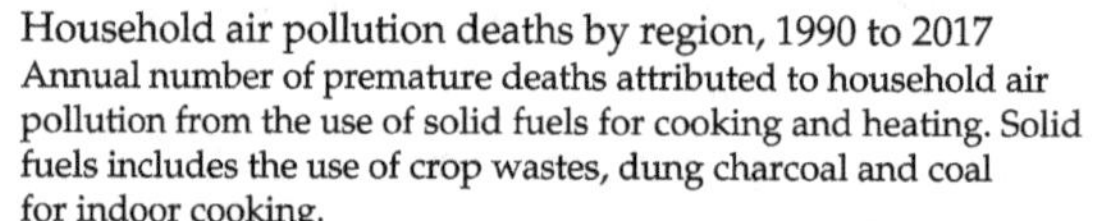

Household air pollution deaths by region, 1990 to 2017
Annual number of premature deaths attributed to household air pollution from the use of solid fuels for cooking and heating. Solid fuels includes the use of crop wastes, dung charcoal and coal for indoor cooking.

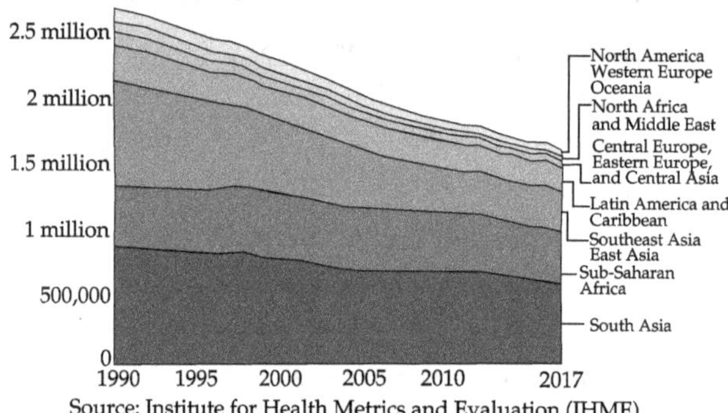

Source: Institute for Health Metrics and Evaluation (IHME)

5. There can be several sources of indoor air pollution. Tobacco smoke is one of the most important air pollutants in closed places. "Passive smoking" or environmental tobacco smoke (ETS) pollution can lead to all the harmful effects of tobacco smoking seen in the smokers in their non-smoking companions. ETS as a health hazard has been unequivocally proven and is also getting social recognition now. One can occasionally see signs displaying the all-important message: "Your smoking is injurious to my health" in offices and homes. The children of smoking parents are among the worst affected persons.

6. The next most important source of indoor air pollution is the allergens. House dust mites (HDM) are very small insects not visible to the naked eye and are the commonest source of allergy in the house. They are ubiquitous and thrive in a warm and moist atmosphere. They breed very fast and are very difficult to eradicate. Modem houses present ample breeding spaces for them in the form of carpets, curtains, mattresses, pillows, etc.

7. Pets form an important part of life for some of us. But they can add plenty of allergens to our indoor atmosphere. Cats are notorious for doing this. Fine particles from feline fur can remain stuck to the upholstery and carpets for a long time, even after the removal of the animal and lead to the worsening of asthma and skin allergies.

8. Moulds, fungi and several other microorganisms thrive in damp conditions and can lead to allergies as well as infections. Humidifiers in the air-conditioning plants provide an ideal environment for certain types of bacteria and have led to major outbreaks of pneumonia. It is important to regularly clean the coolers, air-conditioners and damp areas of the house such as cupboards, lofts, etc., to minimise this risk.

9. Other indoor pollutants are toxic chemicals like cleansing agents, pesticides, paints, solvents and inferior-quality personal-care products, especially aerosols. Very old crumbling pipes, boilers, insulation or false roofing can also be important sources. Asbestos is a hazardous product that can cause cancer in humans.

10. It is important to realise that the air we breathe at home may not be clean always and we must try to eliminate the source of pollution. We should give due consideration to ventilation.

10.1 On the basis of your understanding of the passage, answer any ten of the following questions by choosing the most appropriate option:

(a) The Almighty wants that human beings....................

(i) should try to breathe clean air
(ii) should not pay attention to pollutants
(iii) must ignore ETS
(iv) should become passive smokers

(b) Pick the option that lists statements that are NOT TRUE according to the passage.

1. Moulds, fungi and several other microorganisms thrive in dry conditions.
2. Air pollutants that are generally present in very low concentrations can assume significance in closed ill-ventilated places.
3. Fine particles from feline fur can remain stuck to the upholstery and carpets for a long time.
4. Tobacco smoke is one of the most important air pollutants in open areas.

(i) 1 and 4 (ii) 2 and 3 (iii) 2 and 4 (iv) 1 and 3

(c) Air conditioning plants become the cause of ....

(i) allergies (ii) pneumonia (iii) heart attack (iv) infection

(d) Based on the graphical chart in the passage, choose the option that correctly represents the number of deaths that took place in South East Asia and East Asia from 1990 to 2017.

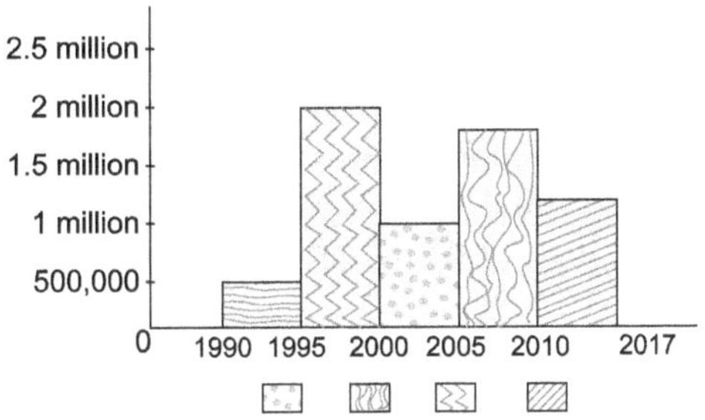

2.5 million
2 million
1.5 million
1 million
500,000
0
1990 1995 2000 2005 2010 2017

(1) (2) (3) (4)

(i) Option 1 (ii) Option 2 (iii) Option 3 (iv) Option 4

(e) Which countries have the least rate of deaths in the year 1990 as per the chart?

(i) East Asian (ii) African (iii) NorthAmerican (iv) South Asian

(f) Based on the given graphical representation of data in the passage, choose the option that lists the statements that are TRUE with respect to the household air pollution deaths from 1990 to 2017.

1. 1 million deaths took place in Sub-Saharan African countries.
2. More than 500,000 people die in South Asia.
3. Latin American countries accounts for less than 500,000 deaths.
4. North America tops the list of deaths due to household air pollution.

(i) 2 and 3 (ii) 1 and 4 (iii) 3 and 4 (iv) 1 and 2

(g) Which of the following is not a source of indoor air pollution?

(i) Air conditioners (iii) Vehicle emission
(ii) Animal dusts (iv) Tobacco smoke

(h) According to the chart, which country has shown the steep decline in the death rate due to the household pollution?

(i) Central European (ii) North American (iii) Latin American (iv) East Asian

(i) How much air do we breath in a year?

(i) 10,000 litres air. (iii) Four million litres.
(ii) More than four million litres. (iv) 90,000 litres.

(j) Which word in the passage means same as 'make impure'? (para 2)

(i) exhausts (ii) contaminate (iii) noxious (iv) harmful

(k) Arrange the given sources of indoor air pollution in the order in which they cause harm from higher to lower risk.

1. Allergens through dust mites
2. Pets
3. Tobacco smoke
4. Moulds and fungi

(i) 3, 1 ,2, 4 (ii) 1, 3, 4, 2 (iii) 2, 4, 3, 1 (iv) 3, 4, 1, 2

ANSWERS

(a) (i) should try to breathe clean air
(b) (i) 1 and 4
(c) (ii) pneumonia
(d) (ii) Option 2
(e) (iv) South Asian
(f) (ii) 1 and 4

(g) (iii) Vehicle emission

(h) (ii) North American

(i) (ii) More than four million litres.

(j) (ii) contaminate

(k) (i) 3, 1, 2, 4

11. Read the passage given below.

1. One can define economic growth as the increase in the inflation-adjusted market value of the goods and services produced by an economy over time. Statisticians conventionally measure such growth as the percent rate of increase in real gross domestic product or real GDP.
2. Growth is usually calculated in real terms - *i.e.*, inflation-adjusted terms – to eliminate the distorting effect of inflation on the prices of goods produced. Measurement of economic growth uses national income accounting. Since economic growth is measured as the annual percent change of gross domestic product (GDP), it has all the advantages and drawbacks of that measure. The economic growth-rates of countries are commonly compared using the ratio of the GDP to population (per-capita income).
3. The, rate of economic growth, refers to the geometric annual rate of growth in GDP between the first. and the last year over a period of time. This growth rate represents the trend in the average level of GDP over the period and ignores any fluctuations in the GDP around this trend.
4. Economists refer to an increase in economic growth caused by more efficient use of inputs (increased productivity of labour, of physical capital, of energy or of materials) as intensive growth. In contrast, GDP growth caused only by increases in the amount of inputs available for use (increased population, for example, or new territory) counts as extensive growth.
5. Development of new goods and services also generates economic growth. As it so happens, in the U.S. about 60% of consumer spending in 2013 went on goods and services that did not exist in 1869.The economic growth rate is calculated from data on GDP estimated by countries' statistical agencies. The rate of growth of GDP per capita is calculated from data on GDP and people for the initial and final periods included in the analysis of the analyst.
6. Living standards vary widely from country to country and furthermore the change in living standards over time varies widely from country to country. Below is a table which shows GDP per person and annualised per person GDP growth for a selection of countries over a period of about 100 years. The GDP per person data are adjusted for inflation, hence they are real. GDP per person (more commonly called per capita GDP) is the GDP of the entire country divided by the number of people in the country; GDP per person is conceptually analogous to average income.

Economic growth by country				
Country	**Period**	**Real GDP per person at beginning of period**	**Real GDP per person at end of period**	**Annualized growth rate**
Japan	1890–2008	$1,504	$35,220	2.71%
Brazil	1900–2008	$779	$10,070	2.40%
Mexico	1900–2008	$1,159	$14,270	2.35%
Germany	1870–2008	$2,184	$35,940	2.05%
Canada	1870–2008	$2,375	$36,220	1.99%
China	1900–2008	$716	$6,020	1.99%
United States	1870–2008	$4,007	$46,970	1.80%
Argentina	1900–2008	$2,293	$14,020	1.69%
United Kingdom	1870–2008	$4,808	$36,130	1.47%
India	1900–2008	$675	$2,960	1.38%
Indonesia	1900–2008	$891	$3,830	1.36%
Bangladesh	1900–2008	$623	$1,440	0.78%

7. Seemingly small differences in yearly GDP growth lead to large changes in GDP when compounded over time. For instance, in the above table, GDP per person in the United Kingdom in the year 1870 was $4,808. At the same time in the United States, GDP per person was $4,007, lower than the UK by about 20%. However, in 2008 the positions were reversed: GDP per person was $36,130 in the United Kingdom and $46,970 in the United States, *i.e.*, GDP per person in the US was 30% more than it was in the UK. As the above table shows,

this means that GDP per person grew, on average, by 1.80% per year in the US and by 1.47% in the UK. Thus, a difference in GDP growth by only a few tenths of a percent per year results in large differences in outcomes when the growth is persistent over a generation.

11.1 On the basis of your understanding of the passage, answer any ten of the following questions by choosing the most appropriate option:

(a) How do Statisticians measure economic growth?

(i) Increase in the inflation-adjusted market value of goods.
(ii) Decrease in the inflation-adjusted market value of goods.
(iii) Percent rate of increase in real GDP.
(iv) Increase in the production of goods and services.

(b) From the tabulated data given below, choose the right option that indicates the CORRECT annualised growth rate.

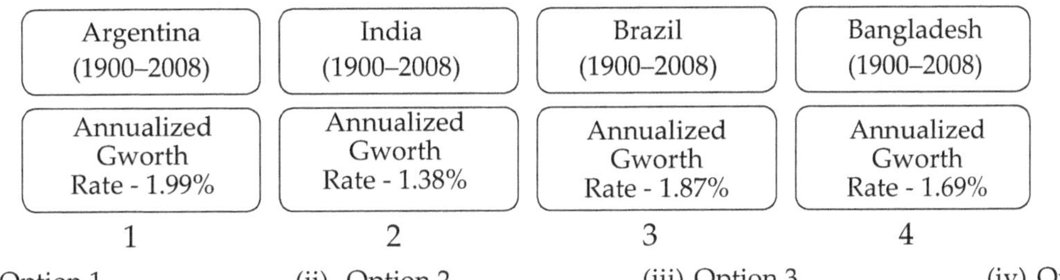

(i) Option 1 (ii) Option 2 (iii) Option 3 (iv) Option 4

(c) Which country's annualised growth rate is 2.05%?

(i) Germany (ii) Canada (iii) China (iv) Brazil

(d) Based on the given table in the passage, choose the option that list the statements that are TRUE with respect to the GDP per person.

1. GDP per person in the US in 1870 was higher than the GDP in the UK.
2. GDP per person in the UK was higher than the GDP in the US.
3. GDP per person in Canada in 2008 was higher than the GDP in Germany.
4. GDP per person in Germany in 2008 was higher than the GDP in Canada.

(i) 1 and 2 (ii) 2 and 3 (iii) 3 and 4 (iv) 1 and 4

(e) Pick the option that lists statement that is NOT TRUE in the passage.

(i) Economic growth rate represents the trend in the average level of GDP over the period including any fluctuations in the GDP around this trend.
(ii) Economic growth is measured as the annual percentage change of gross domestic product (GDP), it has all the advantages and drawbacks of that measure.
(iii) Development of new goods and services also generates economic growth.
(iv) The GDP per person data are unchanged for inflation, hence they are real.

(f) How is the rate of growth of GDP per capita is calculated?

(i) From data on GDP
(ii) Geometrically
(iii) According to change in GDP
(iv) On inflated adjusted terms

(g) According to the 1890-2008 survey, which option CORRECTLY represents real GDP per person in Mexico?

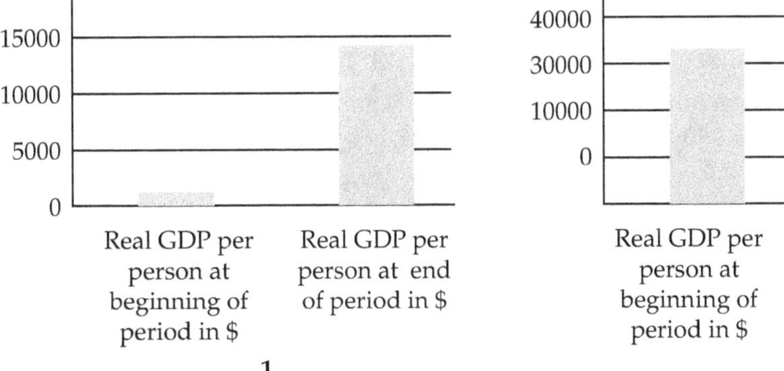

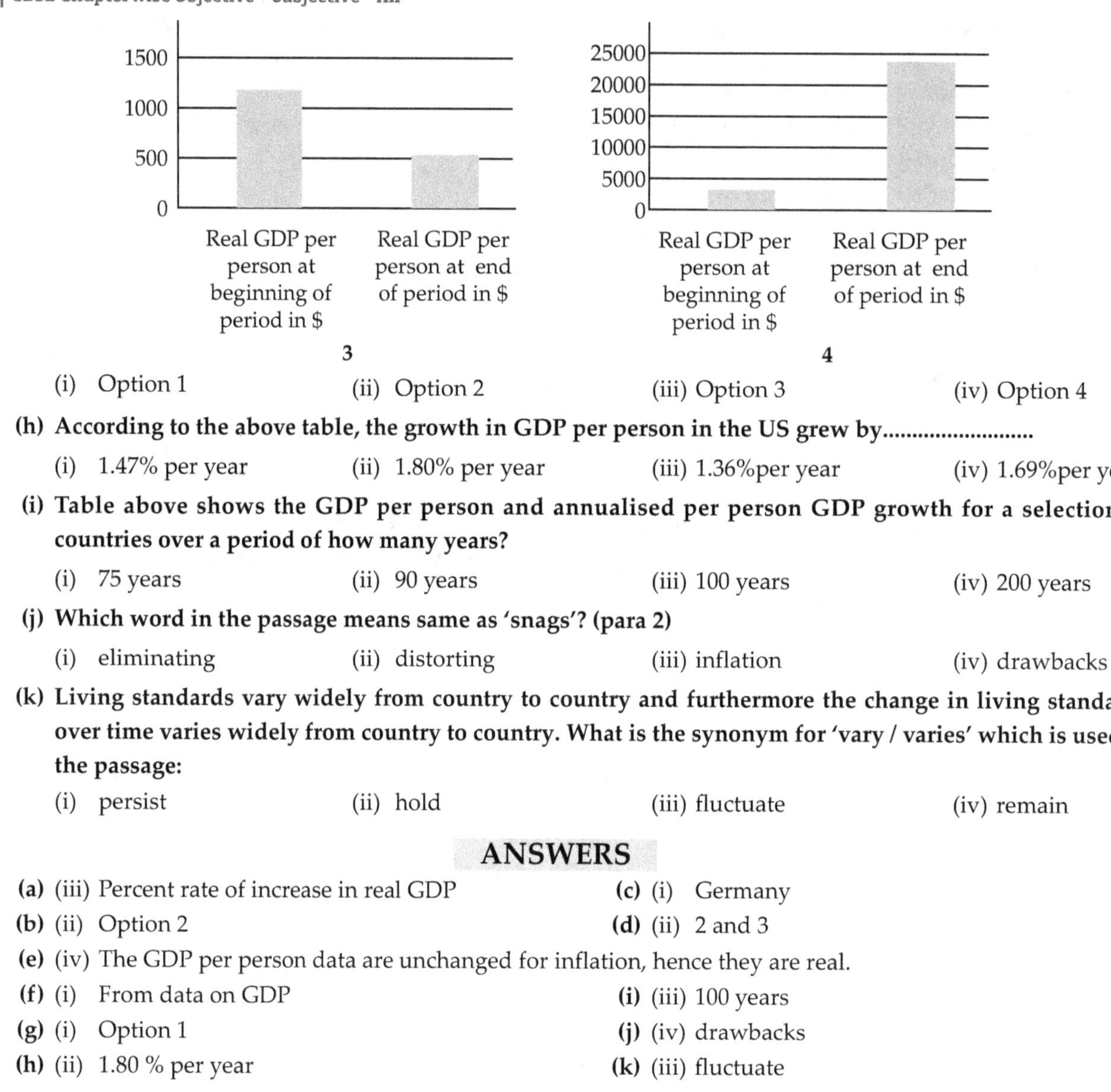

(i) Option 1 (ii) Option 2 (iii) Option 3 (iv) Option 4

(h) According to the above table, the growth in GDP per person in the US grew by.........................

(i) 1.47% per year (ii) 1.80% per year (iii) 1.36%per year (iv) 1.69%per year

(i) Table above shows the GDP per person and annualised per person GDP growth for a selection of countries over a period of how many years?

(i) 75 years (ii) 90 years (iii) 100 years (iv) 200 years

(j) Which word in the passage means same as 'snags'? (para 2)

(i) eliminating (ii) distorting (iii) inflation (iv) drawbacks

(k) Living standards vary widely from country to country and furthermore the change in living standards over time varies widely from country to country. What is the synonym for 'vary / varies' which is used in the passage:

(i) persist (ii) hold (iii) fluctuate (iv) remain

ANSWERS

(a) (iii) Percent rate of increase in real GDP
(b) (ii) Option 2
(c) (i) Germany
(d) (ii) 2 and 3
(e) (iv) The GDP per person data are unchanged for inflation, hence they are real.
(f) (i) From data on GDP
(g) (i) Option 1
(h) (ii) 1.80 % per year
(i) (iii) 100 years
(j) (iv) drawbacks
(k) (iii) fluctuate

12. Read the passage given below.

1. The World Trade Organisation (WTO) Ministerial Conference which commenced in Hong Kong on December 13, 2005 adopted a declaration on December 18, 2005 after six days of acrimonious negotiations between developed and developing countries. Although initially there was a show of unity among developing countries especially on the issue of agriculture, which was reflected in the formation of the G-110, the final outcome of the Ministerial Declaration has been thoroughly anti-development.

2. The Ministerial Declaration has not only failed to address substantially the concerns of developing countries but has actually paved the way for an eventual trade deal by the end of 2006, which is going to be severely detrimental to their interests. It is clear by now that the so-called "Development Round" launched in Doha in 2001 has been manipulated by developed countries, especially the United States and the members of the European Union, to push for further trade liberalization in developing countries while they continue to protect their economies through high subsidies and non-tariff barriers.

3. Far from redressing the asymmetries of the global trading system, the Doha round seems to be heading for another catastrophe for the developing world. The EU stuck to its intransigent position on the deadline of 2013 for the elimination of export subsidies and developing countries gave up their demand for an earlier end date despite the initial collective efforts of the G-110. There has been no concrete commitment on the reduction of domestic support other than export subsidies. The EU can continue to subsidise agriculture to the tune of 55 billion euros a year. The EU budget adopted recently ensures that nothing can be touched in the agriculture budget till at least 2013. The US budget reconciliation process and the final vote in the Congress are set to extend domestic support to agriculture and counter-cyclical support to commodities up to around 2011.

4. Even in the case of cotton, the agreement to eliminate subsidies by 2006 is restricted to export subsidies only and does not include other forms of domestic support. The US refused to give duty-free access to exports from Least-Developed Countries (LDCs) for 99.9 percent of product lines and the final agreement was on 97 per cent of them, which would enable the US and Japan to deny market access to LDCs in product lines such as rice and textiles.

   Much of the Aid for Trade for LDCs, which is being showcased by developed countries as a "development package", is disguised in conditional loan packages that are contingent upon further opening up of their markets. India's prime interest in agriculture was to ensure the protection of its small and marginal farmers from the onslaught of artificially low-priced imports or threats thereof.

5. The proposals for agricultural tariff cuts, which are already on the table, are quite ambitious and the G-20 has already committed itself to undertake cuts to the extent of two-thirds of the level applicable to developed countries. Moreover, India has 100 percent tariff lines bound in agriculture with the difference in the applied level and the bound level not very marked in many lines. In this context, the systemic problem face by India's small and marginal farmers practising subsistence agriculture will only get aggravated as a result of the impending tariff cuts that have been agreed upon. The government claims that the right to designate a number of agricultural product lines as special products based upon the consideration of food and livelihood security and to establish a special safeguard mechanism based on import quantity and price triggers, which have been mentioned in the Ministerial Text, adequately addresses the concerns of Indian farmers.

6. The claim is questionable since the nature as well as the extent of protection under the category of special products remains restricted and the special safeguard mechanism, admittedly, is a measure to deal with an emergency and is of "a temporary nature". Therefore, seen in the light of the insignificant reductions in domestic farm subsidies by developed countries, tariff reduction commitments by developing countries seem to be totally unjustifiable. Developing countries have also agreed on the Swiss formula for tariff cuts under Non-Agricultural Market Access (NAMA). Although the coefficients will be negotiated later, it is unlikely that developed countries will agree upon sufficiently large coefficients for the formula that would ensure adequate policy space for developing countries in future to facilitate development of different sectors of their industries.

7. The Ministerial Text's ritual references to "less than full reciprocity" and "special and differential treatment" fails to conceal the fact that the flexibilities provided by the July framework regarding the nature of the tariff reduction formula, product coverage, the extent of binding and the depth of cuts have been done away with. Moreover, no concrete commitment has been obtained in the Ministerial Text for the removal of the Non-Tariff barriers by developed countries, which is their principal mode of protection, despite developing countries making such major concessions on industrial tariff cuts. The fact of the matter is that developing countries have committed themselves to cuts in both agricultural and industrial tariffs, without getting anything substantial in return from developed countries. And India has facilitated the adoption of this bad deal in the backdrop of an acute crisis faced by Indian agriculture.

12.1 On the basis of your understanding of the passage, answer any ten of the following questions by choosing the most appropriate option:

(a) What type of negotiations took place between developed and developing countries in the Ministerial Conference of the WTO?

(i) Fruitful (ii) Friendly (iii) Bitter (iv) Helpful

(b) Pick the option that lists statements that are NOT TRUE according to the passage.

1. Initially there was a show of unity among developing countries especially on the issue of environment.
2. Developing countries have also agreed on the Swiss formula for tariff cuts under Non-Agricultural Market Access
3. The US agreed to give duty-free access to exports from Least-Developed Countries.
4. India's prime interest in agriculture was to ensure the protection of its small and marginal farmers from the onslaught of artificially low-priced imports or threats thereof.

(i) 1 and 3 (ii) 2 and 3 (iii) 3 and 4 (iv) 1 and 4

(c) How do developed countries like the US and the European Union protect their economies?

(i) By liberalising trade barrier
(ii) By restoring the global trading system
(iii) Through high subsidies and non-tariff barriers
(iv) By subsidising agriculture

(d) Based on the graphical chart in the passage, choose the option that represents the comparative study of Annual Percentage change of Europe and Africa in the year 2018.

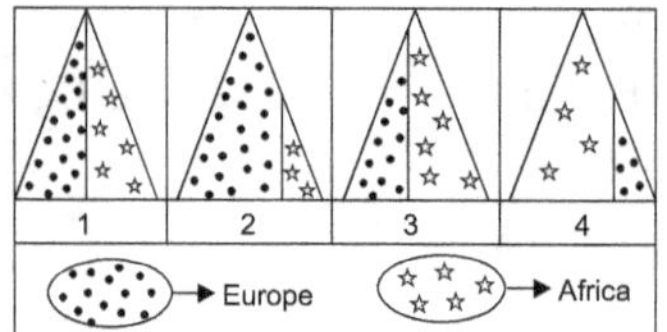

(i) Option 1 (ii) Option 2 (iii) Option 3 (iv) Option 4

(e) The US refused to give duty-free access to exports from which countries?

(i) Developed countries
(ii) Developing countries
(iii) Under developed countries
(iv) Least developed countries

(f) Based on the given graphical representation of data in the passage, choose the option that lists the statements that are TRUE with respect to the usage of email.

1. Annual percentage change in the growth of Middle East and Asian countries is same in 2018.
2. Worldwide growth of commercial services was more in 2017 than in 2018.
3. The growth percentage of commercial services in Asia was more in 2017 but fell down in 2018.
4. Percentage change in the growth in South and Central America goes in negative in the year 2018.

(i) 1 and 3 (ii) 2 and 3 (iii) 3 and 4 (iv) 1 and 4

(g) Which claim of the Indian Government is questionable?

(i) Right to designate agriculture product lines as special products considering food and livelihood security.
(ii) India has facilitated the adoption of a beneficial deal for agriculture at WTO.
(iii) Formation of G-110 proves unity among developing countries.
(iv) Developing countries can negotiate large coefficient on the Swiss formula for tariff cuts.

(h) Why is it that the imbalances of the global trading system appear to be catastrophic?

(i) EU has not moved away from its declared position.
(ii) US refused to give duty- free access to exports from LDCs.
(iii) The collective efforts of G-110 failed.
(iv) All of the above

(i) How much budget the EU has proposed to subsidise agriculture?

(i) 55 million euros a year.
(ii) 55 billion euros a year.
(iii) 65 billion euros a year.
(iv) 75 million euros a year.

(j) Which word in the passage means same as 'intensified'? (para 5)

(i) Impending (ii) Aggravated (iii) Designate (iv) Triggers

(k) Arrange the given statements in the order in which they are featured in the passage.

1. It is clear by now that the so-called "Development Round" launched in Doha in 2001 has been manipulated by developed countries.
2. The EU stuck to its intransigent position on the deadline of 2013 for the elimination of export subsidies.
3. The World Trade Organisation (WTO) Ministerial Conference commenced in Hong Kong on December 13, 2005.
4. India has 100 percent tariff lines bound in agriculture with the difference in the applied level and the bound level not very marked in many lines.

(i) 1, 4, 2, 3 (ii) 2, 1, 4, 3 (iii) 3, 1, 2, 4 (iv) 1, 3, 2, 4

ANSWERS

(a) (iii) Bitter
(b) (i) 1 and 3
(c) (iii) Through high subsidies and non-tariff barriers
(d) (i) Option 1
(e) (iv) Least Developed countries
(f) (iv) 1 and 4
(g) (i) Right to designate agriculture product lines as special products considering food and livelihood security
(h) (iv) All of the above
(i) (ii) 55 billion euros a year
(j) (ii) Aggravated
(k) (iii) 3, 1, 2, 4

❑❑

SECTION - B
WRITING SKILLS

Invitations and Replies

1

Invitations are, generally, printed cards through which we invite our guests on some auspicious occasion like wedding, birthday, anniversaries, house warming, inauguration of a shop / factory etc.

Invitations are of two types: (a) Formal (b) Informal.

- ➢ They can be printed on cards or can be drafted in the form of letters.
- ➢ They are a single sentence presentation in third person in case of a formal invitation and first / second person in case of an informal invitation.
- ➢ An invitation answers the questions of who, when, where, what time and for what *i.e.*,
  - (a) The occasion.
  - (b) Name of the host.
  - (c) Date, time and venue.
  - (d) RSVP.

Formal invitations are formal, polite, pleasant and courteous whereas, informal invitations generally take the shape and form of personal letters. We use these to invite our friends, relatives and dear ones. In informal invitations, the tone and treatment is relaxed, informal and friendly.

Sample Invitations :

1. Your father, Mr. Raj Kumar Gupta, residing at K-18, 13th Cross Malleswaram, Bangalore wants to celebrate the success of your brother Rohan's clearing the IIT-JEE Entrance Examination and securing admission in IIT Powai, Mumbai. He wants you to draft a formal invitation for him on his behalf. Draft the invitation for him.

Mrs. and Mr. Raj Kumar Gupta

request your presence at

UTSAV BANQUET HALL

84-Kamla Road, Rajaji Nagar, Bangalore-5

at 8.00 p.m. on 1st July, 20XX

to celebrate their son's success in the

IIT-JEE ENTRANCE EXAMINATION

RSVP:

Mrs. & Mr. Rajkumar Gupta

271201/973296964

2. You are Rukmini/Raja of R-201, Fort Road, Chennai. You have just purchased a new house. You decide to have a house-warming ceremony and invite your cousin Balaji. Write the invitation in **50 words** giving all necessary details.

R-201, Fort Road,
Chennai
20th October, 20XX

Dear Balaji,

I am glad to tell you that I've purchased a new house and to celebrate the event, we thought of a small get together with our close friends and relatives. Therefore I invite you to our housewarming party on 25th October, 20XX at 7:30 p.m. We will have dinner to commemorate the event. I would be delighted if you would bring uncle along with you.

Yours
Rukmini/Raja

3. On behalf of the principal of your school draft a formal invitation to be sent to the grand parents of the students on the occasion of The Grand Parents Day. Invent other details yourself.

The Principal, Staff & Students

Of

St. Paul's School, Vijay Nagar, Agra

invite you on the occassion of

The Grand Parents Day

On Tuesday, 25th February, 20XX at 8:00 a.m.

in the school auditorium

Shree G.K. Bansal

The Chairman of the school will

to be the chief guest for the event.

RSVP:

Principal

Ph. 0562-272356XX

Sample Replies to Invitation :

1. Write a formal reply to Mrs. and Mr. Chawla accepting the invitation to attend the birthday party of their son. You are Mr. Anil Singh. Invent other details yourself.

Ans. 12th January, 20XX

Mrs. and Mr. Anil Singh thank Mrs. and Mr. Gupta for inviting them on the occasion of the 14th birthday of their son, Sunil, on Monday, 28th January, 20XX at Konark Hotel and assure that they will be glad to attend the function. They will be present to wish the boy many happy returns of the day.

Best wishes

Singhs

2. You are Dr. Stanzin, a certified art therapist from Leh. You have been invited by G. D. Public School. Jammu, to conduct a seminar for students on 'Art Therapy the Way Forward''. This seminar is to introduce students to the usefulness of art in dealing with personal and social problems. Write your reply, in about **50 words** accepting the invitation.

Ans.

The Principal
G. D Public School
Jammu
16th November, 20XX
Dear Sir/Madam

I am extremely grateful to you for inviting me to conduct the seminar for students on 'Art Therapy the Way Forward' and highly appreciate the initiative taken by the school in this arena. This therapy is very useful these days as it will relieve the students from any unwanted stress they have. I will be delighted to attend the function as per the schedule and therefore accept the invitation and confirm my presence at the scheduled venue at 11:00 a.m.

Thanking you
Yours sincerely
Dr. Stanzin

Practice Exercise :

1. For the House Warming Ceremony, you plan to invite your friends, relatives and colleagues. You are Raman and Shanti. Write out the invitation for the same.

2. You are Hemant/Hema. You have been invited to attend a seminar on 'Conservation of Water' organised by department of water supply of your district. Send a formal reply in not more than 50 words accepting the invitation.

Choose the correct option:

1. **Which one is informal expression of inviting someone?**
   (a) Would you like to come to my wedding party?
   (b) Could you like to come to my wedding party?
   (c) I would like to invite you to come to my birthday party.
   (d) Do you want to come to my wedding party?
2. **What is the purpose of invitation expression?**
   (a) To persuade someone to come to occasion/party.
   (b) To tell someone about a celebration.
   (c) To invite someone to come to occasion/party.
   (d) To explain someone about a celebration.
3. **Which one is expression of accepting invitation?**
   (a) I don't think I can join. sorry.
   (b) Sorry, I don't think I can.
   (c) That's sounds great. Thanks.
   (d) I'd loved to but I have appointment with my mother.
4. **Which one is informal invitation?**
   (a) An invitation to the opening of a school.
   (b) An invitation to a graduation ceremony.
   (c) An invitation to a wedding.
   (d) An invitation to a birthday party.
5. **Peter :** We'll throw a small party. Can you join us?
   Mr. Smith : I would love to Peter, but I might be flying to Colorado on Sunday.

Peter : Well, we'll miss you if you can't make it, but I understan(d).

Based on the conversation above, which is statement is true?

(a) Mr. smith declines peter's invitation.
(b) Peter will go to Colorado.
(c) Mr. Smith will go to Colorado on Monday.
(d) Peter got disappointed as Mr. Smith declines to come.

6. **What does R.V.S.P mean?**

(a) Please respond
(b) Please come
(c) Please don't be late
(d) Please call

7.

Please join us
In celebrating the graduation of:
YUNIAR BESTIANA, M.Ed.
Sunday, November 30th, 2017
at 8 p.m.
Abdul Wahid Avenue 56 Bondowoso
Mr. and Mrs. Sudjiatmojo Please
RSVP by November 28th, 2017
Desi - 085739999789

Which statement is true based on the text?

(a) Mr. and Mrs. Sudjiatmojo held this party for themselves.
(b) Yuniar Bestiana has just finished her study.
(c) This party will be held for Desi.
(d) People should call Desi to see Yuniar Bestiana.

8. **Mr and Mrs. Ibrahim invite you to share the joy of the marriage uniting their daughter Alina Ibrahim to Ahmad Ismail on Friday, the 13th of June 2018, at 3 o'clock in the afternoon.**

Venue: At Gajah Wong Restaurant JI. Affandi Yogyakarta

The purpose of the text is to invite you ....

(a) To attend Mr and Mrs Ibrahim's marriage.
(b) To attend Alina and Ahmad's wedding party.
(c) To unite Alina and Ahmad in a wedding party.
(d) To have dinner with Mr. Ibrahim's family.

9.

The Principal, Staff And Teachers
Of
Sunrise Public School
take pleasure in inviting
noted stage artist
MS. NALINI
to grace the one-act play competition
From 8:30 am to 11:00 am RSVP
Awaiting a favourable response from your end
RSVP
Karuna, Cultural Secretary
987xxxxx00

What is missing in the above given invitation?

(a) Venue (b) Time (c) Subscription (d) None of these

10. **Formal invitations are usually written in:**

(a) first person (b) second person (c) third person (d) any of these

11. **A formal invitation generally includes:**

(a) request
(b) solicitation
(c) an attempt to get another person to join a specific event
(d) all of the above

12. **What is not included in informal invitation?**

(a) Sender's address (c) Date
(b) Receiver's address (d) None of these

13. **Informal invitations are usually written in:**

(a) first person (c) both (a) and (b)
(b) third person (d) none of these

14. The sender's address is followed by ____________ in informal invitation.

(a) receiver's address (c) main body
(b) salutation (d) date

15. **The date in invitation card is written on:**

(a) left side of the page. (b) right side of the page.
(c) centre of the page. (d) bottom of the page.

16. **Choose the statement that does not describe the feature of formal invitation.**

(a) A polite and courteous tone should be used.
(b) It is generally enclosed in box.
(c) It is written in simple present tense.
(d) They follow the pattern of ordinary personal letters.

17. **Choose the statement that does not describe the feature of informal invitation.**

(a) They are written to friends, relatives and acquaintance.
(b) The style and tone is relaxed and informal.
(c) They are written in third person.
(d) They follow the pattern of ordinary personal letter.

18. **On the basis of the invitation drafted above, answer the following questions:**

The Management, Staff and Students [1]
of
Government Model Sr. Se(c) School, Chandigarh [2]
cordially invites you to their
ANNUAL FUNCTION
Tarang
at 6.00 p.m. on 4 December 2OXX
in
The National Auditorium
Sh. Promod Kumar
Secretary Higher Education has kindly consented to be the chief guest.

Identify the part of the formal invitation card numbered.

(a) Venue and time (c) Subscription
(b) Name of the host (d) Salutation

19. Identify the part of the formal invitation card numbered.

(a) Name of the host
(b) Name of the institution
(c) Venue
(d) None of these

20. What is the purpose of the invitation drafted above?

(a) To explain about annual function to someone.
(b) To invite someone to attend annual function.
(c) To retell about a program.
(d) None of these

ANSWERS

1. (a) Western countries have a shortage of manpower in this very field.
2. (c) To invite someone to come to occasion/party.
3. (c) That's sounds great. Thanks.
4. (d) An invitation to a birthday party.
5. (a) Mr. smith declines peter's invitation.
6. (a) Please respond
7. (b) Yuniar Bestiana has just finished her study.
8. (b) To attend Alina and Ahmad's wedding party.
9. (a) Venue
10. (c) third person
11. (d) all of the above
12. (b) Receiver's address
13. (a) first person
14. (d) date
15. (a) left side of the page.
16. (d) They follow the pattern of ordinary personal letters.
17. (c) They are written in third person.
18. (b) Name of the host
19. (b) Name of the institution
20. (b) To invite someone to attend annual function.

❑❑

Letter Writing

2

The most common form of a written communication is the letter. Letter writing is an indispensable activity of human society. We write letters to our friends and relatives to maintain contacts with them. However, in the present time with the boom in methods of communication, many of us don't have the time, inclination, or the temperament and the art to write letters, So telephone, fax and e-mail have replaced personal (informal) letters.

However, formal letters are still in vogue, Commerce, trade, official correspondence, public representation, complaints and other dealings, transactions and communication with the people are still conducted through letters.

Formal Letters : They are the letters written using formal language and in a precise manner. It is a means of communication between two parties, within an organisation, or between third parties.

Important Instructions :

- Since CBSE follows the block format, everything should be left aligned.
- Open and close with a salutation.
- Write the letter in at least three paragraphs.
- Use formal language, avoid starting with 'I', keep, sentences short and to the point and do not use contractions.
- End with a short sentence that anticipates the response of the addressee.
- Use polite and impersonal tone.
- Use passive voice where possible.
- Be brief and to the point, do not beat about the bush.
- Be clear and specific; state the purpose clearly and concisely.
- Be positive and polite even if you are writing a complaint.

Business Letters :

They can be primarily classified into :

(i) Letter to the Editor

(ii) Letters of enquiry/asking for information

(iii) Replying to enquiry/giving information

(iv) Placing orders

(v) Cancelling orders

(vi) Complaints

(vii) Requests

(viii) Writing a Job Application

Important Instructions Regarding the Content of the Letter :

- Begin by identifying yourself.
- Clearly state the purpose of writing in the subjects, as well as, in the introduction of the letter.
- Give relevant details such as order date, order number, date of advertisement, letter number, demand draft number etc.
- Make a request for appropriate action but remember the editor cannot do anything to solve your problem. He can only publish your concerns.
- Use polite language and a pleasant tone.
- Convey the message briefly and in a straightforward manner.
- Dont's repeat any point.

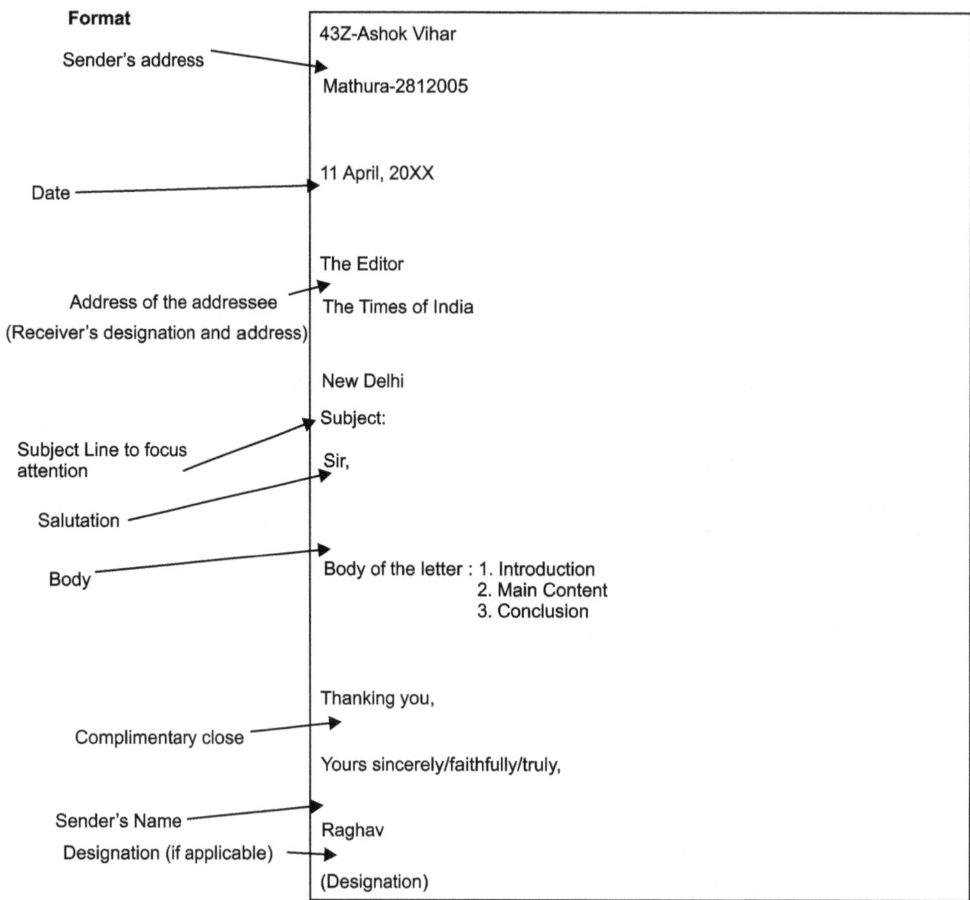

Formal and Informal Invitation Letters

1. *The literary club of your school (A.B.C. Public School) is putting up the play "Waiting for Godot." As secretary of the club, draft an invitation inviting the famous writer Mr S.K. Bansal to be guest of honour at the function. Write the invitation in not more than 50 words. You are Gourav/Gauri.*

(i) The purpose of this letter is to invite S.K. Bansal as___________.

(A) guest of honour at a school function

(B) to take participate in the function

(C) to distribute awards

(D) all of the above

(a) Only (A) (b) Both (A) and (B) (c) Both (B) and (C) (d) Only (D)

Ans. (a) Only (A)

(ii) What is letter writing?

(a) People write a letter to improve their writing skills.

(b) Any written statement id letter.

(c) It is giving information through message writing.

(d) None of the above

Ans. (c) It is giving information through message writing.

(iii) How would you write a salutation in the given letter?

(a) Dear Sir/Madam (b) To The Editor (c) Dear Brother (d) Dear

Ans. (a) Dear Sir/Madam

(iv) Which of the following complimentary closure will you use in the given letter?

(a) Your loving (b) Yours faithfully (c) Yours caring (d) All of these

Ans. (b) Yours faithfully

(v) Which of the following are needed to write a formal letter?

(a) Date
(b) Contact details of receivers
(c) Both (a) and (b)
(d) None of these

Ans. (c) Both (a) and (b)

2. *As the principal of a reputed college, you have been invited to inaugurate a Book Exhibition in your neighbourhood. Draft a reply to the invitation in not more than 50 words, expressing your inability to attend the function. You are Tara/Tarun.*

(i) Select the most appropriate subject for the given letter.

(a) Inability to accept the invitation, sir.
(b) Reply to your invitation.
(c) Rejecting the invitation.
(d) None of these.

Ans. (a) Inability to accept the invitation, sir.

(ii) Why is the "subject" column critical in formal letters?

(A) It tells about the writer's choice.
(B) It makes letters attractive.
(C) Talk about the purpose of the letter.
(D) Is not essential at all.

(a) Both (C) and (B) (b) Only (D) (c) Both (A) and (B) (d) Only (C)

Ans. (d) Only (C)

(iii) If you don't know the recipient's name, how would you address the letter's recipient?

(a) Dear Mr./Ms.
(b) Dear
(c) Hello
(d) Dear Sir/Madam

Ans. (d) Dear Sir/Madam

(iv) Where do you write the central part of the letter?

(a) Body of the letter.
(b) Starting of letter.
(c) At the ending of the letter.
(d) After salutation.

Ans. (a) Body of the letter.

(v) What type of letter leaves the desired effect on the recipient of the letter?

(a) It should be grammatically correct.
(b) It should be in a proper format.
(c) It should be relevant and to the point.
(d) All of these.

Ans. (d) All of these.

3. *You have received an invitation to be the judge for a Literary Competition in X.Y.Z. School. Send a reply in not more than 50 words, confirming your acceptance. You are Mohini/Mohan.*

(i) What is the name given to the address at the top of a formal letter?

(a) Starting lines.
(b) Receiver's address.
(c) Sender's address.
(d) Heading.

Ans. (c) Sender's address.

(ii) The tone and attitude of the writer while writing must be_______.

(a) polite (b) aggressive (c) frustrated (d) sympathetic

Ans. (a) polite

(iii) Select the appropriate subject for the given letter.

(A) Application for invitation.
(B) Application for acceptance.
(C) Acceptance of invitation for judging the literary competition.
(D) Acceptance of participation at the literary competition.

(a) Both (B) and (D)
(b) Both (A) and (C)
(c) Both (B) and (A)
(d) Both (C) and (B)

Ans. (b) Both (A) and (C)

(iv) Select the information mentioned in the body of the letter.

(a) About confirmation of the presence.
(b) About rejection of the presence.
(c) About the date and time of the event.
(d) About contact details.

Ans. (a) About confirmation of the presence.

(v) Select the location where the sender's name and designation are mentioned informal letter.

(a) At the left top corner.
(b) At the right bottom corner.
(c) At the bottom left corner.
(d) At the right top corner.

Ans. (c) At the bottom left corner.

4. *You are the secretary of the Old Students Association, G.V.M. School Ajmer. The 20th Alumni Meet will be held on Saturday, 29th August, 20XX, at Raj Hotel. Write an invitation letter to all the old students of the school to attend the meet.*

(i) Select the appropriate line for closure of this letter.

(a) Commanding to come to the event.
(b) Requesting the students to confirm their seats.
(c) Requesting the students to come early to the event.
(d) None of the above.

Ans. (b) Requesting the students to confirm their seats.

(ii) Which one of the following is the correct subject statement for the given letter?

(a) Application regarding invitation for 20th Alumni Meet.
(b) Organizing Alumni Meet.
(c) Confirming the seats of Alumni students.
(d) All of the above.

Ans. (a) Application regarding invitation for 20th Alumni Meet

(iii) What is the purpose of invitation expression in formal invitation letters?

(A) To persuade someone to come to the event.
(B) To tell someone about the event.
(C) To invite someone to come to the event.
(D) To explain to someone about the event.

(a) Both (A) and (D) (b) Only (C) (c) Only (D) (d) Both (A) and (B)

Ans. (c) Only (C)

(iv) Which one is the formal expression of inviting someone?

(a) Let's go to my party.
(b) It's party time.
(c) I would like to invite you to come to my event.
(d) Can you join to my celebrations.

Ans. (c) I would like to invite you to come to my event.

(v) What would you say in the opening part of the formal letter?

(a) Ask how good the atmosphere is in the recipient's address.
(b) Ask about the health of recipients.
(c) Inform the recipients about the purpose of the letter.
(d) Both (b) and (c).

Ans. (c) Inform the recipients about the purpose of the letter.

5. *You are Sakshi Bansal, the Head Girl of Spring Public School, Haryana. Your school is holding an inter-school T-20 Cricket Tournament from 10th October- 15th October, 20XX. Write a formal invitation to Sh. B.K. Modi, The legendary cricketer, inaugurated the championship on 10th October, 20XX, at 10:00 a.m. at your school playground.*

(i) "Yours faithfully" is used in which part of the formal letter?

(a) Heading (b) Opening (c) Body (d) Closing

Ans. (d) Closing

(ii) To have the desired effect on the recipients, what should a formal letter be?

(a) In the proper format.
(b) Detailed.
(c) Grammatically eroded.
(d) All of these.

Ans. (a) In the proper format.

(iii) If you don't know the recipient's name, how would you close the Formal letter?

(A) With love
(B) Yours sincerely
(C) Yours faithfully
(D) Affectionately yours

(a) Both (A) and (D) (b) Only (B) (c) Only (C) (d) Both (C) and (B)

Ans. (b) Only (B)

(iv) An informal letter, the receiver's address includes.

(a) Sir/Madam (b) Date (c) Receiver's name (d) Sender's Name

Ans. (c) Receiver's name

(v) Informal letter date is placed :

(a) above sender's address.

(b) above receiver's address.

(c) between sender's address and receiver's address.

(d) none of the above.

Ans. (c) between sender's address and receivers address.

6. *Rohit has got success in CBSE-PMT. He wants to celebrate his admission to SRCC College, Delhi, by throwing a party for his friends. Write an informal invitation giving details of the venue, time, and date. Do not exceed 50 words.*

(i) A letter to a friend or relative comes under the _______ category.

(a) formal (b) informal (c) semi-official (d) none of these

Ans. (b) informal

(ii) Which one is the informal invitation?

(A) An invitation to the opening of a school.

(B) An invitation to a graduation ceremony.

(C) An invitation for alumni meet.

(D) An invitation to a birthday party.

(a) Both (A) and (B) (b) Both (B) and (C) (c) Only (D) (d) Only (C)

Ans. (c) Only (D)

(iii) Which one of these forms is not used to address people in friendly letters?

(a) Dear (b) My dear (c) Respected (d) Dearest

Ans. (c) Respected

(iv) Which one of the following complimentary closures can be used for a given letter?

(a) Yours truly (b) Yours faithfully (c) Yours sincerely (d) All of these

Ans. (c) Yours sincerely

(v) Which of these is not prefixed with any form of courteous leave-taking in informal letters?

(a) With best wishes (b) With love (c) With kind regards (d) Your regards

Ans. (d) Your regards

7. *You are Simran. The wedding of your elder sister Sakshi will be held on the 15th June, 20XX, at Hotel Taj View, Udaipur. Write out an informal invitation to your friend Sush requesting him to attend the function.*

(i) Which of the following phrases can be used to start the main body of an informal letter?

(A) All the best.

(B) You will be pleased to know.

(C) Please refer to letter number.

(D) We are pleased to place an order.

(a) Both (A) and (D) (b) Both (C) and (D) (c) Only (B) (d) Only (A)

Ans. (c) Only (B)

(ii) Where should the name of the writer be written in an informal invitation?

(a) Top right corner (b) Bottom left corner (c) Top left corner (d) Body

Ans. (b) Bottom left corner

(iii) Which line would you like to close give letter?

(a) I do hope you will join us.

(b) Kindly assemble.

(c) Both (a) and (b).

(d) None of these.

Ans. (a) I do hope you will join us.

(iv) Which of the following salutation will you use in the given letter?

(a) Respected (b) Dear Sir/Madam (c) Dear friend (d) Dear

Ans. (c) Dear friend

(v) What is the essential information to be mentioned in the body of the letter?

(a) Brief information about the marriage function.
(b) Date and time of the event.
(c) Details of marriage.
(d) All of these.

Ans. (a) Brief information about the marriage function.

8. *You are Ankit. Your friend from Singapore is staying in the hostel. Invite him to join Diwali Celebrations with you at your residence.*

(i) At what location sender's address is mentioned in informal letters?

(a) Top left corner (b) Bottom left corner (c) Top right corner (d) Body of the letter

Ans. (a) Top left corner

(ii) With which line from the following you will end this letter?

(A) Do join us for the event.
(B) Do join us for Diwali Pujan.
(C) Come and enjoy.
(D) None of the above.

(a) Both (B) and (C) (b) Both (A) and (B) (c) Both (A) and (C) (d) Only (D)

Ans. (a) Both (B) and (C)

(iii) How to write an informal letter?

(a) Ignore grammar.
(b) Write legibly simple English.
(c) Leave out the date.
(d) Scribble.

Ans. (c) Write legibly simple English.

(iv) You can help a letter do its job by doing what?

(a) Write it on pretty and coloured paper.
(b) Used colourful pens.
(c) Write it accurate and clearly.
(d) All of these.

Ans. (c) Write it accurate and clearly.

(v) You start an informal letter with________.

(a) sender's address
(b) receiver's address
(c) date
(d) time

Ans. (a) sender's address

9. *Write a letter to your friend inviting him to the house-warming ceremony of your newly constructed house.*

(i) Which of the following is "Not" a part of the Informal letter?

(a) Greetings (b) Heading (c) Materials list (d) Signature

Ans. (c) Materials list

(ii) Which one of the following is an example of a greeting you will use in the given letter?

(A) Love
(B) Dear Vinay
(C) Vinay, I have missed you.
(D) Vinay, can we meet up?

(a) Both (A) and (B) (b) Both (C) and (D) (c) Only (B) (d) Only (C)

Ans. (c) Only (B)

(iii) The writer's message in an informal letter is known as_______.

(a) body (b) closing (c) salutation (d) heading

Ans. (a) body

(iv) Which information will you mention in the body of the given letter?

(a) Date and time of an event.
(b) All vital information about the event.
(c) Request to come for the event.
(d) None of these.

Ans. (b) All vital information about the event.

(v) The salutation used in letter is also known as________.

(a) greetings
(b) complimentary closure
(c) address
(d) heading

Ans. (a) greetings

10. *Your parents have completed 25 years of happy married life. Invite your aunt, living in Hyderabad, to join you in the Silver Jubilee Celebration of their marriage at your residence.*

(i) Which of the following line will you like to close your letter?

(a) Do join us on this auspicious day.
(b) Do not join us on this auspicious day.
(c) Would you like to come?
(d) None of these

Ans. (a) Do join us on this auspicious day

(ii) If writing the letter to your relative, which way of closing a letter would be best?

(a) Yours faithfully
(b) Yours obediently
(c) Yours sincerely
(d) All the best

Ans. (c) Yours sincerely

(iii) What information do you need to add in the body of the letter in the given letter?

(A) Regarding the health of parents.
(B) Regarding the details of the function.
(C) Regarding the weather of the receiver's address.
(D) All of these.

(a) Both (A) and (B) (b) Only (B) (c) Only (C) (d) Both (C) and (B)

Ans. (b) Only (B)

(iv) An informal letter, acknowledge the invitation in ________.

(a) first-person (b) second person (c) third person (d) all of these

Ans. (a) first-person

(v) For informal letter, word limit should be________.

(a) 100-125 words (b) 150 words (c) 50 words (d) 200 words

Ans. (c) 50 words

Sample Letters :

1. You are Suraj/Swati of 102, Shipra Town, Delhi. You have seen an advertisement in The Hindustan Times for the post of Executive Chef in a 5-Star Hotel. Apply for the job with complete biodata in **120-150** words.

The Marriot Hotel, Delhi **Required Executive Chef** Good culinary skills, honest, energetic, innovative, hardworking, at least five years' experience in a 3- Star Hotel. Drop your C.V. on mailing address of The Marriot Hotel.

102, Shipra Town
Delhi

27th January, 20XX

The Managing Director
The Marriott Hotel
Delhi

Subject: Application for the post of executive chef

Dear Sir,

This is with reference to the advertisement published in the esteemed daily 'The Hindustan Times' on 25th January, 20XX, for the post of Executive Chef in your renowned hotel, I intend to apply for the same. I have completed my MBA in Hotel Management from Delhi University. I am painstaking, honest and punctual. I assure you that if selected, I shall work with full devotion and sincerity. For further details, I am enclosing my bio-data.

In anticipation of an early response.

Encl.: Bio-data

BIO-DATA

Name	:	Suraj/Swati
Father's Name	:	Anil Vohra
Date of Birth	:	25th November, 1993
Communication Address	:	102, Shipra Town, Delhi-XXXXXX Phone- 98XXXXXXXX
E-Mail Address	:	Sur123@gmail.com
Marital Status	:	Unmarried
Nationality	:	Indian
Academic Qualifications	:	(i) M.B.A. Anand College with 93% marks (ii) Hotel Management, Delhi University with 92% marks
Experience	:	Trainee at the Taj Hotel, New Delhi.
Strengths	:	Good communication skills, computer literate
Languages	:	Good command over spoken and written Hindi & English.
Hobbies	:	Reading and Sketching
References	:	1. Ashok Gupta, Manager, Taj Hotel, Delhi. Ph-XXXXXXXXXX
	:	2. Kiran Sharma, Associate Professor, Anand College.PhXXXXXXXXXX

Yours sincerely

Suraj/Swati

2. You came across an advertisement in 'The Times of India' regarding the post of an animator in Mumbai. Draft an application in about **120-150** words for the post of the same in response to the advertisement giving your resume. You are Garvita/ Garvit of B-121, Street Park Lane, Kolkata.

Sitaara Edutech
Animator Required
Needed a young and dynamic animator to create engaging and on-brand graphic and animations for various eLearning courses and short films.
Experienced candidates with specialization in animations software and a creative flair preferred. Fluency in Adobe Creative Suit and English is a must.
Apply within five days of the advertisement to the HR Manager.

B-121, Street Park Lane
Kolkata

17th April, 20XX

The Manager
Xentrix Studios
Mumbai

Subject: Application for the post of animator

Dear Sir,

In response to the advertisement published in the newspaper, 'The Times of India' for the post of animator, I would like to apply for the same. After clearing All India Common Entrance Examination for Design (CEED), I did six months certificate program in domains like visual effects (VFX) specialisation, digital composting, and video editing.

I possess the foremost skills required in animation careers i.e. genuine interest in art and design which helps in bringing out the creative and artistic expression that will allow static images to develop visual graphics and movements. I believe that all these qualities will fulfill your requirement you need in a proficient animator.

If selected, I assure you that I would contribute my best to the work for your company. For reference, I am enclosing my resume as under.

Encl.: Resume

RESUME

Name	:	Garvit/Garvita
Father's Name	:	D.K. Gandhi
Date of Birth	:	21st October, 1993
Communication Address	:	B-121, Street Park Lane, Kolkata-XXXXXX
	:	Phone- 98XXXXXXXX
E-Mail Address	:	gar123@gmail.com
Marital Status	:	Unmarried
Nationality	:	Indian
Academic Qualifications	:	(i) Senior Secondary from Tagore Public School, Kolkata
		(ii) Graduation in designing & Arts from Govt. run institute
		(iii) Diploma in Character Animation from Adam College
Experience		2 years at HOBNOB Enterprises, Mumbai
Strengths	:	Sound IT skills and the ability to concentrate
Languages	:	Good command over spoken and written Hindi & English.
Hobbies	:	Drawing and Sketching
References	:	1. Ashok Singh, Manager, Accenture. Pune ,Ph-XXXXXXXXXX
		2. Minal Sathe, Crox, Delhi. Ph- XXXXXXXXXX

Hoping for a favourable response.

Your sincerely
Garvit/Garvita

Practice Exercise :

1. Kim Public School, Una, urgently requires a post-graduate teacher to teach Maths. They have placed an advertisement in 'The H.P. Times' for the same. You are Bharat/Bharti Sharma from 56, Patel Marg, Una. Draft a letter in about **120-150** words including a CV, applying for the advertised post.

KIM PUBLIC SCHOOL

REQUIRES

POST GRADUATE MATHS TEACHER

Candidates having B. Ed degree with experience, excellent communication skills, interest in co-curricular activities and proficiency in computer preferred.

Candidates can apply by 25th April, 20XX through school website.

2. You came across an advertisement in 'The Times of India' regarding the post of a graphic designer in Mumbai. Draft an application in about **120-150** words for the post of the same in response to the advertisement giving your resume. You are Darshan/ Darshana of 34, Thakur Complex, A Wing, Kandivli, Mumbai.

> XYZ Media
>
> **Graphic Designer Required**
>
> Needed young and dynamic graphic designer to create engaging and on-brand graphics for a variety of media at XYZ Media. Candidates should possess a creative flair and the ability to convert requirements into design along with an outgoing personality and good communication skills.
>
> Apply within five days of the advertisement to the HR Manager.

Choose the correct option :

1. **Letter written for searching or seeking a job is called:**
   (a) Resume
   (b) Job Application
   (c) CV
   (d) Prospecting Letter

Ans. (b) Job Application

2. **Job letter is :**
   (a) Formal (b) Informal (c) Both (a) and (b) (d) None of these

Ans. (a) Formal

3. **Job letter contains:**
   (a) A Prospecting letter
   (b) An Application
   (c) A Cover letter
   (d) A Resume

Ans. (c) A Cover letter

4. **A good cover letter will:**
   (a) Create a favourable first impression.
   (b) Demonstrate your professionalism.
   (c) Illustrate your communication skills.
   (d) All of these.

Ans. (d) All of these

5. **The job application letter is:**
   (a) a statement of your job objective.
   (b) a summary of your qualifications and experiences.
   (c) a description of your core strength and suitability for job.
   (d) a foreword.

Ans. (c) a description of your core strength and suitability for job.

6. **Which of the following is NOT something that a cover letter should always contain in its closing paragraph?**
   (a) Request for an interview.
   (b) Statement that you look forward to hearing from the recipient.
   (c) Statement thanking the employer for considering the cover letter.
   (d) None of these.

Ans. (a) Request for an interview.

7. **Which of the following is necessary for successful cover letter_____.**
   (a) opening, body and closing paragraphs
   (b) addressing the letter to a specific individual or department
   (c) connecting your skills to the ones profiled in the job advertisement
   (d) all of the above

Ans. (d) all of the above

8. **What's the best way to make value judgments or claims of personal attributes more credible in a cover letter?**
   (a) Use very positive language in making the claim.
   (b) Substantiate the claims by backing them up with examples.
   (c) There is no good way to make such claims, so omit them.
   (d) None of the above.

Ans. (b) Substantiate the claims by backing them up with examples.

9. **The first paragraph of job application contains:**
   (a) Educational information
   (b) Personal information
   (c) Professional information
   (d) All of these

Ans. (b) Personal information

10. **How can you make the most of your college experience in your cover letter?**
   (a) Describe skills gained in the classroom.
   (b) Describe sports and extracurricular activities.
   (c) Discuss hands-on projects.
   (d) All of these.

Ans. (d) All of these.

11. **How should you start a letter if you do not have a named person to write to?**
   (a) Dear Personnel Department
   (b) To Whom it May Concern
   (c) Dear Sir/Ma'am
   (d) Dear Manager

Ans. (c) Dear Sir/Ma'am

12. **Which of the following should NOT be included in an application letter?**
   (a) Why you are applying for the position.
   (b) Your skills, qualifications and experience that are relevant to the position applied for.
   (c) Details of problems you have had with employers in the past.
   (d) Your interest in / knowledge of the organisation.

Ans. (c) Details of problems you have had with employers in the past.

13. **Long paragraphs are expected in application letters so job-seekers can discuss their skills and qualifications in great detail.**
   (a) True
   (b) False

Ans. (b) False

14. **Your address, phone number, birth day, social security number, and bank account number are all parts of your___________.**
   (a) personal information
   (b) job duties
   (c) education history
   (d) employment history

Ans. (a) personal information

15. **A signature is done in cover letter:**
   (a) at the end
   (b) at the Start
   (c) anywhere
   (d) none of these

Ans. (a) at the end

16. **If you begin a letter with "Dear Sir" you should end it with:**
   (a) Yours sincerely
   (b) From
   (c) Yours faithfully
   (d) Yours

Ans. (c) Yours faithfully

17. Which part of the application letter contains the main content?

(a) Body of the letter
(b) Heading
(c) Complimentary close
(d) None of these

Ans. (a) Body of the letter

18. When you end your cover letter by saying that you will call to follow up within a week or so, you are using what type of ending?

(a) Aggressive
(b) Active
(c) Personal
(d) Complimentary

Ans. (d) Complimentary

19. The length of cover letter should not be:

(a) more than one page.
(b) more than two pages.
(c) more than three pages.
(d) none of these.

Ans. (a) more than one page.

20. Which of the following is not a function of a cover letter?

(a) To inform the employer of the job you are applying for.
(b) To show how well you write.
(c) To inform the reader of what you expect to get out of the job you're applying for.
(d) To entice the reader to want to get to know you better by interviewing you.

Ans. (c) To inform the reader of what you expect to get out of the job you're applying for.

21. When should you send a cover letter?

(a) Only when an ad specifically requests it.
(b) Every time you send out your resume.
(c) When you need to list your salary requirement.
(d) When you need to list references.

Ans. (b) Every time you send out your resume.

22. Which of the following is NOT something that a cover letter writer should always do in his or her opening paragraph?

(a) Inform on why he or she is writing.
(b) Impress the employer with knowledge of the company.
(c) Be specific about the position sought and what they can can offer.
(d) Mention salary specifications.

Ans. (d) Mention salary specifications.

23. The resume and application letter are:

(a) two different tasks.
(b) two same tasks.
(c) overlapping tasks.
(d) the same task.

Ans. (a) two different tasks.

24. A cover letter should be:

(a) crisp
(b) concise
(c) to the point
(d) all of these

Ans. (d) all of these

25. The __________ paragraph should create interest and explain why you are writing. It should state the type of position you are applying for.

(a) closing
(b) introduction
(c) body
(d) salutations

Ans. (b) introduction

26. 483 Apple Street
New York, NY 10001
(212) 555-8965
Lee.jones@email.com

September 15, 2019

The Recruiter
Rogers Consulting
901 Main Street
New York, NY 10001

Subject: Application for the Post of Human Resources Consultant

I am reaching out to you regarding the posting for the human resources consultant position I found on Indeed.com. I have a great interest in this position and would appreciate your consideration as a candidate for the role.

In my previous experience, I worked in human resources departments to provide support across several different industries. I have worked in my current role as a human resources generalist for the past four years. Prior to this job, I worked as a human resources assistant for two years, which shows my ability to advance in my career.

I have a strong passion for helping others, which is why I have found such fulfillment in human resources, providing support to my fellow employees and assisting them in ways that benefit them both personally and professionally. I also enjoy looking for solutions to common HR problems, which I feel would be a great asset in the position with your company. Since this consultant position works directly with multiple clients, assisting them in their human resources needs, I believe my innovative nature and strong skill set will help me succeed.

I have strong communication skills, which are vital to success in the HR field. I also have a bachelor's degree in human resources from Arizona State University. Throughout my education, I worked with skilled human resources professionals who have shared their insights and experience with me. Some of my strongest skills include my ability to increase employee retention through the improvement of company culture and to develop training and education programs to ensure all employees have access to the information they need to succeed and comply with legal requirements.

I appreciate your time in reviewing this letter and hope to hear from you in regard to the next steps in the hiring process. If you have any questions or need any additional information, please don't hesitate to contact me.

Sincerely,
Lee Jimenez

What is missing in the given letter?

(a) Salutation
(b) Subject
(c) Heading
(d) Closing

Ans. (a) Salutation

27. 12 Jones Street

Portland, Maine 04101

555-555-5555

elizabethjohnson@emailaddress.com

August 11, 2020

Human Resources Manager

238 Main Street

Portland, Maine 04101

Dear Mr. Smith,

I was so excited when my former coworker, Jay Lopez, told me about your opening for an administrative assistant in your Portland offices. A long-time Veggies to Go customer and an experienced admin, I would love to help the company achieve its mission of making healthy produce as available as takeout.

I've worked for small companies for my entire career, and I relish the opportunity to wear many hats and work with the team to succeed. In my latest role as an administrative assistant at Beauty Corp, I saved my employer thousands of dollars in temp workers by implementing a self-scheduling system for the customer service reps that cut down on canceled shifts. I also learned web design, time sheet coding, and perfected my Excel skills.

I've attached my resume for your consideration and hope to speak with you soon about your needs for the role.

Best Regards,

Elizabeth Johnson

What is missing in the given letter?

(a) Salutation (b) Subject (c) Heading (d) Closing

Ans. (b) Subject

28. Ashok Vihar

Delhi

August 15, 2020

Paschim Vihar

Delhi

Subject: Job Application for the Post of Graphic Designer

Dear Sir/Ma'am

I am very interested in the position of Graphic Designer at your esteemed organization. I came across the position via your advertisement in Times Of India.

Currently, I am working with XYZ and I have been handling a wide range of high profile projects. I have been working on Adobe Creative Suite for the last 4 years. Please find below a link to my portfolio.

portfolio@example.com

I am confident that my skills perfectly match your requirements. I have attached my detailed profile to this email for your consideration.

Thank you for considering my application. I hope you find it suitable so that we can arrange a meeting.

Looking forward to hearing from you.

What is missing in the given letter?

(a) Heading (b) Salutations (c) Closing (d) Body

Ans. (c) Closing

29. 15 January 20XX,

Subject : Application for the Post of Programmer

Dear Sir/Ma'am,

I am writing to apply for the programmer position advertised in the Times Union. As requested, I enclose a completed job application, my certification, my resume, and three references.

The role is very appealing to me, and I believe that my strong technical experience and education make me a highly competitive candidate for this position. My key strengths that would support my success in this position include:

- I have successfully designed, developed, and supported live-use applications.
- I strive continually for excellence.
- I provide exceptional contributions to customer service for all customers.

With a BS degree in Computer Programming, I have a comprehensive understanding of the full lifecycle for software development projects. I also have experience in learning and applying new technologies as appropriate. Please see my resume for additional information on my experience.

Thank you for your time and consideration. I look forward to speaking with you about this employment opportunity.

Sincerely,

John Donaldson

(a) What is missing in the letter?

(a) Saluation
(b) Subject
(c) Date
(d) Heading

Ans. (d) Heading

(b) What is the error in the given letter?

(a) Sincerely
(b) Too lengthy
(c) Too short
(d) Use of informal language

Ans. (a) Sincerely

❑❑

Report

3

A Report is a written composition or, in other words, a prepared talk about a particular subject. It is a vivid expression of a personal experience on account of something heard, seen, done, studied, etc, that is meant to be published or broadcasted. The most common example is the news reports we read in the newspapers everyday. Reports can be of many types, such as :

1. A newspaper report.
2. A report about an event or function at school/institute/organisation.
3. A report about an accident/happening that you have witnessed.
4. A report about an enquiry or survey.

Important Instructions :

- Be factual and do not add any information on your own that may seem fictitious.
- Write in indirect speech and preferably in passive voice.
- Write in third person form and avoid using pronouns like I, me or you.
- Avoid imposing your personal opinious and do not make any conclusions.
- Answer the questions to 'when', 'where', 'why', 'what', 'who' and 'how'.

Format :

Heading of a Report

by xyz

Place, Date : Yesterday XYZ Public School celebrated its first annual function...........

[body of a report]

Report Writing

Read the given extract to attempt questions that follow:

1. *Recently your school held a seminar on water conservation on the occasion of world water day celebrations. As the school head boy, write a report in 100-125 words for a local daily. Sign as Anil/Anita.*

(i) Select the most appropriate title for the report.

(a) Report writing.
(b) Report writing on the seminar.
(c) Seminar on water conservation.
(d) World water day celebration.

Ans. (c) Seminar on water conservation.

(ii) Report writing by the individual should be written in:

(a) first person (b) second person (c) third person (d) all of these

Ans. (a) first person

(iii) Choose the option with the information points to be included in the body of the report writing.

(A) Opinion about the best method of water conservation.
(B) Content shared by guest speakers.
(C) Management of water.
(D) All of the above.

(a) Both (A) and (B) (b) Both (B) and (C) (c) Both (C) and (A) (d) None of these

Ans. (a) Both (A) and (B)

(iv) Report discussed a particular problem in ________.

(a) brief (b) detail (c) complex (d) horizontal way

Ans. (b) detail

(v) Select the appropriate conclusion for this report.

(a) Benefits of water conservation.
(b) Optimum utilisation of water.
(c) Improving water management.
(d) All of these.

Ans. (d) All of these.

2. *Your students have organized an exhibition-cum-sale of the goods or items prepared under the Work Experience Certificate. There was an overwhelming response from the public in school. Prepare a report in 100-125 words for a local daily. You are the school coordinator of Devi Neaten School, Gurugram.*

(i) Select the most appropriate title for the report.

(a) Seminar on Exhibition.
(b) Exhibition.
(c) An Exhibition-Cum-Sale.
(d) Devi Neaten School.

Ans. (c) An Exhibition-Cum-Sale.

(ii) Which among the following plan is appropriate for given report writing?

(a) Draw invalid conclusion.
(b) Decide on recommendation.
(c) Formulate specific questions.
(d) All of these.

Ans. (c) Formulate the specific question.

(iii) Choose the option with the information points to be included in the body of the report writing.

(A) About the response of public, teachers, management.
(B) About the appreciation from management for the students.
(C) About the school.
(D) About the details of the students.

(a) Both (C) and (D) (b) Both (B) and (C) (c) Both (B) and (D) (d) Both (A) and (B)

Ans. (d) Both (A) and (B)

(iv) Which of the following option does NOT describe this report?

(a) Persuasive (b) Factual (c) Orderly (d) None of these

Ans. (a) Persuasive

(v) Select the appropriate conclusion for this report.

(a) Motivating to encourage for more such events.
(b) Motivating to encourage the student's creativity and talent.
(c) About exhibition.
(d) All of these.

Ans. (b) Motivating to encourage the student's creativity and talent.

3. *Your state administration has banned the use of plastic bags. You are Amrita, a reporter of The National Herald. Write a report in 100-125 words on how the ban is being ignored and what damage the indiscriminate usage of plastic bags is causing to the environment.*

(i) Select the most appropriate title for the report.

(a) Environment unfriendly plastic bags.
(b) National Herald.
(c) Problems associated with plastic bags.
(d) Report writing.

Ans. (a) Environment unfriendly plastic bags.

(ii) Which of the following information is best suited to start the report?

(a) Information regarding the solution for plastic bags.
(b) Information regarding the ban of plastic bags.
(c) Information regarding rules and regulations against the use of palstic bags.
(d) None of the above.

Ans. (b) Information regarding the ban of plastic bags.

(iii) Choose the option with the information points to be included in the body of the report writing.

(A) Problems due to usage and disposal of plastic bags.

(B) Uses of plastic bags.

(C) Ban use of plastic bags.

(D) Awareness about the use of plastic bags.

(a) Both (A) and (B) (b) Only (A) (c) Both (C) and (D) (d) Only (C)

Ans. (b) Only (A)

(iv) While writing the report, identify the location where you have to mention the writer's name according to the format?

(a) At the end of the report.

(b) Below the title of the report.

(c) In the beginning.

(d) No need to mention.

Ans. (b) Below the title of the report.

(v) Select the appropriate conclusion for this report.

(a) Responsibility towards usage of plastic bags.

(b) Responsibility towards disposal of plastic bags.

(c) Both (a) and (b).

(d) None of the above

Ans. (c) Both (a) and (b).

4. *You witnessed a programme performed by differently-abled people on Star T.V. You were very much impressed by their act/performance and emotionally touched seeing their acts and performances. Highlighting their hard work, talent, the reaction of the judges, etc. Prepare a report in 100-125 words for your school magazine. You are Anjali/Arjun, student editor of the magazine.*

(i) Select the most appropriate title for the report writing.

(a) Seminar on programme.

(b) Report writing.

(c) A particular programme on Star T.V.

(d) Special programme.

Ans. (c) A particular programme on Star T.V.

(ii) Select the option with the information points to be included in the body of the report writing.

(A) About the performance and awards for talented students.

(B) About the occasion of republic day celebrations.

(C) About the talent of the students.

(D) Detail on performances of students.

(a) Both (A) and (B) (b) (A), (C) and (D) (c) Only (D) (d) Only (C)

Ans. (a) (A), (C) and (B)

(iii) Select the appropriate opening for the report writing?

(a) Star T.V. organized a ...

(b) On the occasion of Republic Day...

(c) Performance by a differently-abled person...

(d) All of these

Ans. (b) On the occasion of Republic Day...

(iv) What does a good title do in report writing?

(a) Captures the purpose of the report.

(b) Show how the report is organized.

(c) Explains the findings.

(d) None of these.

Ans. (a) Captures the purpose of the report.

(v) Select most appropriate conclusion for this report.

(a) Motivating for organizing more such events.

(b) Encouraging these students only because of disabilities.

(c) About their performance.

(d) About their achievements.

Ans. (a) Motivating for organizing more such events

5. *Your school organized a seminar on 'How to prevent cruelty towards animals, in which 40 city CBSE schools took part. As coordinator of the program, write a report in 100-125 words for the school magazine. You are Ram/Ramika of A.B.C. Senior Secondary School, Gujarat.*

(i) Which of these can be taken as a title for your report?

(a) Report writing on the seminar.
(b) Seminar to prevent cruelty towards animals.
(c) Seminar on animals.
(d) None of these.

Ans. (b) Seminar to prevent cruelty towards animals.

(ii) Select the option with the information points to be included in the body of the report writing.

(A) Stress on the need for compassion and care towards the animals.
(B) About animal cruelty.
(C) About the animal's safety.
(D) About the animals and human relation.

(a) Both (A) and (B) (b) Both (C) and (D) (c) Both (B) and (C) (d) Both (B) and (D)

Ans. (a) Both (A) and (B)

(iii) From the following options, which option defines the "report body" appropriately?

(a) Section where you give your recommendations.
(b) Section where you conclude your report.
(c) Section where you summarize your report.
(d) Section where you present your observations and findings.

Ans. (d) Section where you present your observations and findings.

(iv) Select the appropriate option for the conclusion of this report.

(a) Stop animal cruelty.
(b) Awareness towards animal cruelty.
(c) Prevention of animals from cruelty.
(d) Methods and techniques.

Ans. (b) Awareness towards animal cruelty.

(v) The end of a good report writing should __________.

(a) conclude the report
(b) like a story
(c) an end
(d) restate the beginning

Ans. (a) conclude the report

6. *You witnessed a bomb blast in the Delhi Market when you went there for Diwali shopping with your parents. Write a report in 100-125 words for your school magazine.*

(i) Select the most appropriate title for the report writing.

(a) Bomb explosion in market place.
(b) A report writing.
(c) An accident.
(d) All of these.

Ans. (a) Bomb explosion in market place.

(ii) Select the option with the information points to be included in the body of report writing.

(A) Information regarding the accident witnessed by the writer.
(B) Accident details.
(C) About Diwali.
(D) About Diwali shopping.

(a) Both (A) and (C) (b) Only (A) (c) Only (C) (d) Both (C) and (D)

Ans. (b) Only (A)

(iii) The above report should display the information about:

(a) witnessed accident
(b) investigation
(c) experiment
(d) inquiry

Ans. (a) witnessed accident

(iv) The body of a good report should contain:

(a) excuse with evidence.
(b) examples with evidence.
(c) facts with supporting evidence.
(d) reasons with evidence.

Ans. (c) facts with supporting evidence.

(v) Select the appropriate conclusion for the report.

(a) About the worst nightmare experienced.
(b) Shocking experience.
(c) Incident.
(d) None of these.

Ans. (b) Shocking experience.

7. *You are Jai/ Jaya studying in A.B.C. Memorial Hall, Trichy. Some students of your school attended a first aid training camp for a week at the Red Cross Headquarters of your state. Write a report for your school magazine in 100-125 words on the events of the camp and your participation and performance.*

(i) Select the appropriate title for the report.

(a) Training Camp.
(b) Report writing.
(c) First aid Training Camp.
(d) All of these.

Ans. (c) First aid Training Camp.

(ii) Select the option with the information points to be included in the body of the report writing.

(A) Student learning.
(B) Student experience.
(C) About red cross camp.
(D) About the red cross trainer.

(a) Both (A) and (B) (b) Both (C) and (D) (c) Only (C) (d) Only (D)

Ans. (a) Both (A) and (B)

(iii) While writing a report, different categories of topic become________.

(a) paragraphs (b) stories (c) answers (d) sentences

Ans. (a) paragraphs

(iv) Report writing should preferably be composed in_________.

(a) irregular manner
(b) regular manner
(c) sequential manner
(d) none of these

Ans. (c) sequential manner

(v) Select an appropriate conclusion for the given report writing.

(a) Regarding training of attendees at the training camp.
(b) Perks and benefits of attending the training camp.
(c) Learning during the training camp.
(d) All of the above.

Ans. (b) Perks and benefits of attending the training camp.

8. *On Teacher's day, the badge holders of your schools organized a grand celebration to honour the teachers of our school. As the head boy/ head girl of the school, write a report on the celebration of Teacher's day in 125-150 words.*

(i) Select an appropriate title for the report.

(a) Teacher's Day celebrations.
(b) A school event.
(c) Report writing.
(d) Celebrations to honour teachers.

Ans. (a) Teacher's Day celebrations.

(ii) Select the appropriate opening for the given report writing,

(a) Teachers were overwhelmed.
(b) On the occasion of Teacher's day.
(c) The programmme started with.
(d) None of these.

Ans. (b) On the occasion of Teacher's day.

(iii) Select the option with the information points to be included in the body of the report writing.

(A) About celebrations of Teacher's day.
(B) About the activities held on Teacher's day.
(C) Thanking teachers.
(D) Appraising the efforts of the students.

(a) Only (A) (b) Both (A) and (B) (c) Only (B) (d) Both (C) and (D)

Ans. (b) Both (A) and (B)

(iv) What is the primary purpose of the given report writing :

(a) To describe the teachers and students relations.
(b) To tell people about events organized by the schools.
(c) To describe the successful event held on Teacher's day.
(d) All of the above.

Ans. (c) To describe the successful event held on Teacher's day.

(v) Select an appropriate conclusion for this report.

(a) Emotions of teachers towards students.
(b) Thanks to teachers.
(c) An account of activities held on Teacher's day.
(d) All of these.

Ans. (b) Thanks to teachers.

9. *You had attended a workshop on personality development for students. Many eminent personalities were also present there. Write a report in 125-150 words on how the workshop proved to be beneficial. You are Raj/ Rajni.*

(i) Select the most appropriate title for the report writing.

(a) Report writing.
(b) Workshop for students.
(c) Workshop on personality development.
(d) All of these.

Ans. (c) Workshop on personality development

(ii) Select the option that lists the most appropriate opening for this report.

(a) I feel such workshops should be organized more frequently.
(b) Regular personality development workshops are organized for students.
(c) Through a multimedia presentation.
(d) After attending the one-hour workshop.

Ans. (b) Regular personality development workshops are organized for students.

(iii) Select the option with the information points to be included in the body of the report writing.

(a) About upgrading the skills that the students learned from the workshop.
(b) About workshop structure.
(c) The procedure of conducting a workshop.
(d) All of the above.

Ans. (a) About upgrading the skills that the students learned from the workshop.

(iv) What point should you keep in mind while writing formal reports?

(A) It should not be too long and detailed.
(B) Data should not be biased.
(C) Language should be easy and attractive.
(D) Incomplete information can be their.

(a) Only (A) (b) Both (A) and (C) (c) Only (D) (d) Only (C)

Ans. (b) Only (A)

(v) Select the appropriate option for the conclusion of this report writing.

(A) Valuables students get in the workshop.
(B) Promote organizing more such workshops.
(C) Motivate employees to participate in workshops.
(D) Importance of workshops.

(a) Only (A) (b) Both (C) and (D) (c) Both (B) and (D) (d) Both (C) and (A)

Ans. (a) Only (A)

10. *Write a report in 100-125 words on the Zonal Cricket Tournament held in the playground of A.B.C. School, Laxmi Nagar, last week. Your report should include names of participating teams, exciting, cheerful atmosphere, decorated playground, a large crowd of cheering students, and presentation ceremony. One of the of the student editors of your school magazine.*

(i) Select the most appropriate title for the report writing.

(a) Cricket tournament.
(b) Report writing.
(c) School tournament.
(d) Zonal Cricket Tournament.

Ans. (d) Zonal Cricket Tournament.

(ii) Select the appropriate option for opening the given report.

(a) The winning team was awarded.
(b) Student editor, the Zonal Cricket Tournament, was held.
(c) Both these teams were cheered.
(d) None of the above.

Ans. (b) Student editor, the Zonal Cricket Tournament, was held.

(iii) Select the option with the information points to be included in the body of the report writing.

(A) About winning and losing of match.

(B) About the teams.

(C) About the performance of the teams.

(D) About the details of the team's members.

(a) Both (C) and (D) (b) Both (B) and (C) (c) Both (A) and (B) (d) Both (D) and (A)

Ans. (c) Both (A) and (B)

(iv) According to the format of the report, select the appropriate location to mention the designation of the writer :

(a) at the end of the report.

(b) in the body of the report.

(c) below the title of the report.

(d) no need to mention.

Ans. (c) below is the title of the report.

(v) Select the appropriate option for the conclusion of report writing.

(a) About the winning of the team.

(b) About the prize distribution ceremony.

(c) Both (a) and (b).

(d) None of these.

Ans. (c) Both (a) and (b).

Application For A Job

1. *Shah Modern High School, Delhi, urgently requires a Postgraduate Teacher to teach Political Science for which they have placed an advertisement in the A.B.C. express. You are Atul/Alina from 21, Vasant Marg, Delhi. Draft a letter including a CV, applying for the advertised post. (125-150 words)*

(i) Letter written for searching or seeking a job is called:

(a) Resume (b) Job application (c) Letter (d) CV

Ans. (b) Job application

(ii) Select the appropriate subject for this letter :

(A) Application for the post of Postgraduate Teacher.

(B) Job application.

(C) Postgraduate Teacher.

(D) Requesting a job.

(a) Both (A) and (B) (b) Only (A) (c) Only (B) (d) Both (C) and (D)

Ans. (b) Only (A)

(iii) Job letter falls in ________ category.

(a) informal (b) formal (c) technical (d) all of these

Ans. (b) formal

(iv) Sender's address must be mentioned in the Job application or not?

(a) Yes (b) No (c) Sender's choice (d) May be

Ans. (a) Yes

(v) Job letter is also known as:

(a) Prospecting letter (b) Application (c) Cover letter (d) Resume

Ans. (c) Cover letter

2. *You are Ram/Rani, Living at 2, Rana Pratap colony, Delhi. Read the advertisement given below and apply for the job that suits you giving Biodata separately. Sun University requires a lecturer in English and Demonstrates in Physics, Chemistry, and Botany for their new campus at Panipat. Candidates with the minimum experience of 5 years can apply. Excellent command over English is a must. Excellent package and compensation for experienced persons.*

(i) Select the most appropriate subject for the letter.

(A) Application for the post of lecturer in English/Hindi/ Demonstrator in Physics/Chemistry/Botany.

(B) Job Letter.

(C) Application for Job.

(D) Job for Teacher.

(a) Both (C) and (A) (b) Both (B) and (D) (c) Both (A) and (D) (d) Both (B) and (C)

Ans. (a) Both (C) and (A)

(ii) A good cover letter should:

(a) make a good impression.

(b) answer the question – why should we hire you?

(c) present your qualifications directly.

(d) all of these.

Ans. (a) make a good Impression.

(iii) Select the most crucial information mentioned in the body of the letter:

(a) about the qualifications.

(b) answer the question – why should we hire you?

(c) experience.

(d) all of these.

Ans. (d) all of these.

(iv) Select the appropriate option to be emphasize in on a job application letter.

(a) Candidate's qualifications and key qualities.

(b) Strength and weakness.

(c) Only qualification.

(d) None of these.

Ans. (a) Candidate's qualifications and key qualities

(v) The job application letter is ________.

(a) a statement of your job objective

(b) a summary of your qualifications and experiences

(c) a description of your core strength and suitability for the job

(d) a forward

Ans. (c) a description of your core strength and suitability for the job

3. *You are Arti /Arav of 15, Model Town, Delhi. You have seen an advertisement in the Hindu for the post of chief chef in a 5-Star Hotel. Apply for the Job with your complete Biodata. Write in 125-150 words.*

(i) The job application and biodata perform:

(a) the same tasks.

(b) different tasks.

(c) two opposite tasks .

(d) overlapping tasks.

Ans. (b) different tasks.

(ii) Select an appropriate option with the information points to be included in the body of the application.

(a) Candidate's experience and qualifications.

(b) Candidate's Biodata.

(c) Candidate's weakness.

(d) Candidate's strength.

Ans. (a) Candidate's experience and qualifications.

(iii) Which of the following is NOT something that a cover letter should always contain in its closing paragraph?

(a) Request for an interview.

(b) A statement that you look forward to hearing from the recipient.

(c) Statement thanking the employer for considering the cover letter.

(d) None of the above.

Ans. (a) Request for an interview.

(iv) Which of the following is necessary for a successful Cover letter?

(a) Opening, body, and closing paragraphs.

(b) Addressing the letter to a specific individual.

(c) Connecting your skills to the ones enlisted in the job advertisement.

(d) All of the above.

Ans. (d) All of the above.

(v) Select the most appropriate subject for the application.

(A) Application for the post of chief chef.

(B) Application for job.

(C) Job application.

(D) Request for job.

(a) Both (A) and (B) (b) Both (B) and (C) (c) Both (D) and (C) (d) All of these

Ans. (a) Both (A) and (B)

4. *You are Parul/Priti of 25/3, T.M. Nagar, Bhopal. You are willing to apply for the post of Marketing Manager in a reputed firm in Mumbai. Write a letter to the Public Relations Officer, X.Y.Z. Enterprises, Mumbai, applying for the job. Write the letter in 125 – 150 words giving your Biodata.*

(i) What's the best way to make value judgments or claims of personal attributes more creditable in a cover letter?

(a) Use positive language in making the claim.

(b) Make sustainable the claims and back them up with the examples.

(c) There is no good way to make such claims, so omit them.

(d) None of the above.

Ans. (b) Makesustainable the claims and back them up with the examples.

(ii) Select the most suitable subject for applying this letter.

(a) Application for requesting job.

(b) Application writing.

(c) Application for the post of Marketing Manager.

(d) All of the above.

Ans. (c) Application for the post of Marketing Manager.

(iii) Select the essential points to be added to a biodata.

(A) Qualification, experience, contact details.

(B) Qualification, personal information.

(C) Personal information of the candidates.

(D) Experience and references.

(a) Only (A) (b) Only (C) (c) Both (A) and (C) (d) Both (C) and (D)

Ans. (c) Both (A) and (C)

(iv) In the above application, should the receiver's address be mentioned compulsorily?

(a) Yes (b) No (c) May be (d) None of these

Ans. (a) Yes

(v) How can you make the most of your college experience in your cover letter?

(a) Describe skills gained in the classroom.

(b) Describe sports and extra curricular activities.

(c) Discuss hands-on project.

(d) All of the above.

Ans. (d) All of the above.

5. *You are Chetan/Chetna, a commerce graduate from Delhi University. You are seeking a suitable job. You came across an advertisement in The Times of India, inviting young and dynamic fresh graduates as sales assistance in a reputed company. Apply for the said job to box No. 8365, C/O The Times Of India, New Delhi.*

(i) The length of the cover letter should not be:

(a) more than one page.

(b) more than two pages.

(c) more than three pages.

(d) none of these.

Ans. (a) more than one page.

(ii) According to the format of a job application, the spacing should be:

(A) Single spaced (B) Double space (C) Triple space (D) Tab

Ans. (a) Single spaced

(iii) The font size should be:

(a) 10.5 (b) 12 (c) 13 (d) 14

Ans. (d) 14

(iv) Select the appropriate starting information for the body of the job application.

(a) Advertisement reference.

(b) Personal information.

(c) Qualifications of the candidate.

(d) Address.

Ans. (a) Advertisement reference.

(v) Select the most appropriate ending for the job application.

(A) Requesting for job consideration.

(B) Thanking for the job opportunity.

(C) Pointing out strength.

(D) Pointing out weakness.

(a) Only (A) (b) Only (C) (c) Both (A) and (B) (d) Both (C) and (D)

Ans. (a) Only (A)

6. *Pramod Suri, a resident of 245, Tilak Nagar, Delhi, reads an advertisement for young school boys and girls to market the products of a renowned company in Delhi. So he decided to apply for the same. Write Pramod's application to Personnel Manager, Harrisons and Simpson Ltd. 237, Nehru Place, New Delhi.*

(i) How many types of job applications are there?

(a) 2 (b) 3 (c) 4 (d) 5

Ans. (a) 2

(ii) Do you think mentioning your experience and expertise in job application leaves a good impression?

(a) Yes (b) No (c) May be (d) May not be

Ans. (a) Yes

(iii) The body of the cover letter contains:

(a) Personal information or why you are applying for the job.

(b) Educational information.

(c) An account of experience or expertise.

(d) All of the above.

Ans. (d) All of the above.

(iv) When you are sending your cover letter saying that you will call to follow up within a week or so, you are using what type of ending?

(a) Aggressive (b) Active (c) Personal (d) Complimentary

Ans. (d) Complimentary

(v) Select the most appropriate subject for this job application.

(A) Job application for the post of Outdoor Marketing Manger.

(B) Resume.

(C) Cover letter.

(D) None of the above.

(a) Both (A) and (C) (b) Both (B) and (C) (c) Only (A) (d) Only (D)

Ans. (c) Only (A)

7. *A pharmaceutical company has opening for sale officers at various locations in north India. The candidate should be a science graduate below 28 years of age. 3-4 years of experience is desirable but not essential. The job requires selling the company's products to hospitals, private practitioners, and institutions. Apply for the above job stating your qualifications and experience. Write to Sales Manager, North I.C.I. India Ltd., Ansari Road, New Delhi.*

(i) ____________ is purposed to help the student with the cost of his/her studies.

(a) Resume (b) Scholarship (c) Both (a) and (b) (d) None of these

Ans. (b) Scholarship

(ii) Which of the following are the types of job application forms?

(A) E-mail job application.

(B) Online job application.

(C) Paper job application.

(D) None of the above.

(a) Both (A) and (C) (b) Both (B) and (C) (c) Both (A) and (B) (d) Only (D)

Ans. (a) Both (A) and (C)

(iii) Do not use job titles that are:

(a) misleading. (c) interesting and descriptive.

(b) vague. (d) both (a) and (b).

Ans. (d) both (a) and (b).

(iv) A signature is done ______ of the cover letter. Fill in the blank with appropriate choice.

(a) at the end (b) at the start (c) anywhere (d) none of these

Ans. (a) at the end

(v) Select the most appropriate starting line for this job application.

(a) I would like to work for your firm.....
(b) This is in response to your advertisement......
(c) Hope my particulars meet your requirements.....
(d) I wish to apply for the same post.....

Ans. (b) This is in response to your advertisement......

8. *You are Rajan/Rajni. Write an application in response to the following advertisement in a National Daily. Consider yourself suitable and eligible for this post. Applications are invited for the post of nursery teacher in A.K national school, UP. The candidate must have a minimum 3 years of teaching experience at the primary and pre-primary levels. The candidate must have a pleasant and energetic personality. An attractive salary is being offered. Interested candidates should apply to the Principal with a detailed resume.*

(i) Which of the following is not the function of a job application?

(a) To show how well you write.
(b) To inform the employer of the job you are applying.
(c) To inform the reader what you expect to get out of the job you're applying for.
(d) All of the above.

Ans. (c) To inform the reader of what you expect to get out of the job you're applying for.

(ii) When should you send a cover letter?

(a) Only if specifically requested.
(b) Every time you send your resume.
(c) When you need to list the reference.
(d) All of these.

Ans. (c) Every time you send out your resume.

(iii) Select the most appropriate subject for the job application.

(A) Application for the post of a nursery teacher.
(B) Request for job.
(C) Job application.
(D) Application for leaving the job.

(a) Both (A) and (D) (b) Both (A) and (C) (c) Both (B) and (D) (d) Both (C) and (D)

Ans. (b) Both (A) and (C)

(iv) Select the appropriate complimentary closing used in the job application.

(a) Yours faithfully (b) Your loving (c) Both (a) and (b) (d) None of these

Ans. (a) Yours faithfully

(v) While sending or uploading the job application, the candidate should end with their signature followed by_________.

(a) their name in typing
(b) complimentary closure
(c) biodata
(d) all of these

Ans. (a) their name in typing

9. *Draft an application for the post of an accountant in A.B.C. Ltd. Co. Hyderabad, in response to their advertisement that appeared in The Times of India dated 1st June, 20XX. Prepared Biodata to be enclosed. You are Nitin/Nicky.*

(i) Select the location where the name and address can be mentioned in a job profile.

(a) Bottom left corner
(b) Top left corner
(c) Top right corner
(d) Bottom right corner

Ans. (b) Top left corner

(ii) What is the total number of references usually given in Biodata?

(a) Two (b) Three (c) Four (d) Five

Ans. (a) Two

(iii) A summary of the applicant at the start of the CV acts as a:

(a) Letter of recommendation.
(b) Statement of objectives.
(c) Synopsis.
(d) Preface.

Ans. (d) Preface.

(iv) Which of the following is mentioned in a resume?

(a) Personal information. (b) Experience. (c) Qualification. (d) All of these.

Ans. (d) All of these.

(v) Which of the following not compulsory to mention in a job description CV?

(a) References (b) Name (c) Nationality (d) Education

Ans. (c) Nationality

10. *X.Y.Z. Industries, Mumbai has given an advertisement in The Hindustan Times for the recruitment of management trainee to be groomed as a manager of their company. To apply for the same, give your detailed Biodata. Furnish all necessary details. You are Atul/Anita, 55-K Gulab Road, Lucknow.*

(i) Which of the following is not revealed in the Biodata?

(a) Career aim (b) Address (c) Qualification (d) E-mail

Ans. (a) Career aim

(ii) Should references not be mentioned in a resume?

(a) True (b) False (c) Not known (d) Both (b) and (c)

Ans. (b) False

(iii) The ideal way to apply for a job vacancy is to submit a resume that is:

(a) full of personal information.
(b) suitable for any job.
(c) self-recommended.
(d) specially written for that job.

Ans. (d) specially written for that job.

(iv) Select the most appropriate subject for this job application.

(A) Job application for the post of Management Trainee.
(B) Requesting job on urgent basis.
(C) Enclosing Biodata.
(D) Job seeking application.

(a) Both (A) and (B) (b) Only (A) (c) Both (C) and (D) (d) Both (A) and (C)

Ans. (b) Only (A)

(v) Do not indicate _________ on the resume.

(a) birthdate (b) marital status (c) religion (d) all of these

Ans. (c) religion

Sample Newspaper Report :

1. A super speciality hospital was inaugurated in your by the Health Minister. As a reporter from 'The Hindu'. Write a brief report on the same to be published in the newspaper.

Super Speciality Hospital Inaugurated

by Neha Singh, Staff Reporter, The Hindu

New Delhi, 8th Aughst 20XX : 'Swasthya Surabhi;, a super speciality hospital was inaugurated by the Minister of State for Health, on Friday. The 400-bed hospital seemed to be equipped with the most advanced and state-of-the-art machines and equipments with the latest infrastructure to back up exigencies. It employs internationally trained physician in the field of emergency medicine. Fully equipped, advanced cardic. Life-support ambulances has been made a available round the clock. Besides having an in-house blook bank, its information system has been linked to the other major blood banks in the country to enable the right group of blood made available at a short notice.

The hospital covered an area of 8,000 square metres and the total expenditure in building the hospital had come around thirty-five crore rupees.

Addressing the people, Dr Prakash the Medical Superintendent, reinforced the need for dedicated and committed staff. He sincerely hoped that the hospital would provide the best health services to the people at a nominal cost.

A blood donation camp was also organised to mark the auspicious occasion. The authorities also announced free treatment for the poor patients on every weekend from 11 to 2 noon.

2. You are Meenu Kumar, a correspondent of 'The Hindu' Chennai. Write a report on the rescue of twenty children from the clutches of child-labour from a fire cracker manufacturing unit in Sivakasi.

Twenty Children rescued from Sivakasi

by Meenu Kumar, Staff Correspondent, The Hindu

Chennai, December 5th, 20xx : Twenty children, between 9 and 12 years of age, were rescued from a firecracker manufacturing unit in Sivakasi, a place about 76 kms from Chennai. The children were rescued from a godown of the unit. They were made to work 12-14 hours a day in a dingy factory. They were kept in dismal conditions with two paltry meals a day and were made to work seven days a week. Many of them are suffering from skin and respiratory infections. The owner of the manufacturing unit has been taken into custody. The police are contacting the parents of the children who come from neighbouring villages. The children have been housed in an ashram for the time-being and are being looked after by an NGO. The police are yet to take action against the factory owner and record the children's statements. Officials said that their parents will have to produce age certificate to take back their words. "We have rescued all the children and they are now in safer hands. Soon, the criminals will be behind the bars." said Ramanand Iyer, Chief Investigation officer.

3. Write a news report on a road accident you have witnessed in Delhi on 20th August.

24 Killed in a Road Accident

Report By-Prakash, Staff Correspondent

Delhi, August 20xx; Twenty-four people, including a woman and a two-month old baby, were killed in a tragic road accident involving a truck and a bus at Najafgarh, a village at 14 km from here. The ill-fated bus was carrying people for a wedding party from Delhi to Mathura. The truck was carrying industrial goods to Noida when it collided head-on with the bus, killing twelve of them on the spot. The injured were immediately rushed to Dr. RML Hospital where eight were succumbed to injuries.

The Police have registered a case against the truck driver as it claims the driver to be drunk while driving. During this may them, some tumultuous elements tried setting the truck ablaze. The police controlled the commotion caused after the accident and are searching for the accused everywhere.

4. You are Antriksh/Anisha of Daisy Public School, Delhi. Recently your school organised an educational tour for the students. Write a report of this in **120-150** words to be published in your school magazine. Use the given cues along with your own ideas to write a report about the same.

- 75 students from class VI-XII went on the tour.
- Four days long tour.
- Children enjoyed Kempty Falls and went for shopping.
- Visit to IMA and Indian Forest Research Institute.
- Parents expressed gratitude to the Principal and the teachers.

An Educational Excursion to Mussorie and Dehradun

By Antriksh/Anisha

Recently, our school organised an educational tour for a group of 75 students from class VI to XII. It was a four-day long tour to Mussorie and Dehradun and the children were accompanied by seven teachers. The children were asked to assemble at the school playground at 7 O'clock in the morning and from there, three buses were hired to take them. By the evening,the children reached Mussorie where there was an arrangement in a three star hotel for stay. Early in the morning they were taken for sightseeing and they had a thrilling experience at Kempty Falls. After spending a good time over there, they did bunjee jumping from a height of 30 feet under the supervision of trained experts. In the evening, they were taken to the shopping mall where the teachers along with students did a good shopping.

Next day, the buses headed for Dehradun. In Dehradun, the children visited Indian Military Academy and had an interaction with the trainees. They learnt about their lives and their duties. At the Indian Forest Research Institute, they got the knowledge of the various ways of forest conservation. The children gathered knowledge in one or the other form from the places wherever they visited. In the following evening, the children were taken for some shopping to the popular market there. Next day after that, the buses started back to their destination. At the school, parents had already gathered to welcome their young tourists. The children as well as parents showed their gratitude towards the teachers and the Principal for organising this wonderful trip.

Sample Magazine Report :

1. A seminar on Water Conservation was held in Mary Land School. As Preetam, the school leader, write a report for the school magazine.

Water Conservation Seminar at Mary Land School

by Preetam, School Leader

As a part of the World Water Day celebrations, Mary Land School organised a seminar on 'Water Conservation' in the school premises on 21st October, 20XX. The seminar was attended by students of six different schools from the city. The judges panel comprised of eminent people of the Municipal Water Board and some social workers of the city. The Mayor of the city was the Chief Guest who delivered the opening address. It was followed by a small documentary showing various ways how man wastes water. Then one by one, the speakers focused on the various ways of conserving water, namely rainwater harvesting, optimal use of water, taking shorter showers, turning off the faucets and pipes when not in use, etc. It was a very enlightening seminar with all the students learning a lot. The students also took an oath at the end of the seminar to contribute to the water-saving efforts of the community.

2. You are the Sports Captain of your school. The annual sports were conducted last month. Write a report in **120-150** words on the conduct of the same. You are Rohan/Ruhi of Delhi Public School, Mall Road, Amritsar.

Annual Sports Meet

by Rohan/Ruhi Chauhan, Sports Captain

Delhi Public School, Mall Road, Amritsar organised its Annual Sports Meet on 20th December, 20xx in its Saina Nehwal as the Chief Guest who was warmly welcomed by the Principal and the staff members. The event started with welcoming the eminent personalities, followed by the march past organised by the senior students of the school. It also included various jumps, races and drills. The winners were awarded the medals by the chief guest. After the award ceremony, Saina gave a speech wherein she congratulated the winners and encouraged the students to take up sports and make it their career options for the glory of the nation.

The event was a huge success where students and parents felt delighted. After the event was over, Saina was surrounded by a multitude of students who waited for long to take autographs and pictures with her.

Practice Exercise :

1. You are Sanjay/Sanjana. Recently when you were going to office in the morning, you witnessed a road accident. Write a report in **120-150** words for the local newspaper. Use the given cues along with your own ideas to write a report about the same.
   - 15 killed in Road Accident
   - The accident took place around 9:00 a.m.
   - Speeding truck rammed a tempo and then hit another car
   - Injured taken to the local medical college
   - The Chief Minister expressed his condolences
   - A magisterial enquiry has been ordered, said by the ADG of Police

2. Your School's N.S.S. Unit went on a cycling campaign creating awareness against plastics. As the leader of the team prepare a report to be read out.

Choose the correct option:

1. A report or account is an:

(a) informational work
(b) technical work
(c) professional work
(d) none of these

Ans. (a) informational work

2. **Report are often used to display the result of:**
   (a) experiment (b) investigation (c) inquiry (d) all of these

Ans. (d) all of these

3. **Report use features as:**
   (a) mobile
   (b) graphics and Images
   (c) method
   (d) account

Ans. (b) graphics and Images

4. **Types of Report:**
   (a) formal (b) research (c) resume (d) revision

Ans. (a) formal

5. **Which thing we need to do in writing report:**
   (a) record the survey not carry out
   (b) record deleted data
   (c) record the object
   (d) none of these

Ans. (c) record the object

6. **In report writing, the language should be:**
   (a) clear (b) unclear (c) vague (d) complicated

Ans. (a) clear

7. **Report writing should be written in:**
   (a) first person (b) second person (c) third person (d) none of these

Ans. (c) third person

8. **A report should be:**
   (a) clear (b) self- explanatory (c) comprehensive (d) all of these

Ans. (d) all of the above

9. **A well written report has:**
   (a) clarity of thoughts
   (b) proper date and place
   (c) both (a) and (b)
   (d) none of these

Ans. (b) proper date and place

10. **In report writing which one clearly states the purpose of the report?**
    (a) Letter transmittal (b) Title (c) Appendices (d) Bibliography

Ans. (b) Title

11. **In report writing which one tells where the story is originated?**
    (a) Placeline (b) Byline (c) Lead (d) Title

Ans. (a) Placeline

12. **What is the report body?**
    (a) It is the section where you present your research findings.
    (b) It is the section where you summarize the entire report.
    (c) It is the section where you give your recommendations.
    (d) It is the section where you make your conclusion.

Ans. (a) It is the section where you present your research findings.

13. **What are the 5W's of report writing?**
    (a) What, When, Why, Where, Who
    (b) What, When, Why, Where, With
    (c) What, When, Why, Where, How
    (d) What, When, With, Where, Who

Ans. (a) What, When, Why, Where, Who

14. **What should be included in the title page of the report?**
    (a) Title, writer's name
    (b) Title, report,
    (c) Title, side headings, date
    (d) Title, references, reports

Ans. (a) Title, writer's name

15. **What is a Lead in a News Article?**
    (a) Answers the questions who, what, where, when, why, and how.

(b) Is a long introduction to the article.
(c) Has quotations from authority figures.
(d) Contains who wrote the article.

Ans. (a) Answers the questions who, what, where, when, why, and how.

16. What is the byline?

(a) The title of the article.
(b) Contains the name of the place where the story took place.
(c) The secondary heading for the article.
(d) Contains the name of the person who wrote the article.

Ans. (d) Contains the name of the person who wrote the article.

17. What is a "quotation"?

(a) Dialogue which has ' ' symbols surrounding it
(b) The lead of the story.
(c) Another name for the headline of the article.
(d) Dialogue that has " " symbols surrounding it and a statement delivered by prominent personality

Ans. (d) Dialogue that has " " symbols surrounding it and a statement delivered by prominent personality

18. Who should the quotation be from?

(a) A random person
(b) A witness or authority figure
(c) A child
(d) The author

Ans. (b) A witness or authority figure

19. The order of a report is:

(a) lead, headline, byline, and summary paragraphs.
(b) headline, summary paragraphs, lead, and byline.
(c) headline, byline, lead, and summary paragraphs.
(d) headline, summary paragraphs, byline, and lead.

Ans. (c) headline, byline, lead, and summary paragraphs.

20. Where does this sentence belong in a report: Learning moving online as COVID crisis continues

(a) Headline
(b) Lead paragraph
(c) Body paragraph
(d) Summary / ending

Ans. (a) Headline

21. VILLAGE ADOPTION-A STEP TOWARDS BEING SOCIALLY RESPONSIBLE

L.M. Memorial Public School

5th March, 20XX

Dwarka

On the occasion of World Literacy Day, L.M. Memorial Public School, Dwarka has taken an oath to embrace the village named Rajpur.

The school has taken the responsibility of educating the people residing in the village. Selected students from each standard are taken there every weekend, during school hours to impart knowledge.

The first 6-month motive is to make each and every person capable of reading and writing. Free books and stationery are being provided for quality education.

Children are given time to spend with each other, play games, and interact.

Apart from educational needs, special care is devoted to hygiene and sanitation. Girls are being given awareness of the importance of menstrual hygiene as well.

Various talent hunts have been organized which left everyone overawed. The immense enthusiasm and zeal in the people to learn is the main driving factor.

A family kind of environment is being created. The school treats the people of the village as its own students and is unbiased. By adopting a village, the school is making its students sensitive towards the needs of the environment at a young age. It is committed to raising the leaders of tomorrow.

What is missing in the given report?

(a) Headline (b) Byline (c) Lead (d) Placeline

Ans. (b) Byline

22. By: Preeti
Maryland School,
16th March, 20XX
Gurgaon

Our school organised a seminar on 'Water Conservation' as part of the World Water Day Celebrations on 13th August, 20XX. The main aim of this seminar was to remind us all about the need to save the government and the non-governmental organisations in providing help water as it is a precious source imperative for our survival.

Distinguished environmentalists and eminent personalities were our guest speakers and they reiterated the need not only of conserving water but also spoke at length on how to conserve water by stressing upon the fact that each drop of water is precious. Dr. Yashraj, an eminent environmentalist, suggested rain-water harvesting as one of the best ways to conserve water.

Using visual aids to highlight his discourse, he suggested that to ensure availability of water for the future generations the withdrawal of fresh water from an ecosystem should not exceed its natural replacement rate. The seminar concluded on the note that water conservation is the most cost-effective, environmentally sound way to reduce our demand for water and so each one of us must do our bit towards improving water management to enhance optimum use of water.

What is missing in the given report?

(a) Lead (b) Headline (c) Date (d) Byline

Ans. (b) Headline

23. Inter-School Twenty
Over Cricket Match
By: Ramesh, Sports Secretary,

17th January, 20XX.

Last Monday an inter-school twenty over cricket match played in our school grounds between Kendriya Vidyalaya, Sector-4 and Central School, Sector-37. It was one of the most thrilling match that we all had seen as the winner was decided only after the last ball of the match had been bowled. Kendriya Vidyalaya won the toss and chose to bat. They set a target of 130 runs in twenty overs for the opposition team who beat them in the last ball of the match by hitting a boundary which took their score to 131 runs. Central School had to make ten runs in the last two balls in order to win. Their star batsman ABC scored a six followed by a fantastic boundary to take his team to victory. It was a great match with a nail-biting finish and all the spectators present there thoroughly enjoyed watching it.

What is the missing part in the given report?

(a) Date (b) Byline (c) Lead (d) Placeline

Ans. (d) Placeline

24. Music And Dance Fiesta
Poorva, Cultural Secretary

D.B. Senior Secondary School, Ambur:

Our school organised a week-long Music and Dance festival, which commenced on the 18th of August and ended on the 26th of August, in which 15 schools of our town participated. It was a great music and dance extravaganza which saw a wide variety of Indian classical music and folklore and western music and dance forms. During this week-long festival, many competitions and programmes were organised in our school and these were graced by illustrious musicians and reputed dancers. On the concluding day of this festival, a two-hour-long programme displaying a unique fusion of classical and western dance and music was put up. This was a treat and delight for all music and dance lovers and was also the highlight of our festival. Seeing the huge success of this fiesta our principal assured us that attempts would be made to organise it on a regular basis.

What is missing in the given report?

(a) Date (b) Headline (c) Placeline (d) Byline

Ans. (a) Date

❑❑

SECTION - C
LITERATURE

Prose–Flamingo

4. The Rattrap–by Selma Lagerlof

Summary :

There was a poor man who sold rattraps and earned his livelihood. His income from the traps was not enough so he begged and stole petty things at times. He used to sleep at night in the houses of people if they allowed him or sometimes in a factory like Ramsjo Iron-Works. Once, an idea struck him that the world was like a rattrap full of temptations. If a man was tempted by the baits of wealth, power, etc. he was supposed to be trapped like a rat in a rattrap. The man selling rattraps lived in poverty without enough food or shelter. So he looked upon the world in the light of his own sufferings. Once, he took shelter in the house of a man who was the crofter in Ramsjo Iron-Works. The man was lonely without any family. He welcomed the rattrap seller as he would get rid of his loneliness at least for a night.

The crofter told him about his life and showed him the thirty kronor that the crofter had kept near the window. The peddler stole the money. Initially, he was happy to get the money but soon he began to work. He feared detection and avoided the highway. He walked through the forest and lost his way there. He then saw the forge of the Ramsjo Iron Works and went there to spend the night. At that time, the iron-master, the owner of the factory, came in. The iron-master mistook him to be his old friend, Nils Olof, with whom he had served in the regiment. To help his friend in his bad days, he invited the peddler to his house. The peddler realized that the iron-master was making a mistake but he preferred to stay quiet.

But he did not like to go into his house as he feared that he might be exposed and identified. The kind-hearted daughter of the iron-master, Edla Willmansson was too compassionate and loving to be resisted. She even suspected that the stranger might have committed some crime. But she ignored that and thought that the man, haunted by fear and security, must have lived a miserable life. She wanted to give him some relief. She assured the peddler that in her house, he would be safe from any interference and would be free to leave anytime. She persuaded him to be her guest on the Christmas Eve. The genuine compassion of Edla gave the man a sense of peace and security. He slept all the while as if he wanted to make up for the sleepless nights he had spent throughout his life.

He ate the Christmas delicacies. The daughter gave him a suit and she invited him for the next Christmas and assured him of secrecy and security. The rattrap seller was overwhelmed. The next morning, he left the manor house. But before leaving, he left the packet containing the thirty kronor of the crofter. He wrote a letter to Edla asking her to return the money to the crofter. He wrote that she had treated him with respect as if he was a real captain. She had treated him as a man and not as a thief. That genuine regard had induced him to be a better man and to give up stealing. Thus, the genuine compassion and kindness of Edla changed the life of a thief and turned him to a better man.

Text Book Questions :

Notice these expressions in the text. Infer their meaning from the context.

(a) Keep body and soul together—to survive/live.

(b) Plods along the road—walk wearily along the road.

(c) Impenetrable prison—inescapable prison (here forest).

(d) Eased his way—easily made his way.

(e) Things have gone downhill—to fall in fortune.

(f) Hunger gleamed in his eyes—starvation reflected in his eyes.

(g) Unwonted joy—unusual joy.

(h) Nodded a haughty consent—arrogantly agreeing for something.

(i) Fallen into a line of thought—possess a particular idea or way of thinking.

Think as you Read :

Q. 1. From where did the peddler get the idea of the world being a rattrap?

Ans. During one of his usual plodding, the peddler thought on the subject of rattraps. It presented him with the idea of the world being a rattrap and he grew fond of thinking this way.

Q. 2. Why was he amused by this idea?

Ans. The peddler was amused by the idea of the world being a giant rattrap as he was never treated very kindly by the world. Therefore, he developed hard feelings for this harsh world and loved 'to think ill of it' by comparing it with a giant rattrap.

Q. 3. Did the peddler expect the kind of hospitality that he received from the crofter?

Ans. No, the peddler did not expect the kind of hospitality that he had received from the crofter. This was because he was generally greeted by harsh, sour and unfriendly faces whenever he had knocked on doors and requested for shelter.

Q. 4. Why was the crofter so talkative and friendly with the peddler?

Ans. The crofter was a lonely fellow who lived alone in a little gray cottage by the roadside. He had no wife or children, so he longed for a company or friends. So, when the peddler reached his doorstep, he was happy to find someone to talk to and felt happy to be relieved of his boredom and monotony. This is the reason he was so talkative and friendly with the peddler.

Q. 5. Why did he show the thirty kroner to the peddler?

Ans. The crofter was a simple and trusting man who craved for a company more than anything else. He wanted to share his joy of earning the money with someone. He got this chance when the peddler turned up at his house one day. Moreover, thinking that the peddler did not believe him, he showed the peddler the thirty kronor bills that he had kept in a leather pouch.

Q. 6. Did the peddler respect the confidence reposed in him by the crofter?

Ans. No, the peddler did not respect the confidence reposed in him by the crofter. In fact, he betrayed his trust by robbing the thirty kroner. But somehow, later in the story, his conscience was awakened by his stay with the Willmanssons and he decides to return the money.

Q. 7. What made the peddler think that he had indeed fallen into a rattrap?

Ans. After stealing the money from the crofter, the peddler tried to escape through the forest but soon lost his way. He was left in despair and he recollected his own thoughts on the world being a giant rattrap. A sudden realization came upon him and he felt as if he had finally got himself caught in the rattrap because he had allowed himself to be tempted by the bait, the thirty kronor bills. Similarly, on his way to the ironmaster's home, he felt himself caught in the trap. He was again haunted by such thoughts when the ironmaster, after coming to know about the truth of the peddler, threatened to get him arrested. The rattrap seller strongly realized that the worldly bait had, once more, tempted and trapped him.

Q. 8. Why did the ironmaster speak kindly to the peddler and invite him home?

Ans. The ironmaster of the Ramsjö Ironworks spoke kindly to the peddler because he had mistaken him for an old regimental comrade, Captain Von Stahle. So, the ironmaster wanted to help the peddler, not only in regaining his health but also in taking up a new vocation. Moreover, the ironmaster was a lonely fellow who lived with his oldest daughter after the death of his wife and the departure of his sons. As he longed for someone's company on the Christmas Eve, he invited the peddler to his home.

Q. 9. Why did the peddler decline the invitation?

Ans. The peddler was alarmed at the idea and request of the ironmaster of spending the night at the manor of the ironmaster, of the Ramsjö Ironworks, who also happened to be an ex-army man. He did not make any attempt to correct the ironmaster when he was mistaken for an old acquaintance. Moreover, he was more worried about the fact that he had the stolen thirty kronor bills with him, and accepting the invitation would be like throwing himself voluntarily into the lion's den. Therefore, the peddler thought it better to decline the invitation.

Q.10. What made the peddler accept Edla Willmansson's invitation?

Ans. Looking at the frightened expressions on the peddler's face, Edla guessed that the peddler had either stolen something or had escaped prison. So she hinted an assurance that he would be free to leave whenever he wanted. Reassured by Edla's guarantee, he accepted the invitation.

Q.11. What doubts did Edla have about the peddler?

Ans. When Edla went to the iron mill to fetch the peddler, she noticed that he was frightened. She had doubts that either the peddler had stolen something or had escaped prison. His appearance and behaviour also left her in doubts whether he was actually an educated man, as claimed by her father.

Q.12. When did the ironmaster realize his mistake?

Ans. The ironmaster realized his mistake the next day when the peddler turned up for breakfast. The valet had bathed the peddler, cut his hair, shaved him and given him clothes. The ironmaster thought that he had been deceived in recognizing the person because of the shade of the furnace the previous night.

Q.13. What did the peddler say in his defence when it was clear that he was not the person the ironmaster had thought he was?

Ans. The peddler defended himself by arguing time and again that he never said that he was a captain or the old comrade of the ironmaster. In fact, he had repeatedly declined the ironmaster's invitation to spend the Christmas night at his manor.

Q.14. Why did Edla entertain the peddler even after she knew the truth about him?

Ans. Edla was a lady with a kind and sympathetic heart and was moved by the plight of the peddler. She had requested her father to allow him to spend one day in peace as a respite from the struggle he had endured round the year. Her principles did not allow her to throw the man out of her house especially when they had promised him a Christmas cheer. Moreover, she had been in high spirits that morning, thinking of the ways to help the tramp. Therefore she entertained the peddler even after knowing the truth about him.

Q.15. Why was Edla happy to see the gift left by the peddler?

Ans. Edla had shown great trust in the peddler by letting him stay at their manor on the Christmas Eve but the news about the robbery of thirty kroner at the crofter's cottage had left her dejected. So she was overjoyed when she reached home to find the package and the letter, left by the peddler. This gesture of appreciation from the peddler made her happy.

Q.16. Why did the peddler sign himself as Captain Von Stahle?

Ans. The peddler had never received respect throughout his life. He was always treated coldly by the world. For the first time in his life, he was being honored and respected. Even after the truth was exposed, the daughter of the ironmaster treated him as she did before. The treatment he received, encouraged him to behave in the similar manner. He signed as Captain Von Stahle so as to underline the impact of Edla's goodness to him.

Understanding the Text :

Q. 1. How does the peddler interpret the acts of kindness and hospitality shown to him by the crofter, the ironmaster and his daughter ?

Ans. The different ways in which he repaid the three people corresponded to the way he interpreted the kindness of the three people. The peddler realized that for the crofter it was his craving for a company that made him offer his hospitality. The ironmaster's hospitality was limited to his acquaintances. It was only the daughter who showed genuine goodness. He was touched by Edla's kindness and it made him act differently. He repaid her good act with a gesture of true gratitude.

Q. 2. What are the instances in the story that show that the character of the ironmaster is different from that of his daughter in many ways?

Ans. Edla and her father were individuals of different natures. Edla had more convincing power than her father and was able to persuade the peddler to accept the invitation. We also read that the ironmaster's hospitability was limited to his old comrade. But, the daughter was from her deep heart pained by the plight of the peddler and continued to treat him well even after the truth about his identity was revealed. Again, after coming to know about the robbery of the crofter's money at the prayer service at church, while the ironmaster was more concerned with the possibility of the peddler robbing them as well, the daughter is more pained by the betrayal of her trust. We also find that while the father was impulsive and reckless in nature, the behaviour of the daughter was more mature and controlled.

Q. 3. The story has many instances of unexpected reactions from the characters to other's behaviour. Pick out instances of these surprises.

Ans. The first instance is the hospitality of crofter. The rattrap seller who was in a habit of being shoed away was surprised at the friendly behaviour of the crofter. He was also surprised at the sudden invitation of the ironmaster (at his mill where the peddler had put up to take shelter at night) to spend the Christmas Eve at his manor. Later, the ironmaster was also shocked to realize his mistake in recognizing the peddler, the next day. Another unexpected reaction was that of Edla, who in spite of knowing the truth of the peddler intervenes to seek the peddler's presence on Christmas Eve. The most unexpected reaction is from the peddler when he leaves an envelope and a letter for Edla showing gratitude for the girl's kindness and hospitality.

Q. 4. What made the peddler finally change his ways?

Ans. The experience of the peddler at the manor of the Willmanssons made him change his ways. Earlier, he had neither known nor come across a true sympathizer or well-wisher. He had no friend to steer him on the right path. Though the crofter had been very hospitable to him and even the ironmaster had almost offered him help, they both failed to leave any impact on him. It was Edla who, through her genuine care and understanding was finally able to change the peddler for the better.

Q. 5. How does the metaphor of a rattrap serve to highlight human predicament?

Ans. The metaphor of a rattrap signifies that the world exists only to trap people by setting baits for them. Whenever someone is tempted by some luxury, he ends up being caught in a dangerous trap. The author makes a deeper comment on the woeful plight of those in pursuit of worldly pleasure which often leads them to unpleasant situations. The story helps in realizing the importance of general goodness and kindness. The peddler is saved from the snare of the trap of the world when he appreciates the kindness extended to him by Edla.

Q. 6. The peddler comes out as a person with a subtle sense of humour. How does this serve in lightening the seriousness of the theme of the story and also endear him to us?

Ans. The peddler doesn't come across as a humorous person, although one can easily find a subtle sense of humour in the way he thought about the world as being a giant rattrap. He was singularly pleased by this thought of his because it provided him with the opportunity of thinking ill of the world that was not kind to him. It is clearly visible that whenever he got caught unaware in the web of deceit spun by his scheming mind, he hid himself behind the thought that the world was a rattrap and he was merely a prey. Thus, he lightened the mood and theme of the story and made us endear him.

Talking about the Text :

Discuss the following in groups of four. Each group can deal with one topic. Present the views of your group to the whole class.

Q. 1. The reader's sympathy is with the peddler right from the beginning of the story. Why is this so? Is the sympathy justified?

Ans. From the beginning, the rattrap seller is shown as a victim of situations and circumstances and not a downright evil character. The peddler had to resort to beggary and stealing because his business was not profitable enough to make both ends meet. His condition of penury did not allow him to be fully righteous. Moreover, we find that he lacked friends and a guide to steer him towards the right path. The sympathy was justified because in the end we find out that the peddler was capable of appreciating genuine goodness and hospitality. When he was treated with respect and kindness by Edla, the daughter of the ironmaster, he reciprocated in the best way he could.

Q. 2. The story also focuses on human loneliness and the need to bond with others.

Ans. The Rattrap deals with the issues of human loneliness and the need to bond with others. Not only the peddler but also other characters like the crofter, the ironmaster and Edla emphasize upon this fact.

The peddler's conscience had left him because he had been lonely in his predicament, for a long time. But Edla's kindness and hospitality changed him. The crofter, on the other hand, was a lonely fellow whose craving for company led him to give shelter to a vagabond, and he ended up getting robbed. Even the ironmaster and his daughter suffer from loneliness. They crave for a company on Christmas Eve and were excited when they got the opportunity to serve a guest.

Q. 3. The story is both entertaining and philosophical.

Ans. The story was told in the form of a fairy tale with a happy ending. The narrative was interesting with many surprises and attention-grabbing dialogues. The twists and the unexpected reactions of the characters often astonished the reader, making the story entertaining. However, the author has carefully managed to weave philosophical elements into the storyline. The rattrap peddler's comparison of the whole world with a giant rattrap makes this an interesting commentary on how such people end up getting trapped in the giant chasm. The story also makes an observation on the inherent goodness of people. It also showcases how goodness and kindness shown by some people can change others' perspective.

Working with words :

Q. 1. The man selling rattraps is referred to by many terms such as "peddler, stranger" etc. Pick out all such references to him. What does each of these labels indicate of the context or the attitude of the people around him?

Ans.

Labels	Contexts
Peddler	As he peddles or sells the rattraps.
Vagabond	Used to describe his nomadic lifestyle.
Stranger	Used to refer to the peddler when he was at the crofter's place, possibly to emphasize the fact that the crofter was compassionate to an unknown man.
Guest	He is treated with compassion, especially at the iron-master's house where he was invited to spend the Christmas.
Intruder	When the peddler trespasses and enters the iron mill.
Tramp	When the peddler asks for lodgings at the iron mill; also when the ironmaster, mistaking him for his old regimental comrade plans of helping him drop his tramp ways and begin a new vocation.
Ragamuffin	When the ironmaster first notices him wrapped in rags and in the state to utter destitution.
Old regimental comrade	The ironmaster mistakes him for his old friend when he first meets the peddler at his iron mill.
Rat	The peddler calls himself a rat and thanks Edla for helping him escape the rattrap with her kindness and compassion.
The poor hungry wretch	Used only once when the author mentions the fact that Edla was excited about the prospect of getting a chance to help an unfortunate fellow on Christmas.

Q. 2. You came across the words, plod, trudge and stagger in the story. These words indicate movement accompanied by weariness. Find five other such words with a similar meaning.

Ans. Other words are lurch, stumble, slog, hike, clump, traipse and stomp.

Noticing Form :

1. He made them **himself** at odd moments.
2. He raised **himself.**
3. He had let **himself** be fooled by a bait and had been caught.
4. A day may come when **you yourself** may want to get a big piece of pork.

Notice the way in which these reflexive pronouns have been used (pronoun + self)

- In 1 and 4, the reflexive pronouns 'himself' and 'yourself' are used to convey emphasis.
- In 2 and 3, the reflexive pronoun is used in place of personal pronoun to signal that it refers to the same subject in the sentence.

Pick out other examples of the use of reflexive pronouns from the story and notice how they are used.

Ans.

Examples	Usage
"...would be like throwing himself voluntarily into the lion's den."	used in place of personal pronoun to signal that it refers to the same subject in the sentence.
"...except my oldest daughter and myself."	used in place of personal pronoun to signal that it refers to the same subject in the sentence.
"...he laughed to himself."	used in place of personal pronoun to signal that it refers to the same subject in the sentence.
"...better powers of persuasion than he himself."	used to convey emphasis.
"...stretched himself out on the floor."	used in place of personal pronoun to signal that it refers to the same subject in the sentence.
"...He could not bring himself to oppose her."	used to convey emphasis.

Thinking about Language :

Q. 1. Notice the words in bold in the following sentence.

"The fire boy shovelled charcoal into the maw of the furnace with a great deal of clatter." This is a phrase that is used in the specific context of an iron plant.

Pick out other such phrases and words from the story that are peculiar to the terminology of ironworks.

Ans. Other such phrases could be as follows:

1. 'A hard regular thumping'
2. 'Hammer strokes'
3. 'A large plant with smelter, rolling mill and forge'
4. 'Pig iron'
5. 'Coal dust'
6. 'Put on the anvil'

Q. 2. Mjolis is a card game of Sweden.

Name a few indoor games played in your region. 'Chopar' could be an example.

Ans. Some indoor games are chess, ludo, table-tennis, playing cards, billiards, etc.

Q. 3. A crofter is a person who rents or owns a small farm especially in Scotland. Think of other uncommon terms for 'a small farmer' including those in your language.

Ans. Some other terms are peasant, cultivator, krishak, kisan etc.

Additional Questions :

Q. 1. What kind of host was the old crofter?

Ans. The old crofter was an affectionate and generous host. He warmly welcomed the peddler as he got someone to talk to, in his loneliness. He served him porridge for his supper and offered a pipe with tobacco roll to smoke and also played Mjolis with him till his bedtime.

Q. 2. Who do you think was at fault-the ironmaster or the peddler? Give two reasons.

Ans. I think the ironmaster was at fault because it was he who invited the tramp to his house for that Christmas thinking him to be his old acquaintance; but on knowing that he was not his acquaintance, he could not oppose his daughter's decision to offer him Christmas cheer. Also, the iron master mistook the peddler for his old friend without establishing his identity.

Q. 3. Did the peddler respect the confidence reposed in him by the crofter?

Ans. No, the peddler did not respect the confidence reposed in him by the crofter. In fact, he betrayed the crofter by stealing 30 kronors from him. However, later in the story, his conscience was awakened during his stay with the Williamnsson and he returned the money.

Q. 4. Did the peddler expect the hospitality he receive from the crofter?

Ans. No, the peddler did not expect the hospitality he received from the crofter. This was because he was usually greeted by sour and unfriendly faces whenever he knocked on doors and requested for shelter.

Q. 5. Why was the crofter so talkative and friendly with the peddler?

Ans. The crofter was a lonely fellow and lived on his own in a small gray cottage by the roadside. He had no wife or partner, so he craved for company of friends. So, one day when the peddler turned up at his doorstep, he was happy to find someone to talk to, and be free from his boredom and monotony.

Q. 6. What made the peddler think that he had indeed fallen in a rattrap?

Ans. After stealing the money, the peddler thought of escaping through the forest but he lost his way. Left in despair, he recollected his own thought on the world being a rattrap. A sudden realization came to him that he has finally got himself into the rattrap because he had allowed himself to be tempted by the 30 kronor bills;. Similarly, on his way home to the ironmaster, he felt himself caught in the trap. He was again haunted by the thoughts when the ironmaster on knowing the truth about the peddler, threatened to get him arrested. The rattrap seller strongly felt that the worldly bait has once more tempted and trapped him.

Q. 7. Why did the peddler decline the invitation?

Ans. The peddler was alarmed at the idea of spending the night at the ironmaster's house who was an ex-army man. He did not make any attempt to correct the ironmaster when he mistook him for an old acquaintance. Moreover, he was anxious of the thought that he had the stolen 30 kroner bills with him and accepting the invitation would be 'throwing himself voluntarily into the lion's den'. Therefore, the peddler thought it better to decline the invitation.

Q. 8. How did the peddler defend himself?

Ans. He defended himself by arguing that he never said that he was a captain or the old comrade of the ironmaster. In fact, he had repeatedly declined the invitation of the ironmaster to spend the Christmas night at the manor.

Q. 9. Why did the peddler sign himself as Captain Van Stahle?

Ans. The peddler had never known respect throughout his life. He was always treated coldly by the world. For the first time in his life, he was honoured and respected. Even after the truth was exposed, the daughter of the ironmaster treated him like before. The treatment he received encouraged him to behave in the similar manner. He signed as Captain Von Stahle so as to underline the impact of Edla's goodness to him.

Q.10. Why did the Crofter repose confidence in the peddler? How did the peddler feel after betraying the Crofter?*

Ans. The Crofter reposed confidence in the peddler because he was a lonesome man who used to live alone. He wanted someone with whom he could share his feelings, so he trusted him to the extent of showing him where he had kept his money. Despite the Crofter treating the peddler with hospitality, the peddler robbed him and was quite pleased with his smartness. However, the fear of getting caught haunted him. So, he avoided the public highway and turned into the woods. It was a big and confusing forest, and due to darkness, he lost his way. He got exhausted moving around the same place, and was filled with despair. He began to feel that the forest was like a big rattrap and the thirty kronors he had stolen were like a bait set to tempt him. He felt helpless like a rat who had no way out of the trap in which he had fallen.

Q.11. How did the Crofter entertain the peddler?*

Ans. Crofter entertained the peddler with his talks and friendly gestures. The crofter was so talkative and friendly with the peddler because he was leading a lonely life in the cottage. He had no one with whom he could talk to and due to this, his life was so boring and monotonous. He was an old man who was living there without a wife or child. So, he was happy to get someone to talk to in his loneliness.

Previous Years' Questions :

Q.1. The peddler believed that the whole world is a rattrap. How did he himself get caught in the same ?

Ans. The peddler believed that the whole world was nothing but a big rattrap. It baited people in the form of riches and joys. The peddler could not make ends meet, so he had to take to both begging and petty theft. As he got lured by the bait of thirty kronors, the world closed in on him and trapped him. He got lost in the forest. At that moment, he realised that his end was near.

Q.2. The peddler thinks that the whole world is a rattrap. This view of life is true only of himself and of no one else in the story. Comment.

Ans. This view of life is universal. It is not true for just the peddler. It relates to everyone who was ever a victim of circumstances. The Peddler, a poor vagabond, marks and sells rattraps to make both ends meet. He even found a parable between the world and the rattrap. He had been living a despicable life of misery, poverty and frustation, visualising the whole world to be a rattrap ready to engorge anyone who succumbed to the bots of its riches and joy. The world had been rather unkind to him, so he felt happy to think ill about it. Despite the Crofter's kindness and hospitality, he betrayed his trust and stole his money. But Edla's compassion and understanding finally brought about a transformation in his nature. So, this situation cannot be judged in case of the Peddler only, rather in everyone who has been victim to this cruel and unkind society.

Q.3. What do we learn about the crofter's nature from the story, 'The Rattrap' ?

Ans. The crofter was a lonely old man who had no wife or a child. He wanted someone to talk to, therefore, he allowed the peddler to spend the night at his house. He not only gave him shelter, but also gave him food to eat and tobacco to smoke. He started a conversation with him and told him everything about himself and his earnings.

Q.4. Why did the iron master speak kindly to the peddler and invite him home ?

Ans. The iron master took the peddler for an old regimental comrade, Nils Olof. He considered the peddler as an old acquaintance who had fallen on evil days so he talked to him kindly and invited him to come home to help him.

Q.5. What hospitality did the peddler receive from the crofter ?

Ans. Unlike the indifferent attitude of the others towards him, the peddler was whole heartedly welcomed by the crofter in his cottage. The crofter at once put the porridge pot on the fire and gave him supper. He gave him a roll of tobacco for his pipe. He also played a game of cards with him.

---

* are board exam questions from previous years

Q.6. Why did Edla plead with her father not to send the vagabond away ?

Ans. Edla was a kind hearted woman. She was pained by the plight of the poor Peddler. She requested her father to allow him to spend one day with them in peace as a respite from the struggle he had to endure round the year.

Q.7. Why did the peddler derive pleasure from his idea of the world as a rat trap?

Ans. The peddler was never treated kindly by the world, which was why he was amused by the idea of the world to be a rat trap. He nurtured hard feelings towards the world by comparing it to a giant rat trap.

Q.8. How did the peddler feel after robbing the crofter ? What course did he adopt and how did he react to the new situation ? What does his reaction reveal ?

Ans. The peddler robbed thirty kronor from crofter's house, who gave him shelter for the whole night in his cottage showing him kindness and hospitality. The peddler felt very happy after that and believed, that it was not safe to walk along the public highway. So, he went into the woods but lost his way and when he could not get out of it, he thought the whole world, with its lands and seas, its cities and villages is nothing but a big 'rattrap' and he was the victim of it. He felt that the bait in his case was the money that he had stolen from crofter's house. It was now his turn to be caught in the world's rattrap. Whenever we become the victim to temptations, we get trapped in this vicious circle.

Peddler could not help but think, and was trying to prove his act of robbery that crofter had put the money to trap him and given to temptation, he was also caught. He was not the only one who was tempted, but almost everyone; some or the other day gets trapped.

Reference to Context :

Read the given extract to attempt questions that follow:

1. *"The rattrap is a Christmas present from a rat who would have been caught in this world's rattrap if he had not been raised to captain, because in that way he got power to clear himself. "Written with friendship and high regard, "Captain von Stahle."*

(i) Why did the Captain want "to clear himself"?

(a) He felt guilty of his past deeds and wanted to make a new start.

(b) He was expecting a promotion for which he had to clear his name from past offences.

(c) He was moving to a new city and wanted a final clearance of his work.

(d) He was applying for a loan and required a clearance for the same.

Ans. (a) He felt guilty of his past deeds and wanted to make a new start.

(ii) The figurative meaning of "Rattrap" refers to:

(a) Desires (b) The world (c) The people (d) Life

Ans. (b) The world

(iii) Identify the figure of speech in the line, *"The rattrap is a Christmas present from a rat"*.

(a) Simile (b) Metaphor (c) Oxymoron (d) Personification

Ans. (b) Metaphor

(iv) Who is 'Captain von Stahle'?

(a) A thief. (c) An impersonator.

(b) A regimental comrade. (d) Nils Olof.

Ans. (c) An impersonator.

(v) What does being "raised to Captain" means?

(a) Assuming new responsibilities. (c) Having a change of heart.

(b) Getting promoted. (d) Transitioning into a newer sense of selfhood.

Ans. (c) Having a change of heart.

Read the given extract to attempt questions that follow:

2. *"No one can imagine how sad and monotonous life can appear to such a vagabond, who plods along the road, left to his own meditations. But one day this man had fallen into a line of thought, which really seemed to him entertaining. He had naturally been thinking of his rattraps when suddenly he was struck by the idea that the whole world about him — the whole world with its lands and seas, its cities and villages — was nothing but a big rattrap. It had never existed for any other purpose than to set baits for people. It offered riches and joys, shelter and food, heat and clothing, exactly as the* *rattrap offered cheese and pork, and as soon as anyone let himself be tempted to touch the bait, it closed in on him, and then everything came to an end."*

(i) What does the phrase "left to his own meditations" means?

(a) To follow own exercise regime.
(b) To meditate at night.
(c) To do as one pleases.
(d) To be left on their own.

Ans. (d) To be left on their own.

(ii) What does the phrase "line of thought" mean?

(a) A particular way of thinking.
(b) A line with different thoughts.
(c) To think about a line.
(d) To ponder.

Ans. (a) A particular way of thinking.

(iii) The reason behind falling for the "bait" is?

(a) Gluttony (b) Envy (c) Greed (d) Anger

Ans. (c) Greed

(iv) The paragraph is________.

(a) self-explanatory (b) non-fiction (c) symbolic (d) figurative

Ans. (c) symbolic

(v) The author draws a parallel reference between:

(a) rich and poor.
(b) thieves and vagabonds.
(c) riches, joys and cheese, pork.
(d) bait and greed.

Ans. (c) riches, joys and cheese, pork.

Read the given extract to attempt questions that follow:

3. *"The next day both men got up in good season. The crofter was in a hurry to milk his cow, and the other man probably thought he should not stay in bed when the head of the house had gotten up. They left the cottage at the same time. The crofter locked the door and put the key in his pocket. The man with the rattraps said good bye and thank you, and thereupon each went his own way. But half an hour later the rattrap peddler stood again before the door. He did not try to get in, however. He only went up to the window, smashed a pane, stuck in his hand, and got hold of the pouch with the thirty kronor. He took the money and thrust it into his own pocket. Then he hung the leather pouch very carefully back in its place and went away"*

(i) What does "getting up" in good season mean?

(a) Getting up in winter
(b) Getting up late
(c) Getting up early
(d) Getting up in a timely manner

Ans. (d) Getting up in a timely manner

(ii) The bait for the rat was?

(a) Pork (b) Cheese (c) Kronor (d) Food

Ans. (c) Kronor

(iii) The crofter was a __________ Host.

(a) kind (b) cunning (c) shrewd (d) trustworthy

Ans. (a) kind

(iv) What is the figurative meaning of "each went on his own way"?

(a) Both men went in opposite directions.
(b) Crofter went north and the stranger went south.
(c) Crofter went east and the stranger went west.
(d) Each went as per their nature of earning a livelihood.

Ans. (d) Each went as per their nature of earning a livelihood.

(v) Who is the head of the house?

(a) Crofter (b) Thief (c) Landowner (d) Elizabeth

Ans. (a) Crofter

Read the given extract to attempt questions that follow:

4. *"First of all we must see to it that he gets a little flesh on his bones," he said to his daughter, who was busy at the table. "And then we must see that he gets something else to do than to run around the country selling rattraps." "It is queer that things have gone downhill with him as badly as that," said the daughter. "Last night I did not think there was anything about him to show that he had once been an educated man."*

(i) What does adding "flesh on his bones" means?

(a) Surgery
(b) Providing food
(c) Providing animal skin
(d) Providing clothes

Ans. (b) Providing food

(ii) Which country is being talked about?

(a) Sweden (b) Switzerland (c) London (d) USA

Ans. (a) Sweden

(iii) Who is being talked about here?

(a) The old man
(b) Captain von Stahle
(c) The ironman
(d) Vagabond

Ans. (d) Vagabond

(iv) Select the correct option to fill in the blank.

Going downhill implies________.

(a) things not going well
(b) going downstream
(c) avoiding other routes
(d) going down the hill

Ans. (a) things not going well

(v) Select the correct option to fill in the blank.

The daughter is _________.

(a) persuasive (b) outspoken (c) friendly (d) good hearted

Ans. (a) persuasive

Read the given extract to attempt questions that follow:

5. *As he walked along with the money in his pocket he felt quite pleased with his smartness. He realised, of course, that at first he dared not continue on the public highway, but must turn off the road, into the woods. During the first hours this caused him no difficulty. Later in the day it became worse, for it was a big and confusing forest which he had gotten into. He tried, to be sure, to walk in a definite direction, but the paths twisted back and forth so strangely! He walked and walked without coming to the end of the wood, and finally he realised that he had only been walking around in the same part of the forest. All at once he recalled his thoughts about the world and the rattrap. Now his own turn had come. He had let himself be fooled by a bait and had been caught. The whole forest, with its trunks and branches, its thickets and fallen logs, closed in upon him like an impenetrable prison from which he could never escape.*

(i) Which figure of speech does the "forest" denote?

(a) Metaphor (b) Simile (c) Personification (d) Hyperbole

Ans. (a) Metaphor

(ii) Which emotion is the thief going through?

(a) Nervousness (b) Fear (c) Bravery (d) Excitement

Ans. (b) Fear

(iii) Which other adjective is used for rattrap in the extract?

(a) Forest
(b) World
(c) Impenetrable prison
(d) Wood

Ans. (c) Impenetrable prison

(iv) How would you describe the character of the rattraper from the extract?

(a) Smart
(b) Cunning
(c) Courageous
(d) Brave

Ans. (b) Cunning

(v) "Now his turn had come." Do you think that everyone's turn will come in the rattrap?

(a) Maybe (b) None of these (c) No (d) Yes

Ans. (d) Yes

6. *The young girl opened the package, which was so badly done up that the contents came into view at once. She gave a little cry of joy. She found a small rattrap, and in it lay three wrinkled ten kronor notes. But that was not all. In the rattrap lay also a letter written in large, jagged characters ....*

(i) Who was the young girl referred here?

(a) Crofter's daughter.
(b) A worker at Rmasjo ironworks.
(c) Ironmaster's daughter.
(d) Captain von Stahle's daughter.

Ans. (c) Ironmaster's daughter.

(ii) The story uses the word 'rattrap' as what form of literary device?

(a) allegory (b) irony (c) alliteration (d) metaphor

Ans. (d) metaphor

(iii) Where did the young girl find kronor notes?

(a) In the package. (b) In the rattrap. (c) In the wallet. (d) In the envelop.

Ans. (b) In the rattrap.

(iv) What does the 'jagged characters' in the letter show about the writer?

(a) He was drunk.
(b) He wrote in a hurry.
(c) He was an illiterate.
(d) He wrote with.

Ans. (c) He was an illiterate.

7. *No one can imagine how sad and monotonous life can appear to such a vagabond, who plods along the road, left to his own meditations. But one day this man had fallen into a line of thought, which really seemed to him entertaining.*

(i) What kind of life did the rattrap seller lead?

(a) Cheerful (b) Contented (c) Monotonous (d) Distressed

Ans. (c) Monotonous

(ii) Identify the figure of speech used in the sentence 'sad and monotonous life can appear to such a vagabond'.

(a) irony (b) pun (c) satire (d) humour

Ans. (a) irony

(iii) How did his thoughts seem to him?

(a) entertaining (b) very dull (c) boring (d) appealing

Ans. (a) entertaining

(iv) In what manner was the peddler walking?

(a) quickly
(b) slowly
(c) dejectedly
(d) both (ii) and (iii)

Ans. (d) both (ii) and (iii)

8. *But just as he laid his head on the ground, he heard a sound–a hard regular thumping. There was no doubt as to what that was. He raised himself, "Those are the hammer strokes from an iron mill", he thought.**

(i) Who is he?

Ans. 'He' in the extract is the rattrap peddler.

(ii) Where was 'he' at that moment?

Ans. At that moment, the rattrap peddler was trapped in a forest.

(iii) Why did he lay his head on the ground?

Ans. The rattrap peddler was stuck in the forest and could not find his way out. As darkness was settling around him, he gave up and laid his head on the ground tired.

(iv) Did he feel comfortable on hearing the thumping sound? Why?

Ans. Yes, he felt comfortable on hearing the thumping sound as it gave him hope that there was a way out from the forest and he would not remain trapped.

Multiple Choice Questions

1. **Where has the story "The Rattrap" been set up?**

(a) Jewellery shops (b) Forests of Sweden (c) Roads of Sweden (d) Mines of Sweden

Ans. (d) Mines of Sweden

2. Why did the Peddler have to resort to begging and thievery?
(a) He was habitual of it.
(b) Miserable life.
(c) Because of non-profitability of his business.
(d) None of these.
Ans. (c) Because of non-profitability of his business.

3. Why was the Crofter so talkative and friendly with the Peddler?
(a) Because he knew him.
(b) He was his friend.
(c) Because he thought of him as his old friend.
(d) Because he was lonely man without friends and family.
Ans. (d) Because he was lonely man without friends and family.

4. The old man was generous with his:
(a) confidence
(b) money
(c) food
(d) guest
Ans. (a) confidence

5. What time of the year was it when the rattrap seller had reached the forest in the?
(a) January
(b) December
(c) February
(d) October
Ans. (b) December

6. What does the 'forge' mean as in the story "The Rattrap"?
(a) A factory.
(b) A shop where metal is heated.
(c) A factory in jungle.
(d) A factory where locks are made.
Ans. (b) A shop where metal is heated.

7. The peddler had various thoughts due to______.
(a) poor circumstances
(b) poverty and loneliness
(c) he was a scholar
(d) he was a traveller
Ans. (b) poverty and loneliness

8. The lesson has a hidden meaning, which is ______.
(a) thieves are everywhere
(b) world is unfair and unkind
(c) one should be wary of strangers
(d) kindness can reform people
Ans. (d) kindness can reform people

9. Edla got the peddler home for Christmas as ______.
(a) she didn't want to be alone for Christmas
(b) he was her friend
(c) he was her father's friend
(d) he was her fiancée
Ans. (c) he was her father's friend

10. The Peddler left the stolen money ______.
(a) as his plan changed
(b) for a new mission
(c) to free himself from the rattrap
(d) none of these
Ans. (c) to free himself from the rattrap

11. The ironmaster realises his mistake after _________.
(a) Edla corrects him
(b) he wears his spectacles
(c) sees an old photograph
(d) he sees peddler in new clothes and after the peddler cleans his face
Ans. (d) he sees peddler in new clothes and after the peddler cleans his face

12. The peddler declined the invitation as ______.
(a) he was scared of being caught
(b) he was on a run
(c) he wanted to hide his identity
(d) he didn't like the hosts
Ans. (a) he was scared of being caught

13. The ironmaster and the daughter learnt about the thief at ________.
(a) the church
(b) the market
(c) the police station
(d) the Christmas party
Ans. (a) the church

14. After the peddler told the ironmaster about the rattrap, the ironmaster______.

(a) screamed at him
(b) laughed at him
(c) threw him out of the house
(d) handed him over to the sheriff

Ans. (b) laughed at him

15. Elda gave the peddler ______ to make him feel warm.

(a) blanket (b) shawl (c) sweater (d) fur coat

Ans. (d) fur coat

16. ______ came to the iron mill for inspection.

(a) The police (b) Ironmaster (c) Peddler (d) Edla

Ans. (b) Ironmaster

17. Peddler noticed ______ in people.

(a) indifference (b) hatred (c) envy (d) hostility

Ans. (a) indifference

18. Who is the author of the story 'The Rattrap'?

(a) Selma Lagerlof (b) Thomas B. Allen (c) Howard Phillips (d) Sudha Murthy

Ans. (a) Selma Lagerlof

19. Sweden mines are rich in which ore?

(a) Brass (b) Copper (c) Steel (d) Iron ore

Ans. (d) Iron ore

20. This story revolves around whom?

(a) Around Crofter and his daughter.
(b) Around crofter.
(c) Around ironman.
(d) Around the peddler- the Rattrap seller.

Ans. (d) Around the peddler- the Rattrap seller.

21. How was the physical appearance of the peddler in the chapter The Rattrap?

(a) His clothes were in rags.
(b) His cheeks were sunken.
(c) Hunger gleamed in his eyes.
(d) All of these.

Ans. (d) All of these.

22. What idea struck the rattrap seller's mind one day?

(a) This world is joyful and wonderful.
(b) He should run away.
(c) The whole world is also like a rattrap.
(d) People are wonderful.

Ans. (c) The whole world is also like a rattrap.

23. Why does the rattrap seller think of this world as a big rattrap?

(a) The world offers us various types of baits in form of comforts of life.
(b) This in return traps us into rattrap of the world.
(c) This leads us to various types of miseries.
(d) All of the above.

Ans. (d) All of the above.

24. Why was he amused by his idea of a rattrap?

(a) It was a bad joke.
(b) It was a good comparison.
(c) It was the exact situation and was humorous.
(d) It was sarcastically true.

Ans. (c) It was the exact situation and was humorous.

25. The peddler often thought about the people:

(a) who had caught rats.
(b) who had been tempted to touch the bait.
(c) were thieves.
(d) were priests.

Ans. (b) who had been tempted to touch the bait.

26. What does the metaphor of rattrap signify?

(a) No freedom to humans.
(b) Thieves.
(c) Attractions of the world.
(d) Human greed and distractions.

Ans. (d) Human greed and distractions.

27. What did the peddler see one dark evening?

(a) A little grey cottage.
(b) An old woman.
(c) A small boy.
(d) All of these.

Ans. (a) A little grey cottage.

28. The peddler and the crofter played a game after the supper the game was ________.

(a) rummy
(b) mjolis
(c) the snake and the ladder
(d) ludo

Ans. (b) mjolis

29. The old man was generous with his:

(a) neighbours (b) friends (c) family (d) guest

Ans. (d) guest

30. Where did the crofter work earlier in the chapter 'The Rattrap'?

(a) At a factory.
(b) At Ramsjo Ironworks.
(c) At a shop.
(d) At cowshed.

Ans. (b) At Ramsjo Ironworks.

31. The crofter had received a payment of:

(a) forty kronor
(b) thirty kronor
(c) twenty-five kronor
(d) ten kronor

Ans. (b) thirty kronor

32. How had the crofter earn the money in the chapter 'The Rattrap' ?

(a) By toiling day and night.
(b) By selling his cows milk.
(c) By selling his cow.
(d) By working at cowshed.

Ans. (b) By selling his cows milk.

33. What was the mistake made by the crofter when the peddler was in his house?

(a) He asked his address.
(b) He called the police.
(c) He showed him the place where he had kept his money.
(d) He abused him.

Ans. (c) He showed him the place where he had kept his money.

34. Where did the old man keep his money?

(a) In the chest (b) In his box (c) In the bank (d) In a leather pouch

Ans. (d) In a leather pouch

35. The rattrap peddler returned to the man's house in order to:

(a) steal the thirty kronor
(b) say thanks to the old man.
(c) take the bag he had left behind.
(d) note down the address of the old man.

Ans. (a) steal the thirty kronor.

36. How did the rattrap seller enter the cottage in order to steal the money?

(a) By breaking the lock.
(b) By smashing the window pane.
(c) By breaking the door.
(d) By entering through the ventilator.

Ans. (b) By smashing the window pane.

37. Why did the Peddler feel like stealing?

(a) Has to repay a loan.
(b) Has to buy a drink.
(c) Habitual of it.
(d) Due to others' indifference to his needs.

Ans. (d) Due to others' indifference to his needs

38. What did the peddler do after stealing the crofter's money in the chapter The Rattrap ?

(a) The peddler chose the path through the forest which was lonely.
(b) He enjoyed a great meal.
(c) The peddler bought more rattraps.
(d) The peddler helped someone who was more needy than himself.

Ans. (a) The peddler chose the path through the forest which was lonely

39. What happened when the rattrap seller left the mainroad and went into the forest?

(a) He was happy there although he lost his way out.

(b) He took rest there after being lost in it.

(c) He enjoyed the forest and its greenery.

(d) He became confused and lost his ways.

Ans. (d) He became confused and lost his ways.

40. Why was the rattrap seller trapped in the forest in the chapter The Rattrap?

(a) Because it was a dense forest.

(b) Because he could not find his way out.

(c) Because it was dark.

(d) Both (a) and (b).

Ans. (b) Because he could not find his way out.

41. "When the rattrap seller had lost all the hopes, he heard a sound." From where was the sound coming?

(a) From a school

(b) From a mill

(c) From a lake

(d) From a shop

Ans. (b) From a mill

42. "He summoned all his strength, got up and staggered in the direction of the sound." Who is 'he' referred to in the chapter The Rattrap?

(a) The crofter

(b) The rattrap seller

(c) The ironmaster

(d) All of these

Ans. (b) The rattrap seller

43. Where did the rattrap seller go from the dense forest in the chapter The Rattrap?

(a) He went to a forge.

(b) He went towards the bank of the river.

(c) He went back to the crofter.

(d) None of these.

Ans. (a) He went to a forge.

44. For what did the rattrap seller ask permission?

(a) To stay there for the night.

(b) To dance in the factory.

(c) To help the blacksmiths.

(d) To build a wall.

Ans. (a) To stay there for the night.

45. Who sat in the dark forge near the furnace?

(a) The master smith

(b) His helper

(c) Both (a) and (b)

(d) None of these

Ans. (c) Both (a) and (b)

46. What was master smith wearing?

(a) A short shirt and a pair of wooden shoes.

(b) A long shirt and a pair of wooden shoes.

(c) A long shirt and a pair of leather shoes.

(d) A short shirt and a pair of leather shoes.

Ans. (b) A long shirt and a pair of wooden shoes.

47. Who came to the iron-mill on a round of inspection?

(a) The security guard

(b) The caretaker

(c) The ironmaster

(d) The policeman

Ans. (c) The ironmaster

48. The ironmaster mistook the rattrap peddler for:

(a) an old cousin of his wife.

(b) an old employee.

(c) an old servant.

(d) an old regimental comrade.

Ans. (d) an old regimental comrade.

49. Where did the ironmaster invite the rattrap seller?

(a) To the dance party.

(b) To the hospital.

(c) To his house for the Christmas eve.

(d) To a marriage party.

Ans. (c) To his house for the Christmas eve.

50. The peddler was invited by the ironmaster to stay at his house. This made the peddler:

(a) feel alarmed
(b) feel guilty
(c) feel uncomfortable
(d) jump up with joy

Ans. (c) feel uncomfortable

51. The ironmaster lived in the manor with his:

(a) old mother
(b) eldest daughter
(c) wife
(d) sons

Ans. (b) eldest daughter

52. Why did the Peddler decline the invitation?

(a) Because he had stolen money.
(b) Because he wanted to run.
(c) Because he wanted to hide money.
(d) Because he wanted to remain at the mill.

Ans. (a) Because he had stolen money.

53. Why did the Peddler feel that he had fallen into The Rattrap?

(a) Because he fell into a pit.
(b) Because he fell in love with Edla.
(c) Because his heart is changed.
(d) Because of his pitiable circumstances.

Ans. (d) Because of his pitiable circumstances.

54. Who was finally able to convince the peddler to go to the ironmaster's house as a guest during Christmas?

(a) The guard at the iron mill.
(b) The ironmaster's daughter.
(c) The apprentice.
(d) The blacksmith.

Ans. (b) The ironmaster's daughter.

55. The purpose of her visit to the iron-mill was to:

(a) advise him to give up stealing and start living a better life.
(b) counsel him about what he did was wrong.
(c) propose to him to stay at their house forever.
(d) persuade the rattrap seller to spend Christmas Eve at their house.

Ans. (d) persuade the rattrap seller to spend Christmas Eve at their house.

56. The girl had brought with her the following article to make him feel warm:

(a) a fur coat
(b) a sweater
(c) a woollen shawl
(d) a blanket

Ans. (a) a fur coat

57. Sitting in the carriage with the young girl, the rattrap seller was deep in thought. He felt:

(a) confident.
(b) nervous and tense.
(c) ashamed at coming with the girl.
(d) guilty at having stolen the crofter's money.

Ans. (d) guilty at having stolen the crofter's money

58. The first move of the ironmaster was to make sure that the guest could:

(a) be given some clothes.
(b) be given some money.
(c) have verification done.
(d) gain some flesh on his body.

Ans. (d) gain some flesh on his body.

59. The second thing of priority for the rattrap seller was to:

(a) to marry him to someone.
(b) feed him some food.
(c) take him to a doctor.
(d) make him sleep comfortably.

Ans. (b) feed him some food.

60. The reason for ironmaster's unhappiness was that:

(a) he hated the way he looked.
(b) he had made a mistake in recognizing him.
(c) he came to know he was a thief.
(d) he looked ugly now.

Ans. (b) he had made a mistake in recognizing him.

61. The tramp argued with the ironmaster saying that:

(a) he did not want to marry Edla.
(b) he could celebrate Christmas.
(c) he was smarter than them.
(d) he could just go back.

Ans. (d) he could just go back.

62. The rattrap peddler gave the ironmaster a lecture on:

(a) how to be professional.
(b) how to be ethically correct.
(c) how to be honest.
(d) how the world is a rattrap.

Ans. (d) how the world is a rattrap.

63. The reaction of the ironmaster to the peddler's lecture was that:

(a) he slapped him.
(b) he laughed.
(c) he made fun of him.
(d) he shouted at him.

Ans. (b) he laughed.

64. The daughter wanted the peddler to stay so that he could:

(a) play a game of poker with them.
(b) play cards with them.
(c) eat a meal with them.
(d) enjoy at least Christmas with them.

Ans. (d) enjoy at least Christmas with them.

65. At the church next day what did the ironmaster and his daughter come to know about the rattrap seller?

(a) That he was a rich man.
(b) That he had stolen the old crofter's money.
(c) That the rattrap seller had run away.
(d) That he had been arrested.

Ans. (b) That he had stolen the old crofter's money.

66. What did the package left for Edla contain?

(a) A diamond ring
(b) A necklace
(c) A small bangle
(d) A small rattrap with 30 kronor on it

Ans. (d) A small rattrap with 30 kronor on it

67. The rattrap peddler left a note with the package. The note was signed as:

(a) Captain von Stahle
(b) The Rattrap
(c) The Vagabond
(d) The Peddler

Ans. (a) Captain von Stahle

68. Why did the peddler want to be nice to Edla?

(a) Because she was kind and benevolent.
(b) Because he had decided to change.
(c) Because she treated him like a real Captain.
(d) Because basically he was a nice person.

Ans. (c) Because she treated him like a real Captain.

69. Why did the peddler leave the stolen money in a Rattrap?

(a) Because of his guilt.
(b) Because he didn't want to deceive them any more.
(c) Because of fear of Iron master.
(d) To repay the love and care given by Edla.

Ans. (d) To repay the love and care given by Edla.

70. What would have happened if Edla would have gone by her father's decision?

(a) The peddler would have gone back to his old ways.
(b) The peddler would have changed any way.
(c) The peddler would have never got out of the forge..
(d) The peddler's perception would have changed.

Ans. (a) The peddler would have gone back to his old ways.

71. In what manner has the story been narrated?

(a) Non-fictious style
(b) Realistic manner
(c) Fairy tale manner
(d) None of these

Ans. (c) Fairy tale manner

72. What lightens the seriousness of the lesson?

(a) Peddler's greed
(b) Peddler's gossip
(c) Peddler's tricks
(d) Peddler's sense of humour

Ans. (d) Peddler's sense of humour

73. Why was the ironmaster so talkative and friendly with the Peddler?

(a) Because he knew him.

(b) He was his friend.

(c) He was his neighbour.

(d) Because of his resemblance to one of his old friend.

Ans. (d) Because of his resemblance to one of his old friend.

74. Why did the Peddler not reveal his true identity?

(a) Because of fear.

(b) He didn't want to hurt them.

(c) In the greed of getting money.

(d) None of these.

Ans. (c) In the greed of getting money.

75. From where did the Peddler get the material to make rattraps?

(a) Shops (b) Roads (c) Streets (d) Stores

Ans. (d) Stores

76. Why did Peddler sign himself as Captain Von Stahle?

(a) He didn't want to hurt them.

(b) Because he forgets his name.

(c) Because he wants to meet Edla's expectations of him being an armyman.

(d) None of the above.

Ans. (c) Because he wants to meet Edla's expectations of him being an armyman.

❑❑

5. Indigo–by Louis Fischer

Summary :

Gandhiji had gone to attend the December 1916 Annual Convention of the Congress. One "emaciated" peasant named Rajkumar Shukla from Champaran, came up to him. He was illiterate and wanted Gandhiji's help in context to the injustice done to the peasants of Champaran. Gandhiji told Shukla that he had appointments in Kanpur and had to go to other parts of India too. Shukla followed him for weeks which impressed Gandhi.

Gandhi asked Shukla to meet him in Calcutta. Shukla met Gandhiji and took him to Bihar. He took Gandhi to Rajendra Prasad's house, but he was out of town. The servants mistook Gandhi as another peasant and did not allow him to draw water from the well thinking him to be an untouchable. Gandhiji went to Muzzafarpur, where J.B. Kripalani received him at the station with a large body of students. It was extraordinary, because J.B. Kripalani was a government professor and Gandhiji advocated home-rule, which was anti-government.

News of Gandhiji's arrival spread. People and lawyers came to see him. He scolded the lawyers for collecting large fees from peasants especially from the "sharecroppers". He realized law courts were useless, unless the peasants were freed from the fear of their oppressors. At that time, Germany had developed a synthetic indigo. Therefore cultivation of indigo by British planters was not profitable which forced the British planters to give up the cultivation of Indigo. They tried to make some extra money while going out. They agreed to release the farmers, from the agreement, but only after being paid the compensation. Peasants protested against the demand of compensation. They claimed when the British planters were leaving, then the demand for compensation was unjustified. Gandhjii arrived in Champaran, but the British Landlord Association and the British official commissioner did not co-operate with him at all. However Gandhiji, with the help of several lawyers, continued investigating the facts. Soon he was served a notice by the British authorities to quit Champaran. Gandhiji telegraphed Rajendra Prasad for help. He sent a report to the Viceroy. Soon thousands of peasants demonstrated for Gandhiji, against the authorities. That was the evidence that British might be challenged by Indians. Gandhiji pleaded guilty in court, saying that he had a conflict of duty and he should not be a lawbreaker but should also help the common people. He said he obeyed the voice of conscience. He refused to leave Champaran and asked for the punishment. The magistrate asked Gandhi to furnish bail but when Gandhi refused, the magistrate released him unconditionally. Gandhi told the lawyers about the injustice done to the sharecroppers and advised them to fight for the cause in case he got arrested. The lawyers assured him that they would go to jail if required. Subsequently, the case against Gandhi was dropped. Civil disobedience had won for the first time in India.

Now all negotiations, inquiries, investigations, planning and recording of evidence took place. Gandhi and other lawyers prepared the cases for ten thousand peasants. There were a lot of evidences against the British planters. In the month of June, Gandhi met Sir Edward Gait, the Lieutenant Governor and held series of meetings and subsequently an inquiry was ordered. The inquiry committee consisted of landlords, government officials and Gandhi as a sole representative of the peasants. Gandhiji demanded for fifty percent refund of the entire amount. However, he agreed to accept the refund of twenty-five percent by giving a logical explanation that the amount of money was not important. The prestige of the English landlords was downsized. They no longer behaved like a dictator. The peasants came to know about their rights which was a great achievement.

Then in a few years, the British planters left and Indigo cropping disappeared. Gandhiji said he would make large general solutions that should work for the entire country. They look good on paper, but are difficult to achieve in practice. He wanted to help the backwardness of the Champaran district. He called two of his disciples with their wives. His youngest son Devadas and his wife also came to Champaran to help. They set up primary schools, and taught cleanliness. Gandhiji got a doctor. There were three medicines. Castor oil, quinine and sulphur ointment. His wife Kasturba Bai talked to women about their dirty clothes; women replied that they had only one set of clothes. Champaran was a turning point because basically, Gandhiji declared that the British could not challenge him in his own country. It did not begin as defiance or an anti-British movement; Gandhi was only trying to help the poor peasants. This was Gandhi's working pattern. He didn't like abstract notions, but was loyal to breathing human-beings. His follower Charles Andrews, tried to help him in this movement but Gandhiji refused his help. He said that Indians were strong enough to win it on their own, and just because his follower was an Englishman, they should not want his help. They should be self-reliant.

Text Book Questions :

Notice these expressions in the text. Infer their meaning from the context.

(a) Urge the departure—insist for leaving.

(b) Conflict of duties—dispute of duties.

(c) Harbour a man like me—give shelter to me.

(d) Seek a prop—look for a support.

Think as you Read :

Q. 1. Strike out what is not true in the following :

(i) Rajkumar Shukla was:

(a) a Sharecropper (b) a Politician

(c) a Delegate (d) a Landlord

Ans. (i) (a) a Sharecropper

(ii) Rajkumar Shukla was:

(a) poor (b) physically strong (c) illiterate

Ans. (ii) (c) illiterate

Q. 2. Why is Rajkumar Shukla described as being 'resolute'?

Ans. Rajkumar Shukla is described as being 'resolute' because even after being told about the prior engagements of Gandhi at Kanpur and other parts across the country, he did not quit, rather he continued to accompany Gandhi everywhere. He persistently asked Gandhi to fix a date for his visit to his native district of Champaran. Gandhi, finally impressed by his resolution and determination, complied with his request.

Q. 3. Why do you think the servants thought Gandhi to be another peasant?

Ans. When the servants at Rajendra Prasad's house saw him, they took him to be a simple and humble man as Gandhi was dressed in a plain 'dhoti'. He looked like just another poor farmer of this country, to the servants. As he was accompanied by Rajkumar Shukla whom they knew to be a poor indigo sharecropper, they mistook Gandhi to be another peasant.

Q. 4. List the places that Gandhi visited between his first meeting with Shukla and his arrival at Champaran.

Ans. After his first meeting with Shukla, Gandhi visited Kanpur, his ashram near Ahmedabad, Calcutta, Patna and Muzzaffarpur before he reached Champaran.

Q. 5. What did the peasants pay the British landlords as rent? What did the British now want instead and why? What would be the impact of synthetic indigo on the prices of natural indigo?

Ans. According to the long-term contract, the peasants used to plant fifteen percent of their holdings with indigo and pay the entire harvest as rent. But, with the development of synthetic indigo in Germany, the British landlords who did not want indigo from these plantations, decided to release the peasants of Champaran from the fifteen percent arrangement on the payment of a huge compensation. Development of synthetic indigo would lead to an increase in the price of natural indigo.

Q. 6. The events in this part of the text illustrate Gandhi's method of working. Can you identify some instances of this method and link them to his ideas of Satyagraha and non-violence?

Ans. There are many instances in the narrative that can be linked to Gandhi's idea of non-cooperation and Satyagraha. One such instance was Gandhi's refusal to obey the court order asking him to leave Champaran immediately. Besides that, Gandhi's protest against the delay of the court proceedings was also an instance of his belief in civil disobedience. Gandhi did not flatter to plead guilty in front of the court. He accepted his guilt and presented a rational case as to what made him disobey the law. For him, truth was above everything and he decided to follow the voice of conscience and obey the 'higher law of our being'.

Q. 7. How did the episode change the plight of the peasants?

Ans. The episode of Champaran changed the plight of the peasants of that district. These peasants gained confidence which was evident in their spontaneous demonstration in the morning of Gandhi's trial. The successful refund of the compensation, made the peasants realize, for the first time that; they too had their own rights and were liberated from the fear that had plagued them. This episode also brought an end to the fifteen percent arrangement of sharecropping. The most radical change that the episode brought about was in their social and cultural standard. Gandhi opened schools in six villages. His wife took pains to make the peasants aware of the importance of general sanitation and personal hygiene. Gandhiji even appointed a doctor.

Understanding the Text :

Q. 1. Why do you think Gandhi considered the Champaran episode to be a turning-point in his life?

Ans. Gandhi considered the Champaran episode to be a turning point in his life because it had made him realize that civil disobedience, which had triumphed for the first time, could go a long way in the freedom struggle. The incident had made him successful in making the peasants aware of their rights and becoming confident. This success proved the effectiveness of Gandhi's method of non-violence and non-cooperation.

Q. 2. How was Gandhi able to influence lawyers? Give instances.

Ans. Gandhi was able to influence the lawyers through his conviction, earnestness and pertinent questioning. Gandhi rebuked the lawyers of Muzzaffarpur for charging a large sum of money as fee from the peasants. Later, when the lawyers from Bihar opined that they would return to their own places in the event of his imprisonment, Gandhi made them realize that it would be impudent for them, being lawyers from a neighbouring place, to return when a stranger was ready to get himself imprisoned for the peasants. So, they agreed to follow him to jail. Gandhi also convinced the lawyers not to seek support from an Englishman and be self-reliant.

Q. 3. What was the attitude of the average Indian in smaller localities towards advocates of 'home rule'?

Ans. The average Indian in smaller localities lived in fear of the British. They were afraid of the dire consequences of helping the advocates of "home-rule". Hence, though they were supportive of people like Gandhi, they were afraid of showing it in open and only a few could actually dare to come out. In the story, we find people like Professor Malkani, who had the courage to give shelter to Gandhi on the latter's visit to Muzzaffarpur.

Q. 4. How do we know that ordinary people too contributed to the freedom movement?

Ans. In the chapter 'Indigo', Louis Fischer writes of how a small farmer Rajkumar Shukla (a peasant from a small district, Champaran), helped to bring about a very prominent change. Similarly, many other peasants from the villages fought courageously and contributed in their own way to the movement. Their cumulative effort eventually resulted in their winning the battle of Champaran and they finally freed themselves from the sharecropping arrangement.

Talking about the text :

Discuss the following :

Q. 1. 'Freedom from fear is more important than legal justice for the poor.' Do you think that the poor of India are free from fear after independence ?

Ans. In the story, Gandhi makes it possible for the sharecroppers of Champaran to shed their fear of the British landlords. According to Gandhi, freedom from fear is the first step towards self-reliance. However, it is unfortunate that the poor of the country are not free from fear, even decades after the independence. Their actions, work, etc. are still under pressure; they are under the mercy of the bureaucratic system. Furthermore, the poor live in a continual fear of the police, who instead of taking care, often end up maltreating them. The already poor farmers are becoming poorer, because of globalization and the craze for foreign products. This leaves them in the fear of further destitution.

Q. 2. The qualities of a good leader.

Ans. A good leader is someone who leads the minds of others and convinces them into following his set of ideas and beliefs. As such, there are some qualities inherent in the personna of the leader that sets him apart from the rest. One of these qualities includes dedication to one's work. His enthusiasm is evident in his work and life, and this inspires others to follow him. A good leader is courageous in the face of adversity and is never a quitter. He motivates and encourages others, bringing out the best in them. He appreciates the efforts of others and is not biased or impartial.

Working with words :

Q. 1.
- ◆ List the words used in the text that are related to legal procedures.
  For example: deposition
- ◆ List other words that you know that fall into this category.

Ans.

Deposition	Notice	Summon	Lawyer
Court	Cases	Fee	Agreement
Opposition	Prosecution	Offense	Crime

Compensation	Order	Courthouse	Judge
Prosecutor	Statement	Guilty	Trial
Penalty	Law	Magistrate	Sentence
Bail	Judgment	Inquiry	Evidence
Documents	Imprison	Appeal	Rights
Investigation	Reconvene	Appear	Pleading
Witness	Accused	Proceedings	Adjourn
Verdict	Decree	Accusation	Defense
Impeachment	Charge	Affidavit	Indictment

Talking about Language :

Q. 1. Notice the sentences in the text which are in 'Direct Speech'. Why does the author use quotations in his narration?

Below are some sentences in the text which are in 'direct speech':

"I will tell you how it happened that I decided to urge the departure of the British. It was in 1917."
"I am Rajkumar Shukla. I am from Champaran, and I want you to come to my district!"
"Speak to Gandhi."
"Fix a date,"
"I have to be in Calcutta on such-and-such a date. Come and meet me and take me from there."
"It was an extraordinary thing ... for a government professor to harbour a man like me".
"The commissioner ... to bully me and advised me forthwith to leave Tirhut."
"conflict of duties."
"humanitarian and national service."
"not for want of respect for lawful authority, but in obedience to the higher law of our being, the voice of conscience."
"But how much must we pay?"
"Look, there is no box or cupboard here for clothes. The sari I am wearing is the only one I have."
"What I did," he explained, "was a very ordinary thing. I declared that the British could not order me about in my own country."
"He had read our minds correctly," Rajendra Prasad comments, "and we had no reply... Gandhi in this way taught us a lesson in self-reliance".

Ans. The author uses quotations to indicate the actual words of a speaker. Usually, a quotation is used when a particular passage or sentence is well-written or memorable, is especially relevant in the context under discussion. In 'Indigo,' the author uses quotations when he mentions important commentary or observation, or any pertinent utterance by Gandhi, or for that matter, by any other character.

Q. 2. Notice the use or non – use of the comma in the following sentences:

(a) When I first visited Gandhi in 1942 at his ashram in Sevagram, he told me what happened in Champaran.

(b) He had not proceeded far when the police superintendent's messenger overtook him.

(c) When the court reconvened, the judge said he would not deliver the judgment for several days.

Ans. (a) In this sentence, the comma is used after a long introductory phrase.

(b) Essential clauses do not require commas. In this sentence, the clause 'when the police superintendent's messenger overtook him' is an essential clause because it provides essential information. Hence, a comma is not required in this sentence.

(c) In this sentence again, we have an introductory clause which provides extra information. The second-half of the sentence can stand alone and, therefore, is separated from the introductory clause with a comma.

Things to do :

Q. 1. Choose an issue that has provoked a controversy like the Bhopal Gas Tragedy or the Narmada Dam Project in which the lives of the poor have been affected.

Ans. Fukushima I nuclear accidents in Japan are regarded as one of the largest nuclear disasters in recent years.

Q. 2. Find out the facts of the case.

Ans. On 11th March, 2011, the Tahoka earthquake and tsunami occurred disabling the power supply and cooling of three Fukushima Daiichi reactors. The three cores largely melted in the first three days. This accident, which is rated 7 on the INES scale, led to the release of high radioactive substances, including contaminated water leaking from the three units. Although there were no immediate deaths, over 100000 residents were evacuated from their homes.

Q. 3. Present your arguments.

Ans. The contaminated sea water from such disasters is a potential threat across boundaries. The investigations into the Fukushima disaster have proved some faults in the design of the reactors. Lack of adequate safety measures and response actions in the plant have led to a higher risk.

Q. 4. Suggest a possible settlement.

Ans. A possible way to avert such disasters is by constructing such plants away from residential areas. It is imperative to improve safety measures and take other possible steps to eliminate the release of harmful materials.

Additional Questions :

Short Answer Questions : **(30-40 words)**

Q. 1. Why did the magistrate release Gandhiji?

Ans. Gandhiji pleaded guilty of disobedience. The peasants held a demonstration around the court. The Government was confused and the officials were powerless. The peasants were mounting pressure on the government. So, the magistrate released Gandhiji without bail.

Q. 2. Why did Gandhiji say—: "The battle of Champaran is won"?

Ans. The lawyers had decided to go home~~;~~ if Gandhiji went to prison. But Gandhiji asked them what would become of the injustice to the sharecroppers. The lawyers thought over it and decided that they too would follow Gandhiji. This was the time ~~that~~ when Gandhiji said that the battle of Champaran was won.

Q. 3. Why did Gandhiji agree to the settlement of 25% refund to the peasants?

Ans. Gandhiji had demanded 50 percent refund from the landlords. The landlords offered only 25 per cent. Gandhiji agreed to the settlement of 25 per cent because according to Gandhiji, money was not important. He had made the Britishers bow down before the Indian peasants., which was the primary aim of this struggle.

Q. 4. How did Indigo sharecropping come to an end in Champaran?

Ans. Indigo sharecropping came to an end in Champaran as Germany had developed synthetic Indigo. Sharecropping was no longer profitable for the British planters. They had to surrender their prestige and money to the peasants. So, they gave up their estates which came back to the peasants.

Q. 5. Why was Gandhiji summoned to appear in court?

Ans. Gandhiji went to see a badly treated peasant. He was served with a notice from the Superintendent of Police to quit Champaran. Gandhiji received the notice and wrote on it that he would never quit Champaran. As a result, he was summoned to appear in the court.

Q. 6. Why did Gandhiji rebuke the Muzzaffarpur lawyers?

Ans. Gandhiji rebuked the Muzzaffarpur lawyers because they used to charge very high fees from the poor peasants.

Q. 7. What was the condition of the peasants before Gandhiji's arrival in Champaran?

Ans. The peasants were compelled to plant 15 per cent of their land with indigo crop and surrender the entire harvest as rent. When Germany developed synthetic indigo, they were asked to give compensation for making them free from 15 per cent indigo plantation. Those who disobeyed were beaten by hired criminals.

Q. 8. What was the conflict of Gandhiji?

Ans. Gandhiji's conflict was of discharging ~~the~~ his duties. On one hand, he did not want to set a bad example by breaking the law. On the other hand, he was to listen to the voice of his conscience and serve the human beings.

Q. 9. How did Gandhiji regulate the crowd around the courthouse?

Ans. The officials were powerless as they could not control the crowd outside the courthouse. Gandhiji regulated the crowd in a polite and friendly manner.

Q. 10. Why has Raj Kumar Shukla been described as being resolute?*

Ans. Rajkumar Shukla has been described as being 'resolute' because he wanted Gandhiji to accompany him to his district named Champaran anyhow, Gandhiji was busy at that time and had several engagements. But Rajkumar Shukla never left Gandhiji's side. He followed him whenever he went. At last, Gandhiji had to find time to go with him. It shows how resolute Rajkumar Shukla was.

Long Answer Question : (120-150 words)

Q. 1. 'Non-Violence' and 'Truthfulness' were Gandhiji's tools against the British. He fought with them and won the battle. It proves that 'non-violence' has the power to bring victory over violence. So, write a paragraph on the issue in about 100 words.

Ans. If we meditate~~d~~ deeply and turn the pages of our sacred history, our philosophers, thinkers, saints, rishis and munis have stressed on the need and significance of non-violence. Emperors like Ashoka, Princes like Gautam Buddha and modern sacred souls like our Father of the Nation, Mahatma Gandhi, all have not only preached but also put into practice the act of non-violence. Ashoka the great forbade even the killing of wild animals in his kingdom. Buddha sent his preachers far and wide to sermonize people on the importance of leading a peaceful life. It was Gandhi who brought Independence to India through non-violence, with the help of Indians. It was our concerted effort and sacrifice that brought victorious colours to this nation.

We can very well understand the dictum that we have no right to kill innocent lives. It is a great sin to play with the lives of others. The recent attack of terrorists on Mumbai on 26th November, 2008 will remain a black day in the history of the world. Have these brutal killers ever thought that many families were devastated so many innocent children were orphaned. The nation and the economy are terribly harmed due to their savage activities. Such mean acts are useless and shameful. These bring dishonour, chaos, confusion and trouble. We can do away with these unlawful activities through our concerned efforts. Though the extremists are the traitors but they should be taught the lesson of peace, affection, sympathy, love and selfless service to others since all complicated problems can be solved through mutual understanding and love. It is the need of the hour to bring such strategies into action that may change the lives and ideologies of these forlorn extremists. Let us preach and follow the path of non-violence.

Q. 2. The text 'Indigo' expresses the value of freedom and Indians' fight for freedom. How would you define FREEDOM? Write your views in the form of a speech to be delivered in the morning assembly of your school. Don't exceed 100 words.

Ans. Today, I am going to share my views on the value of freedom for me. Freedom is precious for everyone. 'Only a caged bird can know its importance.' Indians are very well aware of the importance of freedom and the sacrifices at the cost of which we gained it. Our freedom fighters left no stone unturned to get our freedom back from the Britishers. Their long but firm struggle brought us this precious gift of freedom. We have freedom to do anything. We have freedom to live, to express our views, to cast our vote, to religious expression~~s~~ and adaptation~~s~~ and the list continues. Here, the most important thing is that this freedom is priceless for us and we should respect it. This is our duty to keep it up and abiding by social and moral ethics. Freedom is ~~so~~ very important for us and we cannot lose it at any cost.

Q. 3. "He had read our minds correctly." Rajendra Prasad comments. "and we had no reply…Gandhi in this way taught us a lesson in self-reliance". These lines prove that Gandhiji was a true leader in each and every respect. Taking ideas from the lesson about the true leadership skills along with your own views, write a paragraph in about 100 words on "The qualities of a good leader."

Ans. A good leader is a torch bearer who shows the light to his followers and to the masses at large. He brings them from darkness to light, from ignorance to awareness, from fear to self-reliance and from violence to non-violence.

A good leader is a role model for all. He has the personality traits of fearlessness, bravery, initiatives, spot decision making and hard work directed towards public welfare. His feelings of sacrifice for his motherland and for his people make him a charismatic personality for them.

A good leader must be a man of words, of high integrity and truthfulness. He is above all narrow feelings of caste, religion, colour, creed, sex or regionalism and language barriers. His punctuality, love for humanity, patriotism and sincerity to his people, are the examples for others to follow.

* are board exam questions from previous years

At times of national calamity, he sets examples for others and helps all leading them to relief and comfort. He is devoid of selfishness, greed and even comforts. Though he is an advocate of world peace, yet he is ready to sacrifice his life for his motherland.

Q. 4. The lesson 'Indigo' highlights the qualities of leadership shown by Mahatma Gandhi to secure justice for the oppressed people through argumentation and negotiation. Getting a clue from the way Mahatma Gandhi dealt with the Champaran episode, write an article on 'The Qualities of a Good Leader' or 'What makes a Good Leader?'

'What makes a Good Leader?'

Ans. Leadership is the process by which a leader imaginatively directs, guides and influences the work of others in choosing and attaining specified goals by mediating between the individuals and the conflicting organization in such a manner as will satisfy both.

A leader may not be physically strong but he needs to be mentally strong and firm in decisions. For example, Mahatma Gandhi, the greatest of our leaders, had the power of organizing, uniting and attracting people towards him by possessing his intelligence and alertness. A leader has to use his / her brain every time and has to remain alert with eyes and ears open, to avoid being carried away by any fraud or an enemy. Apart from being impartial, a leader needs to be action-oriented. A leader should be effective enough towards himself and encourages everyone through his word to do constructive work while walking on the right path so that everyone can become aware of his / her rights and duties. A leader has to be dedicated. He does whatever it takes to be a role model in every sense of the word.

Q. 5. "In everything, Gandhi did, he tried to mould news free Indian who could stand on his own feet and thus make India Free."

Ans. Instead of choosing a lavish life as a learned advocate, Gandhiji decided to be the pioneer of Independence in India. He gave a new direction to the Indian politics and led us towards freedom. He deliberately recognized the power of youth. In fact, the young generation is needed to be a part of politics even today. Taking reference from the text INDIGO along with your own views, write an article on 'The involvement of students in politics' in about 100 words for your school magazine.

Q. 6. How did Gandhiji use satyagraha and non-violence at Champaran to achieve his goal?*

Ans. Mahatma Gandhi, who was an apostle of peace and non-violence, agitated in Champaran district of Bihar in 1917 and then in Kheda district of Gujarat in 1918. Although the term 'Satyagraha' was coined in 1919, when the Anti - Rowlatt Act protests took place, Champaran witnessed this kind of non-violent protests for the first time.

The protests in Champaran took place as the British introduced farming of cash crops like indigo, which they bought at a low price for export. Opium was also extracted from the seeds of poppy, which was grown to export to China to fill the coffers of the imperialist rulers. The protests were against two decisions of the British, viz., forcing farmers to cultivate cash crops in place of food crops, which they earlier cultivated for sustenance, and payment of abysmally low wages to the growers. Rajendra Prasad, Anugrah Narayan Sinha, Brajkishore Prasad, Acharya Kripalani and many others took part in the agitation with Gandhiji.

Satyagraha was actually a mass civil disobedience movement. Gandhiji set up an ashram and volunteers in scores joined his agitation. He then began cleaning up the villages, built hospitals and schools, induced villagers to remove untouchability and do away with the purdah system. After this, people became conscious of their rights and non-violent protests were all they would do. This culminated in the arrest of Gandhiji. He was later released by an order of the court, after the agitators agitated gathered en masse in front of the police station and the court. Thereafter, Gandhiji was called Bapu across the country. The Champaran movement brought to heel the British rulers and their cohorts, the wealthy landlords; the poor farmers were subsequently paid remunerative wages and their farming right of the desired crops was restored.

Q. 7. How did the court scene at Motihari change the course of India's struggle for freedom?*

Ans. The episode at Champaran was a turning point for India's struggle for freedom. This was when Gandhiji decided to oppose the British rule in India. Gandhiji went to Motihari to gather complete information about the indigo plantation contracts from the peasants; he was accompanied by several lawyers. He was on his way to meet a peasant who was mistreated by some of the indigo planters; he was stopped by a messenger of the police superintendent who served him a notice which asked him to leave. However, Gandhiji ignored the notice and continued his investigation. A case was filed against him and he was arrested. On the day of the trial, unanimously, a large crowd of peasants gathered near the court demanding the release of Gandhiji.

* are board exam questions from previous years

When it became impossible to control them, Gandhiji spoke to them and they all obeyed him. Gandhiji managed to convince the court that he was not there to break laws but he wanted to help the peasants. He was immediately granted bail and later, the case against him was dropped.

Previous Years' Questions :

Q. 1. Though the sharecroppers of Champaran received only one-fourth of the compensation, how can the Champaran struggle still be termed a huge success and victory ?

Ans. The Champaran struggle can be termed as a huge success and victory because of the following reasons.

Gandhiji wanted to break the deadlock. The amount of the refund was not important but the landlords had been obliged to surrender part of the money and with it their prestige also. Lastly, the peasants had developed courage and learnt to amplify themselves. They had overcome their fear.

Q. 2. Why was Gandhiji opposed to C.F. Andrews helping him in Champaran ?

Ans. Gandhiji was opposed to C.F. Andrews helping him in Champaran because he wanted the Indians to be self-dependent and self-reliant in their struggle against injustice. He told him that Indians were strong enough to fight their own battle and had the capability to win it. Therefore, Gandhiji refused his help.

Q. 3. How did Rajkumar Shukla establish that he was resolute?

Ans. Rajkumar Shukla established that he was resolute as he had come all the way from Champaran District in the foothills of Himalayas to Lucknow to speak to Gandhiji. Shukla accompanied Gandhiji everywhere. He also followed him to the Ashram near Ahmedabad. For weeks he never left Gandhi's side till Gandhiji asked him to meet at Calcutta.

Q. 4. How was Gandhi treated at Rajendra Prasad's house?

Ans. When Shukla took Gandhi to Rajendra Prasad's house, he was out of town. The servants knew Shukla as a poor farmer who was pestering their master to help the indigo share croppers. Seeing Gandhi with him they presumed him to be another farmer and allowed him to stay as Shukla's companion.

Q. 5. What were the terms of the indigo contract between the British landlords and the Indian peasants?

Ans. Most of the arable land in the Champaran district was divided into large estates that were owned by Englishmen and Indian tenants worked for them. They got the agreements from the sharecroppers to pay them compensation for being released from the 15% arrangement.

Q. 6. Why is the Champaran episode considered to be the beginning of the Indian struggle for Independence?

Ans. The episode of Champaran was considered to be the beginning of the Indian struggle for Independence because, for the first time, the farmers and peasants rose against the Britishers. The peasants were oppressed by their British landlords, but they lacked the courage to protest. Under the leadership of Gandhiji, they became aware of their rights. A small farmer, Rajkumar Shukla, from a small district, Champaran, helped to bring about a very prominent change. He championed the cause of Champaran movement. Likewise, many other peasants from the villages fought courageously and contributed in their own way to the movement. Their combined effort eventually helped them to win the battle of Champaran and to finally free themselves from 'Share Cropping' arrangement. The success also proved, for the first time, the effectiveness of Gandhiji method of non-violence and non-cooperation. Gandhiji exulted over them and made the villagers feel self-dependant and undaunted.

Q. 7. Gandhiji's was not a loyalty to abstractions; it was a loyalty to living, human beings. Why did Gandhiji continue his stay in Champaran even after Indigo share cropping disappeared?

Ans. Gandhiji was not satisfied with mere political and economic solution so he wanted to bring about a change in the social and cultural conditions of Champaran. He noticed the unhealthy living conditions and poor sanitation in the village. He also realised the need for literacy. He decided to stay in Champaran even after the disappearance of Indigo Share Cropping. A small farmer, Rajkumar Shukla, from a small district of Champaran, helped bring about a very prominent change. He opened up schools in six different villages; and several of his disciples and family members volunteered as teachers. Being a staunch believer of passive resistance, he championed the cause of the Champaran movement. His wife, Kasturba, worked on the personal cleanliness and community sanitation of the place. Gandhiji also hired a doctor for the improvement of the health conditions.

Thus, we can say that Gandhiji was not a loyalty to abstractions. It was loyalty to living, human beings. This also made him keen to eradicate social and cultural backwardness of Champaran. Gandhiji exulted over them and made the villagers feel self-dependent and undaunted.

Q. 8. Why did Gandhiji feel that taking the Champaran case to the court was useless?

Ans. Gandhiji believed that the peasants were under the grip of fear. He felt that taking the Champaran case to the court would be useless because actual relief for the peasants would come when they would be free from fear. So, his ultimate motive was to kill the fear in them.

Q. 9. Why did Gandhiji agree to a settlement of 25 percent refund to the farmers ? How did it influence the peasant-landlord relationship in Champaran ?

Ans : Gandhiji agreed to the settlement of 25 percent because the amount was not important for him but to release the peasants from the indigo raising agreement was much more important. The British planters wanted to prolong the agreement but Gandhiji proved to be wiser. He fought for the poor peasants a long battle for one year and managed to get justice for them. This was a moral victory for them. Even the Britishers had to compromise with their pride and prestige. Peasants now got the courage and became aware of their rights. Their money and time was saved and within few years British planters were forced to give up their estates and these were returned to farmers. They became the owners of their own land. It also ignited the feelings of self-dependence and patriotism among the farmers.

Exploitation is a universal phenomenon. The poor indigo farmers were exploited by the British landlords to which Gandhiji objected. Even after our independence we find exploitation of unorganised labour.

Q. 10. What values do we learn from Gandhiji's campaign to counter the present day problems of exploitation ?

Ans. The conditions that prevailed during the time of Gandhiji are still existing. The weak and the poor are living in the same condition as they used to, prior to the independence, only the ways of exploitation have altered. The poor sharecroppers were exploited by the British landlords and their lands were snatched from them. Gandhiji, fought for them systematically by gathering information and presenting the facts courageously and managed to get justice for the fear stricken peasants. The striking feature of this was that he did not use any form of violence or unfair means.

These methods can be adopted by us also, as we must be aware of our strength and weaknesses and then proceed accordingly as one should not fall into the trap by any means. We should never compromise at the cost of our dignity or self-respect and thus sought out the solutions wisely.

Q. 11. How did Civil Disobedience triumph at Motihari?*

Ans. Gandhiji went to Motihari to gather complete information about the indigo plantation contracts from the peasants. There he was accompanied by several lawyers. He was on his way to meet a peasant who was mistreated by some of the indigo planters; but was stopped by a messenger of the police superintendent who served him a notice which asked him to leave. However, Gandhiji ignored the notice and continued his investigation. A case was filed against him and he was arrested. On the day of the trial, unanimously, a large crowd of peasants gathered near the court demanding the release of Gandhiji. When it became impossible to control them, Gandhiji spoke to them and they all obeyed him. Gandhiji managed to convince the court that he was not there to break the laws but just to help the peasants. He was immediately granted bail and later, the case against him was dropped. An official enquiry was conducted and the landlords agreed to refund the peasants. Although they did not give 50%, the landlords agreed to refund 25%. Thus, Gandhiji won the case for the peasants through Satyagraha and non-violence.

Reference to Context :

Read the given extract to attempt questions that follow:

1. *What about the injustice to the sharecroppers, Gandhi demanded. The lawyers withdrew to consult. Rajendra Prasad has recorded the upshot of their consultations—"They thought, amongst themselves, that Gandhi was totally a stranger, and yet he was prepared to go to prison for the sake of the peasants; if they, on the other hand, being not only residents of the adjoining districts but also those who claimed to have served these peasants, should go home, it would be shameful desertion. "They accordingly went back to Gandhi and told him they were ready to follow him into jail. ''The battle of Champaran is won," he exclaimed. Then he took a piece of paper and divided the group into pairs and put down the order in which each pair was to court arrest."*

(i) What lesson did the lawyers learn from Gandhi?

(a) Unity (b) Being efficient (c) Wisdom (d) Courage

Ans. (a) Unity

* are board exam questions from previous years

(ii) What does Gandhi's action signify?

(a) Power of being an influential lawyer
(b) Effective leadership
(c) Kindness
(d) Intelligence

Ans. (b) Effective leadership

(iii) "The battle of Champaran" was won due to:

(a) The crushing defeat of the British in the courtroom.
(b) Violence by peasants.
(c) Power demonstration by Gandhi.
(d) Different classes of people being fearless and coming together to voice their concerns for the oppressed.

Ans. (d) Different classes of people being fearless and coming together to voice their concerns for the oppressed.

(iv) Rajendra Prasad's role at Champaran was of a:

(a) friend.
(b) recorder of events.
(c) representative of the oppressed.
(d) secretary to Gandhi.

Ans. (c) representative of the oppressed.

(v) Why was Gandhi concerned about the injustice?

(a) To gain popularity.
(b) To represent the oppressed as a lawyer.
(c) Due to his selfless love for the nation and countrymen, and for utmost justice.
(d) It was a farce by Gandhi.

Ans. (c) Due to his selfless love for the nation and countrymen, and for utmost justice.

Read the given extract to attempt questions that follow:

2. *"Presently, the landlords learned that Germany had developed synthetic indigo. They, thereupon, obtained agreements from the sharecroppers to pay them compensation for being released from the 15 per cent arrangement."*

(i) What was the character of landlords?

(a) Generous (b) Exploitative (c) Kind-hearted (d) Friendly

Ans. (b) Exploitative

(ii) What did the peasants grow?

(a) Wheat (b) Rice (c) Indigo (d) Mango

Ans. (c) Indigo

(iii) Select the correct option to fill the blank:

Germany was a _________ market.

(a) competitor (b) friendly (c) underdog (d) dependent

Ans. (a) competitor

(iv) How would synthetic indigo impact the indigo market in India?

(a) Rise in prices
(b) Rise in demand
(c) Decline in prices
(d) Decline in demand

Ans. (b) Rise in demand

(v) Who are the sharecroppers?

(a) Peasants (b) British (c) Lawyers (d) Doctors

Ans. (a) Peasants

Read the given extract to attempt questions that follow:

3. *"Gandhi did not leave. Instead he proceeded to Motihari, the capital of Champaran. Several lawyers accompanied him. At the railway station, a vast multitude greeted Gandhi. He went to a house and, using it as headquarters, continued his investigations. A report came in that a peasant had been maltreated in a nearby village. Gandhi decided to go and see; the next morning he started out on the back of an elephant. He had not proceeded far when the police superintendent's messenger overtook him and ordered him to return to town. Gandhi complied. The messenger drove Gandhi home where he served him with an official notice to quit Champaran immediately. Gandhi signed a receipt for the notice and wrote on it that he would disobey the order."*

(i) How were the peasants treated?

(a) They were given their rights.

(b) They were marginalised.

(c) Some were maltreated while others were treated.

(d) They were respected.

Ans. (b) They were marginalised.

(ii) Animals were used as a mode of:

(a) communication (b) gifts (c) transportation (d) labour

Ans. (c) transportation

(iii) Gandhi was a staunch believer of:

(a) equality and justice for all.

(b) class system.

(c) socialism.

(d) capitalism.

Ans. (a) equality and justice for all.

(iv) The police was represented by:

(a) Indians (b) British (c) British-Indian (d) Local leaders

Ans. (b) British

(v) "Gandhi complied."

(a) Because he believed in non-violence.

(b) Because he was scared of the British.

(c) Because he didn't want to upset the judiciary.

(d) To gain fame.

Ans. (a) Because he believed in non-violence.

Read the given extract to attempt questions that follow:

4. *"Gandhi protested against the delay. He read a statement pleading guilty. He was involved, he told the court, in a "conflict of duties"— on the one hand, not to set a bad example as a lawbreaker; on the other hand, to render the "humanitarian and national service" for which he had come. He disregarded the order to leave, "not for want of respect for lawful authority, but in obedience to the higher law of our being, the voice of conscience." He asked the penalty due."*

(i) What was Gandhi guilty of?

(a) Disobeying the caste system.

(b) Disobeying the local rules.

(c) Disobeying the class system.

(d) Disobeying the court order.

Ans. (d) Disobeying the court order.

(ii) What is the higher law?

(a) The different laws at different levels.

(b) The law of the supreme court.

(c) The law of the British.

(d) The law of one's moral.

Ans. (d) The law of one's moral.

(iii) By following his heart when in "conflict of duties", Gandhi taught us to?

(a) Listen to our consciousness.

(b) Follow materialistic choices.

(c) Follow the orders of superiors.

(d) Follow the order of God.

Ans. (a) Listen to our consciousness.

(iv) Select the correct option to fill the blank:

"He asked the penalty due" shows Gandhi's _________.

(a) shrewdness (b) helplessness (c) courage (d) wisdom

Ans. (d) wisdom

(v) This extract shows Gandhi's character as a:

(a) lawbreaker.

(b) messiah.

(c) representative of the people.

(d) father of the nation.

Ans. (c) representative of the people.

Read the given extract to attempt questions that follow:

5. *"Months passed. Shukla was sitting on his haunches at the appointed spot in Calcutta when Gandhi arrived; he waited till Gandhi was free. Then the two of them boarded a train for the city of Patna in Bihar. There Shukla led him to the house of* *a lawyer named Rajendra Prasad who later became President of the Congress party and of India. Rajendra Prasad was out of town, but the servants knew Shukla as a poor yeoman who pestered their master to help the indigo sharecroppers. So they let him stay on the grounds with his companion, Gandhi, whom they took to be another peasant. But Gandhi was not permitted to draw water from the well lest some drops from his bucket pollute the entire source; how did they know that he was not an untouchable?"*

(i) Select the correct option to fill the blank:

The paragraph shows Shukla's ....

(a) support of Gandhi
(b) persuasive technique
(c) determination
(d) failure

Ans. (c) determination

(ii) Was Gandhi ever mistreated due to the prevalence of caste system in India?

(a) No (b) May be (c) Never (d) Yes

Ans. (d) Yes

(iii) What is the meaning of pester?

(a) Love (b) Care (c) Annoy (d) Misunderstand

Ans. (c) Annoy

(iv) Whom did Shukla approach first?

(a) Rajendra Prasad (b) Gandhi (c) Motilal Nehru (d) Sarojini Naidu

Ans. (a) Rajendra Prasad

(v) What concept is untouchability based on?

(a) Us and them
(b) Pollution and purity
(c) Equality
(d) Harassment

Ans. (b) Pollution and purity

6. *Gandhi told Shukla he had an appointment in Cawnpore and was also committed to go to other parts of India. Shukla accompanied him everywhere.Then Gandhi returned to his ashram near Ahmedabad. Shukla followed him to the ashram. For weeks he never left Gandhi's side. "Fix a date," he begged.*

(i) Why was Gandhiji going to Cawnpore?

(a) To attend his relatives.
(b) To attend some family function.
(c) Due to some appointment.
(d) To his ancestral house.

Ans. (c) Due to some appointment.

(ii) What does Shukla's following Gandhiji everywhere reflect about his nature?

(a) Sheer determination
(b) Obstinate nature
(c) Obsequiousness
(d) Shamelessness

Ans. (a) Sheer determination

(iii) Where was Gandhiji's ashram?

(a) Near Cawnpore
(b) In Lucknow
(c) In Champaran
(d) Near Ahmedabad

Ans. (d) Near Ahmedabad

(iv) For how long did Shukla remain with Gandhiji?

(a) For several weeks.
(b) For few months.
(c) For a year.
(d) For few days.

Ans. (a) For several weeks.

7. *Health conditions were miserable. Gandhiji got a doctor to volunteer his services for six months. Three medicines were available — castor oil, quinine and sulphur ointment. Anybody who showed a coated tongue was given a dose of castor oil; anybody with malaria fever received quinine plus castor oil; anybody with skin eruptions received ointment plus castor oil.*

(i) Where did Gandhiji go to volunteer his services?

(a) Kanpur (b) Calcutta (c) Champaran (d) Delhi

Ans. (c) Champaran

(ii) Which character trait of Gandhiji is revealed through his attitude of extending help to the poor and the miserable ?

(a) He was a compassionate person.
(b) He was a tricky politician.
(c) He was a skillful leader.
(d) He wanted to acquire people's support in this way.

Ans. (a) He was a compassionate person.

(iii) For how long doctor was supposed to render his services?

(a) One year (b) Two years (c) Six months (d) Four months

Ans. (c) Six months

(iv) When was quinine with castor oil given to a patient?

(a) Patient having malaria fever.
(b) Patient with skin eruptions.
(c) Patient having coated tongue.
(d) Patient having pneumonia.

Ans. (a) Patient having malaria fever.

8. *Gandhi chided the lawyers for collecting big fee from the sharecroppers. He said, "I have come to the conclusion that we should stop going to law courts. Taking such cases to the courts does little good. Where the peasants are so crushed and fear-stricken, law courts are useless. The real relief for them is to be free from fear." Most of the arable land in the Champaran district was divided into large estates owned by Englishmen and worked by Indian tenants. The chief commercial crop was indigo. The landlords compelled all tenants to plant three twentieths or 15 per cent of their holdings with indigo and surrender the entire indigo harvest as rent. This was done by long-term contract.*

(i) What do you understand by the word :

(a) Arable (b) Result

Ans. (a) Available for agriculture
(b) Conclusion

(ii) Pick out the names of any two places mentioned in the chapter.

Ans. Muzaffapur and Champaran

(iii) Name the following :

(a) The chief commercial crop (b) Owned of the Estates

Ans. (a) Indigo
(b) Englishmen

(iv) Write the antonyms of the following :

(a) Surrender (b) Courage

Ans. (a) Resist
(b) Fear

Multiple Choice Questions

1. Where was the annual convention of Indian National Congress held?

(a) At Varanas (b) At Mumbai (c) At Bangalore (d) At Lucknow

Ans. (d) At Lucknow

2. From where did the peasant Rajkumar Shukla come to meet Mahatma Gandhi?

(a) Kanpur (b) Champaran (c) Bangalore (d) Chennai

Ans. (b) Champaran

3. Gandhi asked Shukla to meet at:

(a) Bombay (b) Calcutta (c) Madras (d) Delhi

Ans. (b) Calcutta

4. In Patna whose house did Gandhi and Shukla go?

(a) Rajendra Prasad's
(b) Prof. J.B. Kriplani's
(c) Rajkumar Shukla's
(d) Prof. Malkani's

Ans. (a) Rajendra Prasad's

5. Where did Gandhi decide to go first?

(a) Muzaffarpur (b) Champaran (c) Motihari (d) Kanpur

Ans. (a) Muzaffarpur

6. **Who was J.B. Kripalani?**
   (a) Professor of Arts College
   (b) Professor of Science College
   (c) Professor of Commerce College
   (d) Professor of Law College

Ans. (a) Professor of Arts College

7. **Which country had developed the synthetic Indigo?**
   (a) Japan (b) Germany (c) Pakistan (d) Iraq

Ans. (b) Germany

8. **Whom did Gandhiji send a telegram to?**
   (a) Prof. Malkani
   (b) British official commissioner
   (c) Sir Edward
   (d) Prof. J.B Kriplani

Ans. (d) Prof. J.B Kriplani

9. **What was the condition of the Sharecroppers?**
   (a) Forced to give 10% of land for Indigo plantation.
   (b) Forced to give 20% of land for Indigo plantation.
   (c) Forced to give 15% of land for Indigo plantation.
   (d) Forced to give 5% of land for Indigo plantation.

Ans. (c) Forced to give 15% of land for Indigo plantation.

10. **Who was Sir Edward?**
    (a) Lawyer
    (b) British official commissioner
    (c) Magistrate
    (d) Lieutenant-Governor

Ans. (d) Lieutenant- Governor

11. **What did the British official commissioner tell Gandhi in his communication?**
    (a) He asked Gandhi to leave Tirhut.
    (b) He asked Gandhi to leave Motihari.
    (c) He asked Gandhi to leave Champaran.
    (d) He asked Gandhi to leave Muzzafarpur.

Ans. (a) He asked Gandhi to leave Tirhut.

12. **Louis Fischer, the author of Indigo, was ______.**
    (a) Gandhi's friend
    (b) lawyer
    (c) journalist and writer
    (d) editor

Ans. (c) journalist and writer

13. **The story's hidden strength lies in ________.**
    (a) being brave
    (b) being powerful
    (c) freeing oneself from fear of the British
    (d) enrolling lawyers into new roles

Ans. (c) freeing oneself from fear of the British

14. **Gandhi agreed to the planter's offer of 25% refund to the farmers as he was concerned about ________ of farmers.**
    (a) loss (b) profit (c) power (d) prestige

Ans. (d) prestige

15. **Champaran is known for ________.**
    (a) launch of first Satyagraha in India
    (b) launch of Dandi March
    (c) launch of Civil Disobedience Movement
    (d) headquarter of Indian National Congress

Ans. (a) launch of first Satyagraha in India

16. **Sir Edmund was a ________ and was posted at ________.**
    (a) lawyer, France
    (b) doctor, England
    (c) teacher, Delhi
    (d) civil servant, Bengal Presidency of British India

Ans. (d) civil servant and Bengal Presidency of British India

17. **Gandhiji asked ________ to speak to the women about ________.**
    (a) Kasturba, hygiene
    (b) Shukla, food
    (c) Prasad, plantation
    (d) Edmund, education

Ans. (a) Kasturba, hygiene

18. The purpose behind Raj Kumar Shukla's visit to the Annual Congress party session was________.

(a) to get inspiration from Gandhi
(b) to get acquainted with Gandhi
(c) to be a representative of the Congress party
(d) to speak to Gandhi about the injustice of the landlord system in Bihar

Ans. (d) to speak to Gandhi about the injustice of the landlord system in Bihar

19. Gandhi stayed for two days at ________.

(a) Prof. Malkani's house
(b) Sir Edmund's house
(c) Prison
(d) Rajendra Prasad's house

Ans. (a) Prof. Malkani's house

20. By opposing Sir Edmund's stay Gandhi emphasised on:

(a) Unity (b) Trust (c) Self-reliance (d) Equality

Ans. (c) Self-reliance

21. ________ movement was launched in Champaran for upliftment of farmers.

(a) Non-cooperation movement
(b) Independence movement
(c) Self-reliance
(d) Satyagraha

Ans. (d) Satyagraha

22. The result of meeting with the Governor was ________.

(a) appointment of official commission of inquiry
(b) compensation to the farmers
(c) 25% refund
(d) 50% refund

Ans. (a) appointment of official commission of inquiry

23. Where was the author born?

(a) In Philadelphia (b) In Yugoslavia (c) In Scotland (d) None of these

Ans. (a) In Philadelphia

24. When did the author serve in the British army?

(a) 1918-1920 (b) 1909-1910 (c) 1912-1913 (d) 1900-1902

Ans. (a) 1918-1920

25. Which University was the author a member of?

(a) Harvard University
(b) Princeton University
(c) University of Columbia
(d) Oxford University

Ans. (b) Princeton University

26. What is the message conveyed in the lesson Indigo?

(a) Efficient lawyers are good leaders.
(b) Speak aloud and lead.
(c) Wise and courageous leadership can resolve any problem.
(d) Wise leaders are difficult to find.

Ans. (c) Wise and courageous leadership can resolve any problem.

27. Where was the ashram of Gandhiji situated?

(a) Lucknow (b) Patna (c) Sevagram (d) Bombay

Ans. (c) Sevagram

28. At Lucknow Conference, a peasant came to meet Mahatma Gandhi. What was his name?

(a) Rajkumar Shukla
(b) Ram Singh Shukla
(c) Raj Singh Shukla
(d) Rajkumar Singla

Ans. (a) Rajkumar Shukla

29. In Patna whose house did Gandhi and Shukla go?

(a) The lawyer's (b) The magistrate's (c) Shukla's (d) The Governor's

Ans. (a) The lawyer's

30. Why was Gandhiji not permitted to draw water from the well?

(a) Because he was a guest.

(b) Because he was considered untouchable by the servants.

(c) Because he was black.

(d) Because he was a politician.

Ans. (b) Because he was considered untouchable by the servants.

31. Who of the following was both the President of the Congress Party and President of India?

(a) Mahatma Gandhi

(b) Jawaharlal Nehru

(c) Rajendra Prasad

(d) Ram Kumar Shukla

Ans. (c) Rajendra Prasad

32. Where had Gandhi seen Professor J.B. Kripalani?

(a) Shantiniketan School

(b) Vidya Niketan School

(c) Surya Niketan School

(d) Saraswati Niketan School

Ans. (a) Shantiniketan School

33. When did train arrive at Muzaffarpur?

(a) Midnight 15 April, 1917

(b) Morning 15 April, 1917

(c) Evening 15 April, 1917

(d) Afternoon15 April, 1917

Ans. (a) Midnight 15 April, 1917

34. What does Gandhi's fight in Champaran signify?

(a) The power of effective leadership.

(b) The power of lawyers.

(c) The power of farmers.

(d) The power of money.

Ans. (a) The power of effective leadership.

35. What was the condition of the peasants in Champaran?

(a) They were stressed.

(b) They were polite but dominants.

(c) They were self-sufficient.

(d) They were terror-stricken and oppressed.

Ans. (d) They were terror-stricken and oppressed.

36. What was the capital of Champaran?

(a) Calcutta (b) Patna (c) Motihari (d) Lucknow

Ans. (c) Motihari

37. Champaran was located In the foothills of......

(a) Himalayas (b) Aravalli (c) Vindhyachal (d) Nilgiri

Ans. (a) Himalayas

38. What was Gandhiji's demand from the British landlords?

(a) 30% refund as repayment.

(b) 40% refund as repayment.

(c) 50% refund as repayment.

(d) 10% refund as repayment.

Ans. (c) 50% refund as repayment.

39. How did Gandhi address the actions of the people of Motihari?

(a) As liberation from the fear of the British.

(b) By calming down the courages.

(c) By calming down the outrageous.

(d) By chiding the lawyers.

Ans. (a) As liberation from the fear of the British.

40. What did people of Motihari do when they learnt that Gandhi was in trouble with the British authorities?

(a) They surrounded the courthouse.

(b) They did not help him.

(c) They remained in their houses.

(d) They took the side of the British.

Ans. (a) They surrounded the courthouses.

41. What was the statement that Gandhiji read pleading himself guilty?

(a) That he was a law breaker.

(b) That he wanted to command.
(c) That he came to render humanitarian and national service.
(d) That he wanted justice at any cost.

Ans. (c) That he came to render humanitarian and national service.

42. What was the purpose of the advocates of home rule?

(a) To get money and lead a normal life.
(b) To be popular so that they could get their freedom.
(c) To instigate the people so that they could help in bringing liberty.
(d) To encourage people to participate in the freedom movement.

Ans. (d) To encourage people to participate in the freedom movement.

43. What did the Lieutenant-Governor tell Gandhi in his communication?

(a) He asked Gandhi to leave Champaran.
(b) He said that Gandhi would be arrested.
(c) He threatened to deport Gandhi.
(d) That the case against him had been dropped.

Ans. (d) That the case against him had been dropped.

44. Why did Gandhi chide the lawyers?

(a) They were not expert.
(b) They were having Nexus with the British.
(c) They were collecting big fee from the sharecroppers.
(d) All of the above.

Ans. (c) They were collecting big fee from the sharecroppers.

45. Who called Gandhiji as outsider?

(a) Secretary of the British Landlords Association.
(b) Chairman of the British Landlords Association.
(c) Director of the British Landlords Association.
(d) Manager of the British Landlords Association.

Ans. (a) Secretary of the British Landlords Association.

46. Why did prosecutor request the judge to postpone the trial?

(a) Authorities wish to consult their superiors.
(b) Authorities wish to consult their peers.
(c) Authorities wish to withdraw the case.
(d) Authorities wish to consult their subordinates.

Ans. (a) Authorities wish to consult their superiors.

47. Who was Reverend J.Z. Hodge?

(a) British Missionary in Champaran.
(b) British Missionary in Calcutta.
(c) British Missionary in Chennai.
(d) British Missionary in Patna.

Ans. (a) British missionary in Champaran.

48. Gandhiji remained in Champaran for an initial uninterrupted period of.

(a) seven years (b) seven days (c) seven hours (d) seven months

Ans. (d) seven months

49. Quinine plus castor oil was given for.

(a) Malaria (b) Typhoid (c) Dengue (d) Corona

Ans. (a) Malaria

50. Why was Motihari back with peasants?

(a) Because of people's rights.
(b) Because of the oppression of the British.
(c) Because their champion was in trouble.
(d) None of these

Ans. (c) Because their champion was in trouble.

51. Why did Gandhiji protest at Motihari court house?

(a) To be famous
(b) To show his power
(c) To humiliate the British
(d) To protest the court's order to postpone the trial

Ans. (d) To protest the court's order to postpone the trial

❑❑

Poetry–Flamingo

4. A Thing of Beauty–by John Keats

Summary :

The poet, John Keats says that beautiful things will never become 'nothing' as they will continue to hold us in their spell and soothe our soul. Every beautiful thing is like a band that ties us to this earth as it makes us want to live and enjoy these things of beauty. And these things of beauty, according to the poet, are the things that give hope to human-beings and make them want to live, in spite of all the sorrow, ill-health and unpleasant experiences that we face on earth. Some of the beautiful things on this earth that have such an effect on us are the sun, the moon, trees, streams, flowers, forests, beautiful monuments that we have erected for the dead, all the lovely tales that we have heard or read. Finally, he compares all these beautiful things to the immortal drink or nectar given to us by gods or that are gifts of God. Thus, he states his firm belief in the Divine.

Theme :

The theme of the poem rests in the opening line of the poem. A beautiful object is treasured in our mind because it provides us an eternal and an everlasting joy. The happiness never fades into nothingness but multiplies manifold whenever it flashes on our mind's screen.

Message :

The very first line contains the message the John Keats, the great romantic poet, wants to convey. Keats was a worshipper of beauty. For him, beauty was truth. Hence, for him, a thing of beauty is a joy forever. Beauty never fades. Nor is it ever devalued. It never passes into nothingness. When we are full of sorrows and sufferings, to me form of beauty comes to our reserve. It removes the darkness of sadness and sorrows and gives us joy and pleasure. Thus, beauty is a boon for human beings gives us joy and pleasure. Thus, beauty is a boon for human beings.

Text Book Questions :

Think it Out :

Q. 1. List the things of beauty mentioned in the poem.

Ans. Every little or big thing of nature is a thing of beauty and a source of pleasure. The sun, the moon, trees young and old, daffodil flowers are all things of beauty. So are small streams with clear water, mass of ferns and the blooming musk-roses. They are a source of everlasting joy and pleasure.

Q. 2. List the things that cause suffering and pain.

Ans. The things that cause sufferings and pain are : the wicked people outnumbers the good people, and the source of all our sorrows is either ill-health or another human-being.

Q. 3. What does the line, 'Therefore are we wreathing a flowery band to bind us to earth', suggest to you?

Ans. Man has always shared a special bond with nature. Though the world is a beautiful place to live in, there is a lot of pain and suffering too. That could be enjoyed by treasuring the happiness and joy that beautiful things give us. Keats believed that man and nature were woven into an unbroken bond. He believed that beauty around us is like beautiful flowers and we should wreathe them into a flowery band that keeps us connected to the earth.

Q. 4. What makes human-beings love life in spite of troubles and suffering?

Ans. The poet says that the beautiful things on earth lift the pall off our spirits and made life worth living. Each beautiful thing was like a link that formed a chain or wreath that bound us to the earth. The beautiful things in nature like the moon, the sun, the trees, the ferns and the daffodils bring happiness and reduce human's sufferings.

Q. 5. Why is 'grandeur' associated with the 'mighty dead'?

Ans. The sad things become a source of beauty and pleasure when they take the status of art. The poet said that the contemplation of the reminiscences of the mighty persons who were dead gives us same pleasure as we experience in contemplating beautiful things of nature.

Q. 6. Do we experience things of beauty only for short moments or do they make a lasting impression on us?

Ans. Keats believed that beautiful things always have a lasting impression on the human minds. All beautiful objects are a source of joy forever. Beauty survives the trials and tribulations of time and exists continuously in our thoughts.

Q. 7. What image does the poet use to describe the beautiful bounty of the earth?

Ans. The poet used the image of a perennial fountain which poured forth bounties on earth in the form of an immortal drink from the heaven above. He used the expression 'an endless fountain of immortal drink, pouring unto us from the heaven's brink'. Through these lines the poet described the earth and its beautiful bounties that could not be replaced by anything.

Additional Questions :

Read the extracts and answer the questions that follow :

Q. 1. *A thing of beauty is a joy forever:*
Its loveliness increases; it will never
Pass into nothingness; but will keep
A bower quiet for us, and a sleep
Full of sweet dreams,
and health, and quiet breathing.

(a) What is being said to be a joy forever?

Ans. A thing of beauty is said to be a joy forever.

(b) What is peculiar about a beautiful thing?

OR

Explain: "A thing of beauty is a joy forever".

Ans. A beautiful thing leaves a permanent impression on our mind. Its loveliness goes on increasing. It stays in our imagination and becomes a source of joy forever.

(c) What can a beautiful thing do for human-beings?

Ans. A beautiful thing gives us a sound sleep full of sweet dreams, health and a peaceful breathing. It also helps us in achieving peace of mind. It removes sadness and brings happiness to our depressed spirits.

(d) Explain: 'its loveliness increases'

Ans. The joy that we experience on seeing a beautiful object, multiplies, whenever we remember it. Similarly, the loveliness of everything increases and multiplies whenever we visualize it in our thoughts.

(e) What is a bower?

Ans. A bower is a pleasant place in the shade under a tree.

(f) How does a thing of beauty keep a bower quiet for us?

Ans. It reserves a quiet place in our heart. When we are tired, tensed, troubled or disappointed, it heals our sorrows and restores happiness for us again.

(g) Explain: "It will never pass into nothingness".

Ans. A thing of beauty is a perennial thing. Its beauty goes on increasing. It will never be reduced into nothingness.

(h) Explain: 'sleep full of sweet dreams.'

Ans. The joy that beauty gives us is akin to the joy of a blissful sleep full of pleasant dreams.

(i) What does 'quiet breathing' imply?

Ans. It implies the sense of peace and serenity that one experiences on seeing beautiful things. Beautiful sights act as nutrition for a healthy mind and thus refresh and relax us by driving away aggression.

(j) Find words from the passage which mean same as:

(i) of no value (ii) a shady place under a tree (iii) still / silent

Ans. (i) nothingness (ii) bower (iii) quiet

Q. 2. *Therefore, on every morrow, are we wreathing*
A flowery band to bind us to the earth,
Spite of despondence, of the inhuman dearth
of noble natures, of the gloomy days,
of all the unhealthy and o'er-darkened ways
Made for searching:

(a) What are we doing every day?

OR

What according to the poet are we doing every morning?

Ans. The poet felt that we were weaving a flowery band that bound us to the earth and made us live and enjoy our life. Else, life would be a pain without objects of beauty around us.

(b) What evil and bad things do we possess in us?

Ans. We suffer from disappointment. We possess a lack of noble qualities and unhealthy and evil ways.

(c) Explain: 'wreathing a flowery band to bind us to the earth'.

Ans. Keats always felt that life on earth would not have been worth living had it been deprived of beauty. In the above quote, he expressed a similar feeling. He felt that every morning we weave a beautiful string of flowers or memories which helps us to support ourselves and motivates us to live our life to the fullest.

(d) What does 'spite of despondence' imply?

Ans. The poet sees life as a struggle where pain and hopelessness are often faced by man. The expression refers to loss of hope and the sufferings faced by man at various junctures in life.

(e) Why is there an 'inhuman dearth of noble natures'?

Ans. Man is selfish and self-centred. These days, there are only few people on the earth who are noble in character and who put away petty differences by being magnanimous and generous.

(f) What makes our days gloomy?

Ans. Life on earth has always been a struggle for success. We often get obstructed by deceit and selfishness of our fellow-beings. The loss of hope and pangs of defeat that we suffer in our journey of life make our days gloomy.

(g) Explain: 'unhealthy and o'er-darkened ways'.

Ans. The 'unhealthy and o'er-darkened ways' refer to the trials and tribulations of life. They are symbolic of the selfish and jealous methods we adopt to achieve our goals.

(h) Find words from the passage which mean the same as:

(i) malice (ii) morning (iii) disappointment.

Ans. (i) spite (ii) morrow (iii) despondence

Q. 3. *Yes, in spite of all,*
Some shape of beauty moves away the pall
From our dark spirits.
Such the sun, the moon,
Trees old and young, sprouting a shady boon
For simple sheep: and such are daffodils

(a) What does 'in spite of all' refer to?

Ans. The expression refers to all the pessimistic and negative thoughts that obstruct our way to happiness. In spite of the sense of hopelessness and gloom that overshadows and darkens our way, we are able to find our happiness in the beautiful objects of nature.

(b) What sprouts a shady boon for a sheep and how?

Ans. Trees young and old sprout to make a green covering. It becomes a shelter for simple sheep and proves a blessing for them.

(c) What images of beauty has the poet referred to?

Ans. The poet appreciated the simplicity and serenity of beauty through the image of the sun, the moon, the trees, the sheep and the daffodils

(d) What, according to the poet, drives away the sadness from our life?

Ans. Beauty, in any shape or form, helps in driving away the sadness and despair from the dark recesses of our spirit.

(e) How does the poet celebrate the beauty of a tree?

Ans. According to the poet, the trees whether young or old, are a symbol of protection. Nature, through those trees showers on us, her blessings in the form of 'shade', thus, protecting us from heat and rain.

(f) What does the reference 'simple sheep' symbolize?

Ans. Lambs and sheep are envisioned as the embodiments of innocent and serene beauty. Jesus Christ, as an apostle of peace, was a shepherd and was seen surrounded by his flock of sheep, his followers. The poet has made specific reference to the sheep as symbols of 'divine beauty'.

(g) Find words from the passage which mean :

(i) appearance of newly grown plants (ii) blessing (iii) covering

Ans. (i) sprouting (ii) boon (iii) pall

Q. 4. *With the green world they live in; and clear rills*
That for themselves a cooling covert make
'Gainst the hot season; the mid forest brake,
Rich with a sprinkling of fair musk–rose blooms:

(a) Explain: 'with the green world they live in'.

Ans. Nature was at its best in the lush green surroundings of meadows and pastures which provided support to all plants and animals. It was in that green world that they found the true joy and happiness of life.

(b) Describe the role of rills in enriching the environment.

Ans. The small streams, here called rills, with clear water make a cooling shelter for themselves against the hot season.

(c) What does 'clear rills' refer to?

Ans. 'Clear rills' refers to the rivers and streams which are the natural source of water, the elixir of life.

(d) How are they beneficial to mankind?

Ans. The beautiful sight of streams provides a cooling effect that gives respite in the hot season.

(e) Explain: 'the mid forest brake'.

Ans. Nature is beautiful in all its aspects. The poet enjoys its beauty in under-growing thickets that brimmed with the growth of musk-rose.

(f) Find words from the passage which mean same as:

(i) small streams (ii) thickets (iii) shelter.

Ans. (i) rills (ii) brakes (iii) covert.

(g) What is the rhyme-scheme of the poem ?

Ans. The rhyme-scheme is aabbc.

Q. 5. *And such too is the grandeur of the dooms*
We have imagined for the mighty dead;
All lovely tales that we have heard or read;
An endless fountain of immortal drink,
Pouring unto us from the heaven's brink.

(a) Explain: 'the grandeur of the dooms'.

Ans. Growth and decay march hand in hand and are two vital aspects of life. The poet sees beauty in magnificent decay and death of these beautiful creations of nature.

(b) Who are the mighty dead?

Ans. The mighty dead are those who sacrificed their lives for a noble cause and made great achievements in their lifetime.

(c) Why does the poet make this reference?

Ans. The poet refers to those great men and warriors who glorify death by embracing it most gracefully and magnificently.

(d) How is grandeur associated with the mighty dead?

Ans. The mighty dead are honoured and worshipped for their remarkable achievements. Now they are lying buried under their graves. On the day of Judgment, God would also reward them for their noble deeds. It is this dignity that is associated with them.

(e) What lovely tales does the poet talk of?

Ans. He talks of the great myths and the tales of the olden days.

(f) What does the poet call "an endless fountain of immortal drink".

Ans. Beautiful things in all respects, whether in growth or in decay, are a perennial source of motivation. It is an endless fountain from where we could drink the immortal elixir of life.

(g) What image does the poet draw in the last two lines?

Ans. Beautiful things are like an endless fountain which goes on pouring the immortal drink unto us from the heaven. They are a source of immense joy and happiness.

(h) Explain: 'Pouring unto us from the heaven's brink'.

Ans. Beauty is the greatest gift of God to man which has been showered upon us from the heavens above. This beauty is eternal and everlasting in whose glory men, on earth, derive their perennial source of joy and happiness.

(i) Find the words from the passage which mean same as:

(i) magnificence (ii) that never dies (iii) corner/end.

Ans. (i) grandeur (ii) immortal (iii) brink.

Previous Years' Questions :

Q. 1. How can 'mighty dead' be things of beauty ?

Ans. John Keats was the youngest of all Romantic Poets. He was famous for sensuousness, describing the mighty dead as the magnificant warrior who selflessly sacrificed his life for his nation and won grandeur or greatness. So, achieving this is equal to achieving a thing of beauty.

Q. 2. In the hot season, how do man and beast get comfort ?

Ans. John Keats, youngest of all romantic poets, is famous for sensuousness. He says, 'all these beauties are like endless beauties.' The hills or the small stream of clear water make a cooling shelter for themselves against the hot season. These beauties act as a healing balm for both man and beast.

Q. 3. What rich bounty has the heaven given us ?

Ans. John Keats, the youngest of all romatic poets was famous for sensuousness. He described the Earth to have numberless things of beauty. They give joy forever. They are like endles fountains of immortal drink, pouring in from the heaven's brink.

Q. 4. *Its loveliness increases, it will never*
Pass into nothingness; but will keep
A bower quiet for us, and a sleep
Full of sweet dreams, and health, and quiet breathing.

(a) Whose loveliness will keep on increasing ?

Ans. Loveliness of anything that is beautiful keeps on increasing. It gives us immense joy, unending and everlasting pleasure.

(b) Identify the phrase which says that 'it' is immortal.

Ans. "It will never pass into nothingness" is the phrase which says that it is immortal.

(c) What is a 'bower' ?

Ans. "Bower" literary means leafy shelter which here refers to the sweet dreams which consists of all beautiful objects that revive during our sleep when we are tired or troubled. We love to relive these joyous memories.

(d) Why do we need sweet dreams, health and quiet breathing in our lives ?

Ans. We need sweet dreams, health and quiet breathing in our lives as they refresh us and give eternal joy and remove our sorrows and sufferings. Thus, we want to remain bound to the earth.

Q. 5. Mention any four things of beauty that add joy to our life.

Ans. Everything of nature is a thing of beauty and a source of pleasure. Some of them are : the sun, the moon, old and young trees, flowers, small streams with clear water, masses of ferns, blooming musk-rose and lovely tales, etc. all of these are the things of beauty.

Q. 6. Mention any two things which cause pain and suffering.

Ans. The things that cause suffering and pain include the scarcity of people with a noble temperament and the unhealthy and miserable ways in which humanity is searching for meaning in life.

Q. 7. Which objects of nature does Keats mention as sources of joy in his poem ?

Ans. The poet says that, a beautiful thing is a source of ever lasting happiness. The few things that add joy to our life are the sun, the moon, a bower of trees and a clear stream of water.

Q. 8. *Spite of despondence, of the inhuman dearth*
Of noble natures, of the gloomy days,
Of all the unhealthy and o'er-darkened ways
Made for our searching : yes in spite of all,
Some shape of beauty moves away the pall
From our dark spirits.

(a) Name the poem and the poet.

Ans. The lines have been taken from the poem 'A Thing of Beauty' by John Keats.

(b) Why are we 'despondent' ?

Ans. The world we live in is full of depression and despair as there is death of noble souls. These evil and dark emotions leave us despondent and despicable.

(c) What removes 'the pall from our dark spirits' ?

Ans. The poet says that even though the world is not a place worth living in because of the umpteen reasons which gloom and depress, the gusto to live a happy and content life that can be derived from the sight of the beautiful bounties of nature around us. It is the thing of beauty which charms us and makes this world feel like Heaven. These beautiful things remove the pall from our dark spirits.

Q. 9. *All lovely tales that we have heard or read;*
An endless fountain of immortal drink.
Pouring unto us from the heaven's brink.

(a) Name the poem and the poet.

Ans. The above given lines are from the poem 'A thing of Beauty' by John Keats.

(b) What is the thing of beauty mentioned in these lines ?

Ans. The tales of mighty men is the thing of beauty mentioned in the given lines.

(c) What image does the poet use in these lines?

Ans. The poet used the image of 'an endless fountain of immortal drink' to describe the beautiful bounty of the Earth. The Earth, like a fountain, give us numerous beautiful sights like the sun, the moon, flowers, rivers and greenery.

Q. 10. What does Keats consider an endless fountain of immortal drink and why does he call its drink immortal ?

Ans. Beauty, according to Keats is immortal and is continuous source of motivation and inspiration and things of beauty are like endless mountains pouring from heaven. It is an endless fountain of beautiful things so that man can enjoy happiness and peace.

Q. 11. *A flowery band to bind us to the Earth,*
Spite of despondence, of the inhuman dearth
of noble natures, of the gloomy days,
Of all the unhealthy and o'er-darkened ways
made for our searching :

(a) What are we doing every day?

Ans. Every day we are weaving a beautiful string of flowers that would bind us to Earth, and motivate us to live our life happily instead of pains and sufferings.

(b) Which evil thing do we possess and suffer from?

Ans. We possess evils of hatred and jealousy that do not let us live freely and happily. They steal away the joys of life.

(c) What are the cirumstances that contribute towards making humans unhappy and disillusioned with life ?

Ans. There is competition everywhere and the world is full of selfish people. There is dearth of goodness and nobility in human nature. This makes us gloomy, unhappy and disillusioned with life.

Reference to Context :

Read the given extract to attempt questions that follow:

1. *Full of sweet dreams, and health, and quiet breathing.*
Therefore, on every morrow, are we wreathing
A flowery band to bind us to the earth,
Spite of despondence, of the inhuman dearth
Of noble natures, of the gloomy days,

(i) The poet describes all problems in the above extract except:

(a) The sad and stressful days.
(b) The people lacking emotions.
(c) The moments of depression.
(d) The deceitful acts to gain power.

Ans. (d) The deceitful acts to gain power.

(ii) Which option uses imagery as a poetic device in the above extract?

(a) Spite of despondence, of the inhuman dearth.
(b) Of noble natures, of the gloomy days.
(c) A flowery band to bind us to the earth.
(d) Rich with a sprinkling of fair musk-rose blooms.

Ans. (c) A flowery band to bind us to the earth.

(iii) Select the correct option to fill the blank as depicted by the poet in the given extract.

People don't entirely relish the beautiful creations of God because of _________.

(a) the almighty's nobility and magnanimity
(b) their attachment to materialistic things of world
(c) their desire to overpower God
(d) their will to create beautiful things

Ans. (b) their attachment to materialistic things of world

(iv) The literal meaning of 'wreathing' refers to encircling something. What does it signify in this extract?

(a) Paying homage to the lost ones.
(b) Expressing their gratitude to their loved ones.
(c) Bondages to worldly ties.
(d) Having about of fight.

Ans. (c) Bondages to worldly ties.

(v) Which analogy has been used in the extract to depict the beauty of God's creation?

(a) Flowing rivers and streams.
(b) Sound and peaceful sleep.
(c) Canopy of ferns and Daffodils.
(d) Bright sunshine.

Ans. (b) Sound and peaceful sleep.

Read the given extract to attempt questions that follow:

2. *For simple sheep; and such are daffodils*
With the green world they live in; and clear rills
That for themselves a cooling covert make
Gainst the hot season; the mid forest brake,
Rich with a sprinkling of fair musk-rose blooms;
And such too is the grandeur of the dooms

(i) The poet draws attention to which asset of beauty when he writes "grandeur of the dooms"?

(a) The grand canopy of trees making a shade.
(b) The grazing sheep in the backyard.
(c) The mysterious death of our loved ones.
(d) The glorious stories of martyred brave soldiers .

Ans. (d) The glorious stories of martyred brave soldiers.

(ii) Which option uses alliteration as a poetic device in the above extract?

(a) That for themselves a cooling covert make.
(b) Rich with a sprinkling of fair musk-rose blooms.
(c) With the green world they live in; and clear rills.
(d) And such too is the grandeur of the dooms.

Ans. (a) That for themselves a cooling covert make.

(iii) According to the poet, select the correct option to fill the blank.

The cooling effect midst the forest is caused by__________ .

(a) the wild animals
(b) the Daffodils
(c) the rills
(d) the musk rose blooms

Ans. (c) the rills

(iv) The literal meaning of *'brake'* refers to a device for slowing or stopping a moving vehicle. What does it signify here?

(a) The bunch of Daffodils.
(b) The area with thick mass of ferns or bushes.
(c) The streams of flowing waters
(d) The horns of the sheep.

Ans. (b) The area with thick mass of ferns or bushes.

(v) According to the extract, where are the musk roses blooming?

(a) At the banks of flowing rivers and streams.
(b) Along with the Daffodils.
(c) Amidst the canopy of ferns.
(d) In the poet's garden.

Ans. (c) Amidst the canopy of ferns.

Read the given extract to attempt questions that follow:

3. *A thing of beauty is a joy forever*
Its loveliness increases, it will never
Pass into nothingness; but will keep
A bower quiet for us, and a sleep

(i) The poet draws attention to which property of beauty in the above extract?

(a) It slowly fades away.
(b) It aids the sleep.
(c) It stays forever.
(d) It turns to nothingness.

Ans. (c) It stays forever.

(ii) Which option uses rhyme as a poetic device in the above extract?

(a) 'keep', 'sleep'
(b) 'beauty', 'loveliness'
(c) 'forever', 'never'
(d) Both (a) and (c)

Ans. (d) Both (a) and (c)

(iii) Pick the option that is synonymous with a shady place or a leafy shelter?

(a) Sleep (b) Bower (c) Loveliness (d) Beauty

Ans. (b) Bower

(iv) According to the extract, which of the following is a thing of beauty?

(a) Sound sleep with sweet dreams.
(b) Area with thick greenery.
(c) Sleeping under rock shelter.
(d) None of these.

Ans. (d) None of these.

(v) According to the extract, why do the things of beauty "never pass into nothingness"?

(a) The rivers and streams go dry in winters.
(b) Elements of beauty are related to our greed.
(c) Elements of nature are forever available to us.
(d) The Sun never appears in cold regions.

Ans. (c) Elements of nature are forever available to us.

4. *And such too is the grandeur of the dooms*
We have imagined for the mighty dead;
All lovely tales that we have heard or read;
An endless fountain of immortal drink,
*Pouring unto us from the heaven's brink.**

(i) Which two things of beauty are mentioned in these lines?

Ans. The things of beauty mentioned in these lines are the tales we have heard or read about our ancestors describing their sacrifices.

(ii) Why are the 'lovely tales' called an endless fountain?

Ans. The 'lovely tales' are called an endless fountain as they describe the beautiful bounty of the earth.

---

* are board exam questions from previous years

(iii) Where is this fountain situated?

Ans. The fountain is situated on heaven's brink.

(iv) Explain : 'grandeur of the dooms'.

Ans. It is the magnificence that we can imagine for our ancestors on the doomsday.

5. *For simple sheep; and such are daffodils*
With the green world they live in; and clear rills
That for themselves a cooling covert make
'Gainst the hot season; the mid forest brake,
Rich with a sprinkling of fair musk-rose blooms;

(i) Find antonyms of the given words in the extract :

(a) extravagant (b) scorching

Ans. (a) simple
(b) cooling

(ii) Fill in the blanks with appropriate words :

(a) The _______ live amidst greenery. (b) The ______ flowers grow amidst forest brakes.

Ans. (a) daffodils
(b) musk-rose

(iii) Give one word for :

(a) a small stream. (b) a thicket where small animals may hide.

Ans. (a) rill
(b) convert

(iv) Find from the extract, the phrases or words that mean:

(a) full of (b) few here and there

Ans. (a) rich with
(b) sprinkling

6. *A thing of beauty is a joy forever*
Its loveliness increases, it will never
Pass into nothingness; but will keep
A bower quiet for us, and a sleep
Full of sweet dreams, and health, and quiet breathing.

(i) What can a thing of beauty give?

(a) delight
(b) worry
(c) feeling of possessiveness
(d) attitude

Ans. (a) delight

(ii) Loveliness of beautiful things......................... .

(a) are often stolen
(b) remains for a short period of time
(c) multiplies on remembering
(d) ends immediately

Ans. (c) multiplies on remembering

(iii) Which figure of speech is used in 'bower quite'?

(a) Metaphor (b) Antithesis (c) Simile (d) Hyperbole

Ans. (a) Metaphor

(iv) What does 'bower' here means?

(a) leafy shelter (b) health (c) quietness (d) sweet dreams

Ans. (d) sweet dreams

Multiple Choice Questions

1. **What kind of a poet was John Keats?**
   (a) Realistic
   (b) Religious
   (c) Medieval
   (d) Romantic

Ans. (d) Romantic

2. **From where has this poem–A Thing of Beauty been taken?**
   (a) From Keats work - Endymion - A Poetic Romance
   (b) Ode to a Nightingale
   (c) Ode on Melancholy
   (d) Ode on Indolence

Ans. (a) From Keats work - Endymion - A Poetic Romance

3. **Who is Endymion?**
   (a) a worker
   (b) an office boy
   (c) a young child
   (d) a young shepherd

Ans. (d) a young shepherd

4. **Where did the poet and Endymion live?**
   (a) In a hut
   (b) On a hill
   (c) In a tree house
   (d) On mount Latmos

Ans. (d) On mount Latmos

5. **Whom did the enchanted youth resolve to seek?**
   (a) God
   (b) Nature
   (c) Mentor
   (d) Cynthia–the moon goddess

Ans. (d) Cynthia–the moon goddess

6. **Which things cause suffering to human beings?**
   (a) Lack of virtues and in human acts.
   (b) Withering flowers.
   (c) Blooming flowers.
   (d) Flowing streams.

Ans. (a) Lack of virtues and in human acts.

7. **What does Endymion do to seek goddess?**
   (a) Dances
   (b) Sings songs
   (c) Reads scriptures
   (d) Wanders through forests

Ans. (d) Wanders through forests

8. **How is a thing of beauty joy forever?**
   (a) Because it is beautiful.
   (b) Because it is nature.
   (c) Because it is joyful.
   (d) Because its beauty never ends and leaves a lasting impact.

Ans. (d) Because its beauty never ends and leaves a lasting impact.

9. **What is the endless fountain and what is its effect?**
   (a) Moving streams inspires us to keep moving.
   (b) The Sunlight that keeps us energized.
   (c) A thing of beauty is endless fountain and it give happiness.
   (d) None of the above.

Ans. (c) A thing of beauty is endless fountain and it give happiness

10. What does "A Thing of Beauty" is a joy forever mean?

(a) Joy is in memory.

(b) Joy is precious.

(c) Joy is not sold.

(d) It will keep giving happiness for a long time.

Ans. (d) It will keep giving happiness for a long time.

11. What is the concept of beauty?

(a) Beauty is a pleasure.

(b) Beauty is cause of all happiness.

(c) Beauty is nothing.

(d) A quality which always gives happiness.

Ans. (d) A quality which always gives happiness.

12. Do we experience things of beauty only for a short time?

(a) Yes, they are short lived.

(b) Yes, beauty is a temporary thing.

(c) It never lasts forever.

(d) No, they make a lasting impression of happiness.

Ans. (d) No, they make a lasting impression of happiness.

13. How does a thing of beauty provide shelter and comfort?

(a) By giving a sense of joy and happiness.

(b) By removing pain and suffering.

(c) Like a bower.

(d) All of the above.

Ans. (d) All of the above.

14. Write the phrase which means "It is immortal".

(a) It will never fade.

(b) It will never pass into nothingness.

(c) It will never cease.

(d) It will keep giving happiness for a long time.

Ans. (b) It will never pass into nothingness.

15. What is a bower?

(a) A river (b) A stream (c) A big tree (d) A shady tree

Ans. (d) A shady tree

16. Why do we need sweet dreams, health and quiet breathing?

(a) To have a healthy mind and body.

(b) To have sound sleep.

(c) To have peace and happiness.

(d) All of these.

Ans. (d) All of these.

17. What are 'mighty dead' in the poem?

(a) Dead people due to different catastrophe.

(b) Dead relatives who are close to your heart.

(c) Dead plants and vegetation of the forests.

(d) Great respectworthy ancestors specially dead emperors.

Ans. (d) Great respectworthy ancestors specially dead emperors.

18. What does 'brink' mean?

(a) Roof top

(b) A rocky space

(c) Mountain top

(d) An edge at the top

Ans. (d) An edge at the top

19. What image does the poet use to convey that beauty is everlasting?

(a) A bower quiet for us.

(b) Some shape of beauty.

(c) Endless fountain of joy.

(d) Sprouting a shady boon.

Ans. (c) Endless fountain of joy.

20. What is the effect of immortal drink?

(a) No one is thirsty.
(b) Everyone is happy.
(c) Immense joy and happiness.
(d) Beauty never moves away.

Ans. (c) Immense joy and happiness.

21. Pick the words from the poem which mean: stories, magnificance.

(a) Tales and grandeur.
(b) Old and young.
(c) Green world and clear rills.
(d) Sweet dreams and health.

Ans. (a) Tales and grandeur.

22. What is the meaning of gloomy?

(a) All the unhealthy things
(b) Dark spirits
(c) Dull and depressive
(d) None of these

Ans. (c) Dull and depressive

23. How does beauty help us when we are grief "stricken"?

(a) By giving a ray of hope.
(b) Sprouting a shady boon.
(c) By giving daffodils.
(d) None of these.

Ans. (a) By giving a ray of hope.

24. What does poet mean by Some shape of beauty?

(a) Beauty has no shape.
(b) Beauty is abstract.
(c) Beautiful object that gives happiness.
(d) All of these.

Ans. (c) Beautiful object that gives happiness.

25. Which figure of speech is used in the words– Some shape of beauty?

(a) Alliteration (b) Simile (c) Metaphor (d) All of the above

Ans. (a) Alliteration

26. Why are our spirits referreed as dark?

(a) Because of dark clouds and rainy weather.
(b) Because of spirits around that seem evil.
(c) Because of shady trees inducing darkness.
(d) Because of sadness and disappointments.

Ans. (d) Because of sadness and disappointments.

27. What does morrow mean?

(a) Morning time (b) Present time (c) Noon time (d) The next day

Ans. (d) The next day

28. Why do we need a flowery band?

(a) To look beautiful and glamorous.
(b) To smile remembering good old days.
(c) To be joyful and elated.
(d) To have strength and joy inspite of all sadness.

Ans. (d) To have strength and joy inspite of all sadness.

29. What is inhuman in life?

(a) Human inside a river crying for help.
(b) Human inside caves alone and distressed.
(c) Human on trees unable to get down.
(d) Self-centred tendency and inacility to rise above shallow circles.

Ans. (d) Self-centred tendency and inacility to rise above shallow circles.

30. What circumstances make man unhappy?

(a) Chilly cold waves on mountains.
(b) High speed current of flowing rivers.
(c) Crowded places.
(d) Tendency of hopelessness.

Ans. (d) Tendency of hopelessness.

❑❑

6. Aunt Jennifer's Tigers–by Adrienne Rich

Summary :

In the poem 'Aunt Jennifer's Tigers', a woman expresses her suppressed feelings through her art. Aunt Jennifer is the victim of the male-dominated society. She has no one to tell about her mental and physical pain. She makes a picture of a graceful and powerful tiger to convey her deep feelings. The speaker describes the tigers which her aunt produced on the panel. They are set in motion. They are moving quickly by raising the front legs and jumping forward by the back legs. In the green jungle, they look free, bright, brave, fearless and magnificent.

There are men sitting under the tree, but the tigers do not care for them. They move on to their goal boldly and smoothly. Jennifer finds it difficult to make pictures by using the ivory needle. She is tired of doing the household work after she got married. She can't get herself involved in her artistic work. She has to do it in her leisure time. Even then, she has to be sure whether her husband is watching her or not. So her hands are terrified. She will not be free from fear until she dies. She will be dominated by her husband. She will die, but her art will express her desire to move proudly and fearlessly like the tigers she has made.

Theme :

The poem is clearly a feminist poem and revolves around the theme of male chauvinism and gender conflicts. The victimization of the women by their male counterparts has been brought out in the poem. It is a forceful expression of the evils of patriarchy. Aunt Jennifer is victimized and suffers the oppression of her male counterpart even though he is absent. As she is never able to free herself from the oppression of social customs and laws, she creates for herself, an alternate world of freedom for herself, the one which she can only inhabit in her imagination.

Message :

The poem is a struggle of a woman in a male-dominated society where power is defined as masculine. The protagonist of the poem, Aunt Jennifer, represents women all over the world. Particularly the women of America in the 1950's. The women during that period were caught under the oppressive hands of patriarchal society. The poetess, Adrienne Rich, through the poem, delineates a woman's struggle with expression and rebellion.

Text Book Questions :

Think it out :

Q. 1. How do 'denizens' and 'chivalric' add to our understanding of the tigers' attitude?

Ans. Tigers, like all beasts of prey, are the denizens of the forest. The poem attributes the same traits of character and attitude to men, who, like the tigers, prefer to be superior in their domain.

Q. 2. Why do you think Aunt Jennifer's hands are 'fluttering through her wool' in the second stanza? Why is she finding the needle so hard to pull?

Ans. Aunt Jennifer was victimized by the overbearing and dominant nature of her husband. Her life had become a mess due to her suppression by her atrocious husband. The fear of her authoritative husband had gone so deep into her being that she seemed to have lost all her strength and energy. Thus her hands shook and fluttered so much that she could not pull the needle through the tapestry.

Q. 3. What is suggested by the image 'massive weight of Uncle's wedding band'?

Ans. Generally, a 'wedding band' is a symbol of joy and happiness. But in case of Aunt Jennifer, it had become a symbol of torture and oppression. Her relationship with her authoritative husband had become a painful burden to carry. Her 'wedding band' had brought her a world of pain, misery and torture. She had lost her freedom and entered a world of humiliation and oppression.

Q. 4. Of what or of whom is Aunt Jennifer terrified with in the third stanza?

Ans. According to the poet, Aunt Jennifer would carry the marks of injury of her married life to her grave. She would remain afraid of the Uncle and the iron bands of her marriage. The rings of torture, even after her death, would accompany her.

Q. 5. What are the ordeals Aunt Jennifer is surrounded by, why is it significant that the poet uses the word 'ringed'? What are the different meanings of the word 'ringed' in the poem?

Ans. Aunt Jennifer was still mentally surrounded by the ordeals she faced during her married life. The poem narrated the unhappy experiences of her married life. The word 'ringed' is significant. It made it clear that the vicious grip of her unhappy married life was still holding her tightly.

Q. 6. Why do you think Aunt Jennifer created animals that are different from her own character? What might the poet be suggesting, through this poem?

Ans. Aunt Jennifer's animals were so different from her own character as she was greatly experiencing the constraints of her married life. The massive weight of Uncle's wedding band was sitting heavily on her hand. She wanted the animals created by her to move freely in the world. She thought that they would go on prancing, proud and unafraid. She used them as a tool to express her own feelings. She wanted to echo a strong resistance to racism and militarism through them. The poet might be suggesting through that difference, the attitude of Aunt Jennifer as well as that of the tigers. She might have wanted to highlight the feeling of gallantry or dogmatic attitude of the tigers in comparison to the Aunt who was badly terrified.

Q. 7. Interpret the symbols found in this poem.

Ans. The poem is rich in symbolism. *'The massive weight of wedding band'* symbolizes ordeals, hardships and worries of a married life. *'Terrified hands'* and *'ringed with ordeals'* also symbolize unpleasant experiences. *'Topaz'* is a symbol of hardness and brightness. They cling to Aunt Jennifer mentally and physically.

Q. 8. Do you sympathise with Aunt Jennifer? What is the attitude of the speaker towards Aunt Jennifer?

Ans. We sympathize with Aunt Jennifer. Her marriage with Uncle would prove to be fatal. She lived in terror throughout her life. The speaker has no sympathy with her. She wanted that Aunt should have resisted to Uncle's cruelty with courage. But the Aunt could not muster up courage. She suffered in silence. She could express it only with her needlework.

Additional Questions :

Read the extract and answer the questions that follow :

Q. 1. *Aunt Jennifer's tigers prance across a screen,*
Bright topaz denizens of a world of green.
They do not fear the men beneath the tree;
They pace in sleek chivalric certainty.

(a) What are Aunt Jennifer's tigers doing?

Ans. Aunt Jennifer's tigers are jumping across a screen.

(b) How do they look like?

Ans. They looked like shining yellow topaz.

(c) Are they ferocious? Give an example.

Ans. Yes, they are ferocious as they do not fear the men standing under the tree.

(d) What does prancing tigers symbolize?

Ans. Prancing tigers are a symbol of the spirit of freedom within Aunt Jennifer, which remains subdued. They also symbolize the fear of her male counterpart.

(e) Why are they referred to as 'denizens of a world of green'?

Ans. The tigers, which symbolically refer to the male counterpart, are the dwellers of the green forest. Besides the general meaning of the 'wild', the world of green symbolizes the male animal instinct. It also symbolizes the evil and viciousness of male dominance and society.

(f) What qualities of the 'tigers' are highlighted here?

Ans. Fearlessness and ferocity of the tigers are highlighted in the poem. Aunt Jennifer's nervousness and timidity are in sharp contrast to the wild ferocity of the tigers who were not afraid of hunting men. Unlike Aunt Jennifer, the tigers feared nothing.

(g) Explain: 'They pace in sleek chivalric certainty'.

Ans. The movement of the tigers is sleek, stealthy, majestic and elegant. They were sure of their purpose. They move ahead fearlessly undeterred by any obstacles or hindrances.

(h) What does the expression 'Aunt Jennifer's Tigers' imply?

Ans. Aunt Jennifer was embroidering a panel of prancing tigers. The poet referred to the tigers as Aunt Jennifer's Tigers because they were her creation and her work of art.

(i) Find words from the stanza which mean the same as:
(i) jump ahead (ii) yellow precious stone (iii) dwellers.

Ans. (i) Prance (ii) topaz (iii) denizens.

Q. 2. *Aunt Jennifer's fingers fluttering through her wool*
Find even the ivory needle hard to pull.
The massive weight of Uncle's wedding band
Sits heavily upon Aunt Jennifer's hand.

(a) What does the first line of this stanza tell about Aunt Jennifer?

Ans. Aunt Jennifer feels so nervous, fearful and terrified of her male counterpart that even while weaving the tapestry, her fingers shake and flutter. She is a victim of gender oppression at the hands of her husband.

(b) Where are Aunt Jennifer's tigers fluttering through?

Ans. Aunt Jennifer's fingers are fluttering through her wool.

(c) Why did Aunt Jennifer's fingers flutter through her wool?

Ans. Aunt Jennifer lived in constant fear of her husband. She felt so nervous and terrified that her hands shook and fluttered when she sat down to knit.

(d) Why did she find it hard to pull the ivory needle?

Ans. She found it hard to pull the ivory needle more because of mental suppression than of physical weakness.

(e) Explain: 'massive weight of Uncle's wedding band'.

Ans. The expression is symbolic of male authority and power. Matrimony bounds the woman physically as well as mentally. Likewise, Aunt Jennifer was trapped in gender oppression and felt herself burdened by the authority of her husband.

(f) How is Aunt Jennifer affected by the 'weight of matrimony'?

Ans. Aunt Jennifer could not do things freely. She tried to come up to the expectations of her husband and in doing so, she lost her identity. The freedom that she dreamt of through her art was itself symbolic of her oppressed self.

(g) Find words from the stanza which mean same as :

(i) moving about (ii) heavy (iii) strip.

Ans. (i) fluttering (ii) massive (iii) band.

Q. 3. *When Aunt is dead, her terrified hands will lie*
Still ringed with ordeals she was mastered by.
The tigers in the panel that she made
Will go on prancing, proud and unafraid.

(a) What is Aunt Jennifer's death symbolic of?

Ans. Aunt Jennifer's death is symbolic of her complete submission to her suppression.

(b) Explain: 'terrified hands'.

Ans. Aunt Jennifer is terrified by her dominating husband and hence her hands were shivering in his presence.

(c) What does 'ringed with ordeals' imply?

Ans. Aunt Jennifer is so traumatized in her life that the poet imagines that even after her death, she would remain trapped in the struggle of the spirit. Nobody really knows about the terrors Aunt Jennifer has to live with.

(d) Is the society in any way affected by Aunt Jennifer's death?

Ans. Since the society is male-dominated, it would show no concern for Aunt's suffering, even after her death. The loss of her freedom would be her individual loss. The society will not be affected by it and the state of women will still remain the same.

(e) Explain: 'the tigers in the panel will go on prancing, proud and unafraid'.

Ans. The expression is symbolic of the dispassionate and unconcerned attitude of the male towards the desire for freedom among women. Even after her death, the social milieu would remain unaffected, arrogant and ferocious.

(f) Find words from the passage which mean same as:

(i) threatened (ii) surrounded by (iii) board.

Ans. (i) terrified (ii) ringed (iii) panel.

Q. 4. How do the tigers made by Aunt Jennifer look like?

Ans. The tigers, made by Aunt Jennifer on the screen, were jumping and playing about without any fear of the men beneath the tree. They walked with elegance and style displaying the spirit of courage, fearlessness, strength and confidence.

Q. 5. What do the tigers made by the Aunt symbolize?

Ans. The tigers made by Aunt Jennifer symbolized the spirit of courage, strength and fearlessness. Aunt Jennifer, a victim of male oppression, expressed her crushed feelings in the form of art. So, the tigers were symbolic of the fear of male domination which Aunt Jennifer suffered.

Q. 6. Explain 'her terrified hands will lie, still ringed with the ordeals she was mastered by'.

Ans. These lines convey the Aunt's complete submission to the oppressive authority of her husband. The fear of her husband had gone so deep into her being that even death could not liberate her from the chains of her mental suppression. Memories of her husband's tortures and atrocities which bent her into a humiliating slavery would continue to haunt her even after her death.

Q. 7. Explain 'The tigers in the panel .... proud and unafraid.'

Ans. Here, the tigers symbolise the unquestioned authority of man enjoyed by him over his female counterpart. The lines suggest the dispassionate and unconcerned attitude of the male towards the women. Here, Aunt Jennifer tried to escape through her art but ended up portraying an image of her own suppression. While the woman could never free herself from the oppressive authority of her male counterpart, the male, on the other hand would go on enjoying his authoritative arrogance and ferocity without any fear or regrets.

Previous Years' Questions :

Q. 1. *Aunt Jennifer's fingers fluttering through her wool*
Find even the ivory, needle hard to pull.
The massive weight of Uncle's wedding band
Sits heavily upon Aunt Jennifer's hand.

(a) What is Aunt Jennifer doing with her wool ?

Ans. Aunt Jennifer is weaving the image of tigers with her wool.

(b) Why does she find it difficult to pull her ivory needle ?

Ans. She finds it difficult to pull the ivory needle through the tapestry more because of mental suppression by her husband than because of physical weakness.

(c) What does 'wedding band' stand for ?

Ans. Wedding band stands for male authority and power. She is trapped in gender oppression and feels burdened by the authority of her husband-represented by his wedding band.

(d) Describe the irony in the third line.

Ans. The irony is that the wedding band might be small and light but it has burdened her spirit. She seems to have lost her identity under its weight.

Q. 2. *Aunt Jennifer's tigers prance across a screen,*
Bright topaz denizens of a world of green.
They do not fear the men beneath the tree;
They pace in sleek chivalric certainty.

(a) Why are the tigers called Aunt Jennifer's tigers ?

Ans. The tigers are called Aunt Jennifer's tigers because they represent the symbols of strength and self confidence.

(b) How are they described here ?

Ans. They are described as the inhabitant of a dense green forest, prancing unafraid and bright eyed.

(c) How are they different from Aunt Jennifer ?

Ans. They are different from Aunt Jennifer, as the animals created by her displayed chivalry, prancing and unafraid, though, she herself is encircled with the burden of married life which crushed her will.

(d) What does the word, 'chivalric' mean ?

Ans. Chivalric means brave.

Q. 3. What picture of male chauvinism (tyranny) do we find in the poem, 'Aunt Jennifer's Tigers' ?

Ans. In the poem 'Aunt Jennifer's Tigers' we find the picture of a woman oppressed by the male chauvinism. She needs freedom from her burden somehusband, whose ring on her finger is like a handcuff which has snatched all her freedom and happiness. She has a lot of constraints in her life because of her dominating husband and from whom she wants to get free.

Q. 4. How are Aunt Jennifer's tigers different from her ?

Ans. Aunt Jennifer's tigers are proud, free, dauntless and sure of themselves. Unlike them, Aunt Jennifer is terrified and oppressed by her chauvinist husband. She lived her life under constant pressure of duties and responsibilities of a married lady. Living a life on her own terms is a far-fetched dream for her.

Q. 5. What are the difficulties that Aunt Jennifer faced in her life?

Ans. Aunt Jennifer spent her life in accordance to the rules laid down by her husband. Her life was overburdened by the demands and duties and lacked self-expression. She was feeble and had to face oppression by her husband which depicted the age-old tribulations of women's lives.

Q. 6. What lies heavily on Aunt Jennifer's hand ? How is it associated with her husband ?

Ans. The wedding band and the ring lie heavily on Aunt Jennifer's hand. The ring symbolises the weight of her marriage which she has to bear, dead or alive. It reminds her of the pressures of an unhappy and unpleasant marriage.

Q. 7. What will happen to Aunt Jennifer's tigers when she is dead ?

Ans. After Aunt Jennifer's death, she will enter another world and her plight would remain same but her tigers would lead a fearless life and walk with grace, elegance and confidence.

Q. 8. Describe the tigers created by Aunt Jennifer.*

Ans. Aunt Jennifer embroiders tigers on a tapestry. The poet, Adrienne Rich describes the tigers created by Aunt Jennifer as 'bright topaz denizens' of the forest. They are portrayed

Reference to Context :

Read the given extract to attempt questions that follow:

1. *Aunt Jennifer's tigers prance across a screen,*
Bright topaz denizens of a world of green.
They do not fear the men beneath the tree;
They pace in sleek chivalric certainty.

(i) The poet draws attention to which traits of tigers that Aunt Jennifer lacks?

(a) Fearless and Free
(b) Strong and Clever
(c) Striped and Chivalrous
(d) Meek and Afraid

Ans. (a) Fearless and Free

(ii) Which option uses the same poetic device as underlined in the given phrase "Bob is a couch potato"?

(a) Men beneath the tree
(b) Denizens of a world
(c) Bright topaz
(d) Prance across a screen

Ans. (c) Bright topaz

(iii) Pick the option that is synonymous with moving with high springy steps?

(a) Chivalric (b) Pace (c) Screen (d) Prance

Ans. (d) Prance

(iv) According to the extract, what is Aunt Jennifer doing?

(a) Painting on a sheet
(b) Making a drawing
(c) Embroidering on cloth
(d) Printing on cloth

Ans. (c) Embroidering on cloth

(v) According to the extract, which of the following is not true about the tigers?

(a) Tigers are striding in a jungle.
(b) The jungle is green and wild.
(c) The tigers are afraid of hunters.
(d) The tigers are sleek and strong.

Ans. (c) The tigers are afraid of hunters.

2. *Aunt Jennifer's fingers fluttering through her wool*
Find even the ivory needle hard to pull.
The massive weight of Uncle's wedding band
Sits heavily upon Aunt Jennifer's hand.

(i) The poet draws attention to challenges in which facet of human life?

(a) Bachelorhood (b) Married life (c) Youth days (d) Old age

Ans. (b) Married life

(ii) Which option uses the same poetic device as underlined in the given phrase "Lightning danced across the sky"?

(a) Wedding band sits heavily.
(b) Massive weight of Uncle's wedding band.
(c) Fingers fluttering through her wool.
(d) Ivory needle hard to pull.

Ans. (a) Wedding band sits heavily.

---

* are board exam questions from previous years

(iii) The literal meaning of 'ivory' refers to a creamy-white colour. What does it signify here?

(a) A rarely found concrete stone.
(b) A delicate material found in walrus tusk.
(c) A precious stone extracted from oceans.
(d) A hard substance made of elephant tusk.

Ans. (d) A hard substance made of elephant tusk.

(iv) According to the extract, the "massive weight of the wedding band" symbolises?

(a) Adversities of a couple.
(b) Struggles of Aunt's bachelor life.
(c) Marital life pressures on Aunt Jennifer.
(d) The warmth of her married life.

Ans. (c) Marital life pressures on Aunt Jennifer.

(v) According to the extract, why did Aunt Jennifer find the ivory needle hard to pull?

(a) Pressures of her marital life haunted her mind.
(b) The ivory needle was thick and could not penetrate the cloth.
(c) Because her hands were trembling.
(d) She got remembered of her sweet past.

Ans. (a) Pressures of her marital life haunted her mind.

Read the given extract to attempt questions that follow:

3. *When Aunt is dead, her terrified hands will lie*
Still ringed with ordeals she was mastered by.
The tigers in the panel that she made
Will go on prancing, proud and unafraid.

(i) The poet depicts which state of Aunt Jennifer as he writes "her terrified hands"?

(a) Shocked state after seeing the tigers of the forest.
(b) Scared state dealing with problems of her marital life.
(c) Reluctant state after being troubled by her boss.
(d) Gloomy state thinking about her husband.

Ans. (b) Scared state dealing with problems of her marital life.

(ii) Which poetic device does the poet use to compare the state of Aunt and the tigers?

(a) Alliteration (b) Imagery (c) Rhyme (d) Paradox

Ans. (d) Paradox

(iii) The literal meaning of 'panel' refers to a small group of people involved in a discussion or investigation. What does it signify here?

(a) A flat drawing board .
(b) A curved land surface.
(c) A flat embroidery board.
(d) An area of the jungle.

Ans. (c) A flat embroidery board.

(iv) According to the extract, the "ordeals she was mastered by" symbolises?

(a) Aunt Jennifer had a doting husband.
(b) Aunt was happy and excited at work.
(c) Aunt Jennifer was facing youth problems.
(d) Aunt had ill experiences in her married life.

Ans. (d) Aunt had ill experiences in her married life.

(v) According to the extract, complete the following statement with the appropriate option:

On her death, Aunt Jennifer will _________.

(a) get freed from all her worries
(b) live the life as those of the tigers
(c) still be caged with her marital bond
(d) still be a victim of prejudice at work

Ans. (c) still be caged with her marital bond

4. *Aunt Jennifer's fingers fluttering through her wool*
Find even the ivory needle hard to pull.
The massive weight of uncle's wedding band
Sits heavily upon Aunt Jennifer's hand.

(i) Why was it so hard for Aunt Jennifer to pull the ivory needle ?

(a) because needle was heavy.
(b) because Aunt had no energy left.
(c) Aunt Jennifer was under mental pressure.
(d) Aunt was not well.

Ans. (c) Aunt Jennifer was under mental pressure.

(ii) What is 'uncle's wedding band'?

(a) wedding ring
(b) wedding burden
(c) wedding function
(d) wedding bangle

Ans. (a) wedding ring

(iii) The rhyme scheme of the lines is.................. .

(a) abab (b) aabb (c) abba (d) aaba

Ans. (b) aabb

(iv) Uncle's wedding band was like a .... on Aunt's finger.

(a) burden
(b) token of love
(c) reminder of his affection
(d) memoir of good times

Ans. (a) burden

5. *When Aunt is dead, her terrified hands will lie*
Still ringed with ordeals she was mastered by.
The tigers in the panel that she made
Will go on prancing, proud and unafraid.

(i) Why were Aunt Jennifer's hands terrified?

(a) Due to old age
(b) Due to illness
(c) Due to weakness
(d) Due to fear of expressing her desires

Ans. (d) Due to fear of expressing her desires

(ii) Expression 'ringed with ordeals' defines ....

(a) entangled in problems
(b) bitter and unpleasant experiences of her married life
(c) stuck up in ocean
(d) trapped in nightmares

Ans. (b) bitter and unpleasant experiences of her married life

(iii) Name the figure of speech used in 'Still ringed with ordeals'.

(a) Alliteration
(b) Metaphor
(c) Irony
(d) Personification

Ans. (a) Alliteration

(iv) How do Aunt Jennifer's tigers look like?

(a) Terrified (b) Bold (c) Submissive (d) Slave

Ans. (b) Bold

6. *Aunt Jennifer's tigers prance across a screen,*
Bright topaz denizens of a world of green.
They do not fear the men beneath the tree;
They pace in sleek chivalric certainty

(i) Find from the extract, the words closely related to:

(a) horsemen (b) a movie theatre

Ans. (a) chivalric (b) screen

(ii) Complete the statement :

Aunt Jennifer's tigers are afraid ____________ men __________.

Ans. of no, beneath the tree

(iii) Give an example of the following from the extract :

(a) a precious stone (b) a relationship

Ans. (a) topaz (b) Aunt

(iv) Write a phrase from the extract that means :

(a) forest (b) unafraid

Ans. (a) world of green (v) do not fear

Multiple Choice Questions

1. **Who is the poet of the poem, 'Aunt Jennifer's Tigers"?**
   (a) Adrienne Rich
   (b) Jonathan Aaron
   (c) J.H.M. Abbott
   (d) Mark Abley

Ans. (a) Adrienne Rich

2. **How many volumes of poetry has she published?**
   (a) 18 (b) 29 (c) 39 (d) 19

Ans. (d) 19

3. **What does echo through her work?**
   (a) A strong resistance against racism and militarism.
   (b) Her love for poetry.
   (c) Her passion of essay writing.
   (d) Her wish to publish her work.

Ans. (a) A strong resistance against racism and militarism.

4. **What issue does the poem, "Aunt Jennifer's Tigers" address?**
   (a) Constraints of women at professional front.
   (b) Constraints of married life a woman experiences.
   (c) Constraints of women as a poet.
   (d) None of the above.

Ans. (b) Constraints of married life a woman experiences.

5. **What do you understand by the words 'denizens' and 'chivalric' in the poem?**
   (a) The dominant and highly arrogant attitude of the wild animal-tiger.
   (b) Tiger is a wild animal but gets afraid of hunters.
   (c) Tiger is hungry and is chasing the villagers.
   (d) Beauty of the tiger as it strides in the zoo.

Ans. (a) The dominant and highly arrogant attitude of the wild animal-tiger.

6. **What do Aunt Jennifer's fluttering hands through her wool in the second stanza tell us?**
   (a) The lost freedom and fear of Jennifer's mind.
   (b) Her old age and trembling hands.
   (c) Her love for embroidery and knitting.
   (d) Her love for tigers and other cat species.

Ans. (a) The lost freedom and fear of Jennifer's mind.

7. **Why is she finding the needle so hard to pull?**
   (a) Because of fluttering fingers.
   (b) Because of trembling hands.
   (c) Because of her fear for knitting.
   (d) Because of the heavy weight of her marriage ring.

Ans. (d) Because of the heavy weight of her marriage ring.

8. **What does the phrase 'massive weight of the wedding band' mean?**
   (a) Wedding band of hard married life.
   (b) Fatty structure of uncle.
   (c) Fatty body of aunty.
   (d) Heavy body of a tiger.

Ans. (a) Wedding band of hard married life,

9. **Of what or of whom is aunt Jennifer terrified of in the third stanza?**
   (a) That of dangerous tigers around.
   (b) That of her sudden death.
   (c) That of her old age and its challenges.
   (d) That of her dominant husband.

Ans. (d) That of her dominant husband.

10. What is the meaning of the word 'ringed'?

(a) Circles of a ring of fire.
(b) The wedding ring around her finger.
(c) Circles of responsibility of her married life.
(d) None of these.

Ans. (c) Circles of responsibility of her married life.

11. What is the purpose of creating animals which are completely in contrast to aunt's character?

(a) To show her strength and ability of not giving up in the face of difficulties.
(b) Her courage and vulnerabilities.
(c) Her fears and strengths.
(d) None of the above.

Ans. (a) To show her strength and ability of not giving up in the face of difficulties.

12. What is the poet suggesting through the different nature of characters in the poem?

(a) Diversity in nature and its individual constituents.
(b) Everyone has their strengths and unique.
(c) Simultaneous display of aunt's fears and her not giving up attitude.
(d) All of the above.

Ans. (c) Simultaneous display of aunt's fears and her not giving up attitude.

13. Tell and interpret the meaning of 'Denizens of a "world of green".

(a) Forest haters
(b) Forest lovers
(c) Forest dwellers
(d) All of these

Ans. (c) Forest dwellers

14. What is the attitude of the poet or speaker towards aunt Jennifer?

(a) Critic and sceptical.
(b) Very harsh and rude.
(c) Indifferent and analytical.
(d) Full of appreciation and sympathy.

Ans. (d) Full of appreciation and sympathy.

15. Does Aunt Jennifer need sympathy?

(a) Yes, she needs to be consoled.
(b) No, she needs a job.
(c) No, more than sympathy she deserves praise.
(d) None of these.

Ans. (c) No, more than sympathy she deserves praise.

16. What did marriage bring for Jennifer?

(a) Unhappiness at workplace.
(b) Loss of freedom in her old house.
(c) Loss of freedom and burden of responsibilities.
(d) Responsibilities of children.

Ans. (c) Loss of freedom and burden of responsibilities.

17. What is still fresh in Jennifer's mind?

(a) Happy moments.
(b) Early days of marriage.
(c) Uncle's attitude.
(d) The old unhappy memories.

Ans. (d) The old unhappy memories.

18. What did ordeals or tough times do in Jennifer's life?

(a) They made her a hard hearted person.
(b) She developed hatred.
(c) She became weak and vulnerable.
(d) They crushed her artistic personality.

Ans. (d) They crushed her artistic personality.

19. Where do aunt's tigers belong?

(a) To a cage
(b) To a zoo
(c) Mountains
(d) World of green forests

Ans. (d) World of green forests

20. Why did Aunt Jennifer have 'terrified hands'?

(a) They depict the physical condition of aunt.
(b) They show the mental state of aunt.

(c) Reflects tensed, troubled physical and mental state of aunt Jennifer.

(d) Fears of aunt pertaining to her job.

Ans. (c) Reflects tensed, troubled physical and mental state of aunt Jennifer.

21. What is the tone of the poem towards the end?

(a) Happy and cheerful.

(b) Resolved and committed.

(c) Hopeful and elated.

(d) Sad and tensed.

Ans. (d) Sad and tensed.

22. How are Aunt Jennifer's Tigers different from her?

(a) Aunt lives in a city and tigers in forests.

(b) Aunt is old and tigers are young.

(c) Tigers are courageous and carefree and aunt is terrified.

(d) None of the above.

Ans. (c) Tigers are courageous and carefree and aunt is terrified.

23. What lies heavily on aunt Jennifer's hand?

(a) Needles

(b) Embroideries

(c) Work pressure

(d) Wedding ring

Ans. (d) Wedding ring

24. How do the 'Prancing tigers' look?

(a) Just like diamond.

(b) Just like Topaz.

(c) Just like coal.

(d) Just like stone.

Ans. (b) Just like Topaz.

25. Why did aunt embroider tigers on the panel?

(a) To express her supressed feelings.

(b) To express her strengths.

(c) To express her fighting spirit akin to a warrior.

(d) All of these.

Ans. (d) All of these.

26. Why are tigers given the name Aunt Jennifer's Tigers?

(a) Because she created them as an expression to her inner feelings.

(b) Because she brought them and was their caretaker.

(c) Because she bought them from the zoo.

(d) Because she nurtured and caressed them everyday.

Ans. (a) Because she created them as an expression to her inner feelings.

27. What is the meaning of the word 'Chivalric'?

(a) Ferocious and violent.

(b) Fearless and cunning.

(c) Commanding and demanding high respect.

(d) None of these.

Ans. (c) Commanding and demanding high respect.

28. What is presented through uncle's character?

(a) Male strength

(b) Man is powerful

(c) Men are like tigers

(d) Male chauvinism

Ans. (d) Male chauvinism

29. Where are the tigers sleeping?

(a) On the trees

(b) On the mountain top

(c) In the cage

(d) In the caves

Ans. (d) In the caves

30. What is Aunt doing in the poem?

(a) Cooking (b) Embroidery (c) Reading (d) Sleeping

Ans. (b) Embroidery

31. Interpret "terrified hands".

(a) Physical condition of aunt

(b) mental state of aunt

(c) tensed, troubled physical and mental state of aunt Jennifer

(d) fears of aunt

Ans. (c) tensed, troubled physical and mental state of aunt Jennifer

❑❑

Vistas–Flamingo

5. Should Wizard Hit Mommy–by John Updike

Summary :

This story deals with a child's view of the world and the difficult moral questions she raises during the story session with her father.

Jack (Joanne's father) had become accustomed with telling stories to his daughter since she was two years of age. These stories were almost the same except for some slight variations. They all started with a creature usually named Roger (Roger firsh, Roger squirrel, Roger chipmunk), who had some problem and went with it to the wise owl. The owl directed him to go to the magician, who would solve his problem in exchange of money. Then, the Roger creature would be happy and would return home just in time to hear the train whistle that brought his daddy home from Boston.

On that particular Saturday, it was time for Joanne's nap. So Jack had to tell her a story. He began his story and asked Joanne what the creature should be named ? She enthusiastically said, "Skunk, Roger Skunk." The story started with the creature being unable to play and make friends with other creatures because he smelled awful. The creature went to seek the advice of the wise old owl who directed him to go to the magician. The magician, with his magic wand, turned the awful smell that Roger had to a smell of roses. The Roger creature then, as directed, paid the magician's fee.

When Roger Skunk reached home, his mother was disappointed as she thought that it was not right to change one's identity to please his friends. She said real friends are the ones who accept you for who you are and not for who you want to become. She then took Roger back to the magician and hit the magician with the umbrella she had been carrying. The magician then performed his magic and Roger no longer smelled of roses. After that, they returned home just in time to hear the whistle of the train that brought Roger Skunk's father home and from that day on, Roger Skunk was content in being himself.

Throughout this story, Jack wanted to teach his daughter Joanne about moral values, but his daughter Joanne (Jo), who was just a child, reacted differently to the story's ending. She wanted the wizard to hit Roger's mother and let Roger smell of roses. This was a child's perspective of things. To a child, friends mean everything and they do not understand moral values and the importance of things taught by their parents.

Jack was trying to tell Jo that whatever parents say or do for them are in their best interest. But Jo was adamant and wanted another ending for the story.

After the story ended, Jack went down to help his wife, Clare in painting the furniture. When he reached downstairs he saw that the woodwork, a cage of mouldings and rails and baseboards all around them, was half old tan and half new ivory and he felt caught in an ugly middle position, and felt himself to be trapped in the rut of life along with his Life.

Note: Jack had a son named Bobby two years old, Clare was three months pregnant.

Textbook Questions :

Read and find out :

Q. 1. Who is Jo? How does she respond to her father's story telling?

Ans. Jo is the four-year-old daughter of Jack and Clare. For the past two years, she had been hearing stories from her father every evening and on Saturday afternoons. She is an intelligent and inquisitive child who raises questions regarding whatever she heard or see. She is also a very observant listener and tend to correct her father wherever she feels he falters. She likes those stories which have a happy ending.

Q. 2. What possible plot line could the story continue with?

Ans. From the perspective of Jo, the plot line of the story could have ended a happy note with Roger Skunk getting rid of the foul smell forever and being able to play with all his friends. However, Jack's perspective was different. He got carried away by the nostalgic moments of his past and narrated a fictional story to his daughter which reflected his childhood thereby, bringing a sad end to the story which compelled Jo to raise various questions.

Q. 3. What do you think was Jo's problem?

Ans. For Jo, the story could have ended comfortably with Roger Skunk relieved of his foul body-odour and accepted by the other children as their playmate. However, Jack took the story to another level, which created a ruckus in the little and simple world of hers. She was unconvinced with the fact that Roger Skunk's mother did not like the newly acquired smell of roses and wanted him to get his earlier body odour restored. For that little girl, the world was centred around her friends to play with. Therefore, when she noticed that other small animals avoided the poor Skunk, she empathised with him. She could not understand why a mother would want to compromise her child's happiness just to suit her own-self. According to her, Skunk's mommy was wrong and Jo was not ready to accept the fact that mothers are always correct.

Reading with Insight :

Q. 1. What is the moral issue that the story raises?

Ans. The story reveals that moral issues depend on different levels of maturity. There is a sharp contrast between an adult's perspective of life and that of a little child. Children represent innocence. Hatred and injustice have no place in their world. In the story, the baby Skunk was able to make friends only after he smelt of roses. In Jo's perspective, the happiness of making friends was above any other thing. She was unable to understand why mother Skunk pressurized her child to get back to his original foul body-odour. On the contrary, Jack tried to justify the Skunk's mother and wanted Skunk to listen to his mother even if it meant smelling bad again. He wanted his daughter to believe that parents are always correct and they know what is best for their children. Thus, the story raises the question whether parents should always be followed blindly.

Q. 2. How does Jo want the story to end and why?

Ans. Jo was not convinced with the ending of the story and coaxed her father to repeat the story the next day, giving the story a pre-determined climax that she had set. According to her, neither Roger Skunk nor the wizard was wrong in the story. She refused to accept the end where Roger Skunk's mother hits the wizard and demands her son to get his original foul smell back as she believes it is their 'identity'. This is unacceptable for Jo. According to her, the story should have ended where baby skunk smelt of roses and was accepted by his playmates. She believes that mother Skunk was gravely wrong and insensitive to Roger Skunk's feelings for which she should be hit back by the wizard.

Q. 3. Why does Jack insist that it was the wizard that was hit and not the mother?

Ans. Jack had already narrated the story by the time Jo could realize that the story did not get a logical and fair ending for the Mommy not being hit back. Jo's insistence that the wizard should hit Mommy back, angered him. Further, to give into Jo's demand he would have meant disrespecting elders. Jo was very young at that time and Jack believed that it was the time for her to learn to respect elders. Lastly, while narrating the story, he unknowingly got emotionally connected with the memories of his childhood. He imagined Roger Skunk's mother to be his mother and thus could not see his own mother being hit by anyone. Moreover, he personally considered her mother to have made right decisions for him.

Q. 4. What makes Jack feel caught in an ugly middle position?

Ans. As the story of Roger Skunk is unfolded, the impatient and unsatisfied Jo strongly puts forth her point of view. She did not want the story to end the way her father had perceived and narrated. According to her, the wizard should have hit the Skunk's mommy back. Jack knew that from the ethical point of view, what she was asking for was wrong. However, her stubborn stand to change the end of the story, left him in a dilemma. He was caught in a battle between the two perspectives and could not find a way to make Jo understand his point of view that mothers are never wrong.

Q. 5. What is your stance regarding the two endings to the Roger Skunk story?

Ans. Considering the tender age of Jo, both the endings seemed a little irrational. It was certain that she would be learning from whatever she heard and visualized at that age. If the story ended according to Jack, she would never be able to question anything she considered wrong in life since the ending of the story showed that elders were always right at whatever they did. On the contrary, if the story ended as Jo wanted it to, it would stop her from believing and respecting elders. She might even start believing that there was nothing wrong in hitting elders. A balanced view could have been given at the end where the mother either did not hit the wizard or realize her mistake soon.

Q. 6. Why is the adult's perspective on life different from that of a child?

Ans. A child's speech, line of thought, actions and reactions are natural and not guided by any outward influence. He speaks from his heart in accordance with what is ethically right in his perspective. On the other hand, an adult has many things to consider before speaking or reacting since the influence of society governs and dominates their thoughts. In this chapter, Jo speaks what she considers correct but Jack, who is an adult, is caught in a dilemma and keeps thinking on the consequences of accepting his daughter's ending to the story and what the society has made him learn over the time.

Additional Questions :

Short Answer Questions : **(30-40 words)**

Q. 1. What was usually the basic storyline of the tale that Jack told Jo almost daily?

Ans. The stories that Jack used to tell Jo were the slight variations of the basic tale about a small creature usually named Roger who would go to the wise owl whenever in trouble. The wise owl would ask him to go to the wizard who would finally solve his problem.

Q. 2. Describe the wizard's house.

Ans. The wizard had a white house over the crick. Inside it were magical things all jumbled together in a big dusty heap as the wizard did not have a cleaning lady.

Q. 3. How did Roger Skunk's mommy react when he went home?

Ans. When Roger Skunk reached home, his mommy could not stand the smell of rose and asked him about the awful smell. He replied that the wizard had changed the odour of his body. She got angry and went to the wizard to hit his head with an umbrella.

Q. 4. How did Jo react to Jack's storyline?

Ans. Jo did not agree with Jack's storyline in which Roger Skunk's mommy hit that wizard right over his head for changing her son's smell. Instead, Jo wanted the wizard to hit Skunk's mommy and not changing the little Skunk's smell back.

Q. 5. What does Jack want Jo to know and understand in the story?

Ans. Jack wanted Jo to know and understand that parents always love their children the way they are and in return, children should obey their parents. Smelling good or bad was immaterial. Jo refused to accept that. She wasn't ready to accept the fact that parents are always right. She was just a child who wanted happiness all around.

Q. 6. Father has felt empty after two years of storytelling to Jo. What idea do you form about his skill in the art of storytelling?

Ans. It would be wrong to say that Jo's father was a bad story-teller. His only problem was that his stories lacked variety and he ended up telling the same old story again and again with slight variations. He felt empty because he had been telling stories for over two years and was now running short of ideas.

Q. 7. Do you think the father in the story is, more or less, an alter ego of the author, as far as childhood is concerned?

Ans. John Updike in his childhood was a victim of 'psoriasis' and stammering. On account of that, he had to suffer humiliation and ridicule at the hands of his classmates. In the said story, Jo's father too recalled certain moments of humiliation of his own childhood. Thus, Jo's father was more or less, an alter ego of the author.

Q. 8. How was Jo affected by Jack's story telling?

Ans. Jo would get immensely engrossed in the story. She liked the way her father told her the story particularly through body gestures and by changing the tone of his voice. She also liked the predictable way the story would unfold allowing her to make guesses, ask questions and draw conclusions. The whole picture of the story would come alive before her and she would twitch and turn in excitement as the story progress.

Q. 9. 'This was a new phase, just this last month'. What new phase is referred to in the story "Should Wizard Hit Mommy" ?

Ans. The physical and the mental growth of children takes place very fast. The phrase above is referred to the change in Jo and her thoughts. In the past, Jo never questioned her father's story about magic but in later days, she had started raising questions about such spells. She became more inquisitive and less credulous.

Q. 10. Why does the wizard instruct the Skunk to "Hurry up"?

Ans. The wizard asked the Skunk to hurry up, because he used to live alone and did not like anyone company for a long time. Further, he was keen to have his full payment for the task performed. Also, he could not stand the Skunk's foul smell for long.

Q.11. How did the woodland creatures react to the Skunk's new smell? What did the Skunk feel about the new change?

Ans. The woodland creatures found Roger Skunk's new smell aromatic as he smelt like roses. They gladly accepted him as their friend and played with him. He was also happy on being accepted by them as their friend. Eventually, his inferiority complex disappeared.

Q.12. After the Skunk started smelling of roses, Jo thought the story was all over. Why did she think so?

Ans. If a child's emotion is to be taken into consideration, then the Skunk's smelling of roses was a befitting end of the story, because Skunk's long standing desire was fulfilled and he was able to do what was dearest to his heart - play with other woodland creatures.

Q.13. Why in your opinion is the smell of roses obnoxious for the Skunk's mother? "or" how did Skunk's mother react to his new smell?

Ans. Nature keeps its own balance and has its own way. The Skunk's bad body smell was obnoxious for other creatures but certainly not for her mother. Skunks are born with a particular smell and any deviation from it is a violation of nature. So, the mother Skunk did not like the rose-smell of Roger Skunk as she feels the foul smell to be their identity. She believed that the foul smell was natural and was not disgraceful.

Q.14. How did Skunk's mother get him his old smell back?

Ans. Skunk's Mother was furious to learn about the wizard who changed the original smell of her child. She immediately visited the wizard and hit him on his head with her umbrella and asked him to restore Roger's original smell.

Q.15. Who is Jo? How had she changed in the past two years?

Ans. Jo is Jack's 4-year-old daughter. She was no more a patient listener. She did not take things for granted and tried to see things in her own way.

Q.16. How does Jo want the story to end and why?

Ans. Jo understood that Roger Skunk needed to enjoy the company of like his friends as he was all alone. Therefore, she wanted the story to end where Roger started smelling roses due to which, all creatures wanted to be his friends.

Q.17. The Skunk accepts his mom's order like a tame lamb and follows her to the wizard without demur, but Jo chooses to differ from her father with regards to changing the rose smell. How would you account for this difference in attitude between the two?

Ans. Roger Skunk as a character, symbolizes Jack's own personality as a child. He loved and obeyed his mother very much. She in turn, taught him courage and self-regard in dealing with his hurt and humiliation. Thus, the Skunk was as unquestionably obedient as Jack was himself. Jo, on the other hand, was a happy-go-lucky child of four years who had nothing to be upset about and had no humiliation to deal with. She was inquisitive and curious to know more. It was not surprising that she was full of questions. The attitudes of both the Skunk and Jo were shaped by their life experiences.

Q.18. Why did Jo not approve of the Skunk's mother scolding him for his new smell?

Ans. Jo was very happy to hear that the Skunk had got rid of his awful smell and had been accepted by the woodland creatures as their friend. She did not like the Skunk's mother scolding him for his new smell because Jo thought it was pleasant and the one that had won Skunk so many friends. She held the Skunk's mother wrong for scolding him for changing his natural odour.

Q.19. What is the underlying idea behind the wizard's taking the beating and tamely changing the rose smell?

Ans. The author wishes to bring home the idea that mothers are always right and that we should accept what is natural. The wizard also sees the point and tamely changes the Skunk's rose smell into his natural Skunk smell.

Q.20. Why does mother Skunk hug and pat her son as he prepares to sleep?

Ans. The obedience shown by Roger Skunk impressed his mother and she patted and hugged him as he prepared himself to sleep. Moreover, the Skunk's mother was happy because her son got back his original body odour.

Q.21. What inference do you draw from the narrator's statement, "eventually they (woodland creatures) got used to the way he (the Skunk) was and did not mind it at all"?

Ans. The woodland creatures learnt the lesson that what was natural was not disgraceful and should be accepted as an integral part of one's being. One should not hate or avoid others based on their fit or unfit natural features. Instead he should be courageous and tolerant enough to accept nature's creation. This is how the woodland creatures got used to the way the Skunk smelled.

Q.22. How did Jo want the story to end?*

Ans. Jo was not convinced with the ending of the story and coaxed her father to re-tell the story the next day, giving the story a pre-determined path that she had set. According to her, neither Roger Skunk nor the wizard was wrong in the story. Jo refused to accept the end where Roger Skunk's mother hits the wizard and that too without being hit back. She wanted the story to end with the wizard hitting back the mother skunk with his magic wand and chopping off her arms 'force fully'.

Q.23. On seeing Rogar Skunk again with a very bad smell, how did the little animals react first and then later on when he had lost it?*

Ans. On seeing Roger Skunk with a very bad smell, the little animals ran away from him at first. Roger Skunk then went to the wizard who changed his smell to the smell of roses. The little animals became Roger Skunk's friends and played with him when he smelled like roses afterwards.

Long Answer Questions : **(120-150 words)**

Q. 1. What is the moral issue that the story raises?

Ans. Although "Should Wizard Hit Mommy?" reads like a typical bed-time story that elders tell little children, it does raise a moral question. Should parents always decide what is best for their children and should children always obey their parents unquestioningly? Roger Skunk is a very obedient child but he feels very sad and upset because he smells so awful that nobody wants to be friend him and play with him. One day, he gets a chance to change his bad smell with the smell of roses. He feels excited about the change for everyone likes his new smell and readily agrees to play with him. However, Roger's mother does not like the change. For her, Roger was better with his original smell. So, she makes the wizard restore the Skunk's original smell. Roger meekly accepts his mother's decision and later, the other children get used to Roger's awful smell and don't complain about it anymore. The little girl, Jo thinks differently. She feels that the mother is wrong in getting her son's original smell back and wants her to be spanked by the wizard for her mistake regardless of her father who strongly defends the mother Skunk's decision. Thus, the author through this story, raises a moral question of how much authority should parents have in taking children's decisions in life. Since, there are so many views on this subject, the author leaves it for the readers to answer it on the basis of their beliefs, cultures and values.

Q. 2. Why is an adult's perspective on life different from that of a child's?

Ans. As the child grows into maturity, his perspective and vision of life changes gradually. A child views things innocently but a grown up's vision is realistic, full of experience and pragmatic. Going through the story, "Should Wizard Hit Mommy?" Jo, who is four years old, prefers to live in dreams and fantasies like other children of her age. She is hostile by nature and is annoyed because her father refuses to accept her suggestion. Father has a mature perspective and see things with pragmatic perception. He feels that the wizard has unwittingly interfered with nature and had thus, done a great deal of harm and deserves punishment. Hence, the story makes it clear that the perspective of a child and that of an adult is contrasting and absolutely different.

Previous Years' Questions :

Q. 1. At the end of the storytelling session, why does Jack consider himself 'caught in an ugly middle position' ?

Ans. Jack used to tell a story from his own imagination every Saturday night to make Jo sleep. He created a basic plot with a hero named Roger. He had a problem which had to be solved by the wizard who would send him to the wise owl who would then guide him how to get the required pennies. Jo was a precocious child who raised a lot of questions. On that particular day his chief character was a skunk, who wanted to have the smell of roses so that he could relate to his peer group. There was a big controversy at the ending of the story as Jo supported Roger skunk and Jack supported his mother. At the end of the story Jo wanted the ending to be altered and she refused to sleep. Jack went down to help his wife Clare. She was furious as she felt that he had spent too much time with Jo. Jack found himself to be caught in an ugly position as he felt inadequate and helpless, both as a father and a husband.

---

* are board exam questions from previous years

As a father he had not been able to make Jo sleep who was unhappy with the ending of the story and as a husband, his wife was angry at him and he felt like he had nothing to do with her.

Q. 2. What is mother Skunk's role in the story ?

Ans. Mother Skunk's role in the story is to keep a balance. Her act indicates that what is natural is not ungraceful. Taking any deviation is the violation of nature. Moreover, parents quite well know what is best for their children.

Q. 3. What was the basic plot of each story told by Jack ?

Ans. Jack always told a story to his little daughter, Jo, about Roger. Usually, every story had a small creature named Roger fish, Roger squirrel or Roger chipmunk. He had always a problem, he went to the wise owl for advice and the wise owl directed him to go to the wizard. The wizard used his magical spell to solve the problem.

Q. 4. Having got rid of his stink, what problem did Roger Skunk face ?

Ans. He faced the problem from his mother who felt extremely annoyed. She could not stand that smell. She decided to take him right back to that 'awful' wizard and asked him to give back the very original smell to her boy.

Q. 5. What problem did Roger Skunk face he went to play with his friends. How did he solve it ?

Ans. Roger Skunk smelled very bad. Whenever he would go to play, all other little animals would run away from him. Roger would stand there all alone. He went to the wise old owl. The owl told him to go to see the wizard. The wizard solved his problem with some magic spell.

Q. 6. How did Jack end the Roger Skunk story ? How and why did Jo want to change it?

Ans. Jack used to tell his little daughter, Jo, bedtime stories. When she grew older, she began to ask questions to her father. Once her father told her a story of a little animal called Roger Skunk who smelled awfully bad. He, therefore, met with a wizard who solved his problem with a magical wand and made him smell like roses. But Skunk's mother did not like it and took him back to the wizard to make him smell awfully bad once again.

This ending was not acceptable to Jo as she wanted the story to have another end in which the wizard should hit the mommy by his magic wand and leave Roger skunk emitting the pleasant smell of roses. Jo thought that Roger was the hero of the story so he must not look ugly or stinky. Jo's perspective on life was different from her father's. She wanted to change the end of the story to assert her views on her father. She had her own ideals and views which she wanted to be pursued by her father.

Q. 7. Which do you think is a better ending of Roger Skunk's story, Jo's or her father's ? Why ?

Ans. Jo wanted the story to have another end in which the wizard should hit the mommy by his magic wand because for her the smell of roses was awful. Jo thought that Roger was the hero of the story so he must not look ugly or stinky. Jo's perspective on life was different from her father's.

Whereas her father thought the different way. He wanted to convey that for a mother, her son never smells bad. The adults' world is full of hardships and they had to face the reality of life.

His ending may not be very pleasing but is realistic and he wanted to highlight the fact that for a mother, her child is always an object of love. His smell makes no difference.

Thus, the original ending is acceptable.

Q. 8. How was the skunk's story different from the other stories narrated by Jack ?

Ans. Usually, the stories told by Jack were taken well by Jo. But she was not satisfied and convinced with the ending of the skunk's story. She believed that the wizard should have hit back the skunk's mommy and that the skunk should have smelled like roses.

Q. 9. What did Jo want the wizard to do when Mommy Skunk approached him ?

Ans. Jo wanted the wizard to hit Mommy Skunk because she wanted Roger Skunk to smell foul like before and that's why she took him to the wizard. There she hit him with the umbrella and Jo disliked it as according her, the wizard was right.

Q. 10. Why does Jo insist that her father should tell her the story with a different ending ?

Ans. Jo insists that her father should tell her the story with a different ending because she wants that other animals should play with Roger Skunk and for that he the must smell like roses. According to her, the mother is wrong as she made him smell foul again and the wizard should hit his mother. In fact, she wants to assert her views on her father.

Reference to Context :

Read the given extract to attempt questions that follow:

1. *Each new story was a slight variation of a basic tale: a small creature, usually named Roger (Roger Fish, Roger Squirrel, Roger Chipmunk), had some problem and went with it to the wise old owl. The owl told him to go to the wizard, and the wizard performed a magic spell that solved the problem, demanding in payment a number of pennies greater than the number that Roger Creature had, but in the same breath directing the animal to a place where the extra pennies could be found.*

(i) The story being referred to in the first line is narrated to put little girl Jo sleep just before ________. Select the right option from the list.

(a) sunday siesta
(b) everyday evening
(c) crack of every dawn
(d) saturday nap

Ans. (d) saturday nap

(ii) (Roger Fish, Roger Squirrel, Roger __________ Roger Skunk), which animal is missing in the list?

(a) Mangoose (b) Penguin (c) Zebra (d) Chipmunk

Ans. (d) Chipmunk

(iii) Where could the extra pennies be found in this story?

(a) In the middle of a lane
(b) Across the lane
(c) At the end of a lane
(d) Around the bend

Ans. (c) At the end of a lane

(iv) To what family does a skunk belong?

(a) Weasel (b) Amphibian (c) Reptile (d) Primates

Ans. (a) Weasel

(v) Having a fresh hero momentarily stirred Jack to creative ____________. Select the exact word used in the text to fill in the gap.

(a) spirit (b) juice (c) enthusiasm (d) energy

Ans. (c) enthusiasm

Read the given extract to attempt questions that follow:

2. *He paused as a rapt expression widened out from his daughter's nostrils, forcing her eyebrows up and her lower lip down in a wide noiseless grin, an expression in which Jack was startled to recognise his wife feigning pleasure at cocktail parties. "And all of a sudden," he whispered, "the whole inside of the wizard's house was full of the smell of — roses! 'Roses!' Roger Fish cried. And the wizard said, very cranky, "That'll be seven pennies."*

"Daddy."

"What?"

"Roger Skunk. You said Roger Fish."

(i) What was the father doing when he paused at the expression on his daughter's face?

(a) He was talking about skunk.
(b) He was thinking about other animals.
(c) He was thinking about his wife.
(d) He was reciting a story.

Ans. (d) He was reciting a story.

(ii) 'feigning pleasure at cocktail parties'. What does the expression feigning mean?

(a) Pretending (b) Enjoying (c) Loathing (d) Hallucinating

Ans. (a) Pretending

(iii) "And the wizard said, very cranky," Here 'cranky' implies which mood of the wizard?

(a) Bad tempered and irritable.
(b) Eccentric and strange.
(c) Humorous and funny.
(d) None of these.

Ans. (a) Bad tempered and irritable.

(iv) The author refers to the story telling as custom. It implies that it has become a:

(a) habit
(b) ritual
(c) demand
(d) mandatory exercise

Ans. (b) ritual

(v) Roger Skunk's mother reacted to the new smell saying he was:

(a) smelling like roses.
(b) appealingly fragrant.
(c) he should take a bath.
(d) he exuded an awful smell.

Ans. (d) he exuded an awful smell.

Read the given extract to attempt questions that follow:

3. *"That was a long story," Clare said. "The poor kid," he answered, and with utter weariness watched his wife labour. The woodwork, a cage of moldings and rails and baseboards all around them, was half old tan and half new ivory and he felt caught in an ugly middle position, and though he as well felt his wife's presence in the cage with him, he did not want to speak with her, work with her, touch her, anything.*

(i) 'half old tan and half new ivory' captures the essence of what Jack feels. Select the option that lists the correct inference based on the information in the extract.

(a) Caught in the quagmire of emotions.
(b) Caught between two worlds.
(c) Faced with a dilemma of split personality.
(d) Sporting distinct view of circumstances.

Ans. (b) Caught between two worlds.

(ii) Bed time stories are told to put children into peaceful sleep. What does this particular story telling eventually turn out to be?

(a) A discussion of contrasting ideas between adult and child.
(b) An ideological dispute disrupting relationship.
(c) Striking a discordant note in the psyche yet to wake up.
(d) Upsetting the edifice of filial responsibilities.

Ans. (c) Striking a discordant note in the psyche yet to wake up.

(iii) Why cannot Jo digest the idea that wizard was hit by Roger's mother?

(a) Because it was impolite to hit a kind old gentleman.
(b) Because it upset the well set image of a magical figure of childhood fancy.
(c) Because wizard bestowed the skunk with the fragrance of rose.
(d) Because wizards have to be worshipped.

Ans. (b) Because it upset the well set image of a magical figure of childhood fancy.

(iv) Why do you think that Jack just watched Clare labour? Choose the most appropriate answer from the clues given:

(a) He felt detached from all things in the world.
(b) He was angry with his wife.
(c) He thought painting was unnecessary.
(d) He got a sadistic pleasure watching her labour.

Ans. (a) He felt detached from all things in the world.

(v) Why does Jack insist in the story that 'it was the wizard that was hit and not the mother'?

(a) Because he feels he should not give in to the childish demand for change.
(b) Because he wants his growing up daughter to learn the importance of unconditional acceptance.
(c) Because he feels the plot demands such an ending.
(d) Because he feels that Jo will lose trust in him.

Ans. (b) Because he wants his growing up daughter to learn the importance of unconditional acceptance.

Read the given extract to attempt questions that follow:

4. *"And, Roger Skunk said, 'It's me, Mommy. I smell like roses.' And she said, 'Who made you smell like that?' And he said, 'The wizard,' and she said, 'Well, of all the nerve. You come with me and we're going right back to that very awful wizard." Jo sat up, her hands dabbling in the air with genuine fright. "But Daddy, then he said about the other little animals run away!" Her hands skittered off, into the underbrush. "All right. He said,*

(i) The reason why Jo was shocked at the unexpected reaction from Roger's mother was she is:

(a) too naive to realize that sensibilities vary.
(b) a prisoner of her closed mind.

(c) too much of a rebel to accept her father's autocratic way.

(d) a child of rigid mindset.

Ans. (a) too naive to realize that sensibilities vary.

(ii) Pick up the best way you can delineate the title of the story 'Should Wizard Hit Mommy'?

(a) Ambiguous (b) Climactic (c) Open ended (d) Controversial

Ans. (c) Open ended

(iii) What does the author intend to establish by naming the story in the manner he does?

(a) He point out identity crisis is a reality.

(b) He suggest parents should capitulate to their children's wishes.

(c) He suggest a solution to the clash.

(d) He tries to scrutinise the impact of telling fairy tales.

Ans. (a) He point out identity crisis is a reality.

(iv) Why does Jack feel irritated by the frequent questions asked by his daughter? Pick up any two possibilities from the list?

(a) He wants to help Clare after finishing story telling.

(b) He is disturbed to realize his daughter is becoming rather inquisitive.

(c) She is looking and sounding more like her mother.

(d) She is becoming impossible to deal with.

Ans. (b) He is disturbed to realize his daughter is becoming rather inquisitive.

(c) She is looking and sounding more like her mother.

(v) Pick up the best option that conveys the moral of the story.

(a) One should try to change from the way nature has intended.

(b) All creatures in this world should be moulded identically for inclusivity.

(c) One should learn to accept specific qualities as part of their identity.

(d) Friends never accept anyone different from their mould.

Ans. (c) One should learn to accept specific qualities as part of their identity.

Read the given extract to attempt questions that follow:

5. *"Joanne. It's Daddy's story. Shall Daddy not tell you any more stories?" Her broad face looked at him through sifted light, astounded. "This is what happened, then. Roger Skunk and his mommy went home and they heard Woo-oo, woooo-oo and it was the choo-choo train bringing Daddy Skunk home from Boston. And they had lima beans, celery, liver, mashed potatoes, and Pie-Oh-My for dessert. And when Roger Skunk was in bed Mommy Skunk came up and hugged him and said he smelled like her little baby skunk again and she loved him very much. And that's the end of the story."*

(i) "And that's the end of the story." There is a tone of finality in Jack's tone. What can we interpret from it?

(a) He is not going to discuss it further.

(b) A tone of censure that his daughter is being disrespectful.

(c) His verdict as a story teller is supreme.

(d) He is being irrational.

Ans. (c) His verdict as a story teller is supreme.

(ii) The reason why the skunk meekly submitted to his mother's will was he:

(a) feared his mother.

(b) respected and loved his mother.

(c) he started disliking the new smell.

(d) he wanted another fragrance.

Ans. (b) respected and loved his mother.

(iii) 'What possible plot line could the story continue with?' This question suggests a potential clash of ideas and attitudes. Select the right option from the list to identify the clash.

(a) Harshness and understanding.

(b) Fantasy and reality.

(c) Obstinancy and meekness.

(d) Childishness and relenting attitude.

Ans. (b) Fantasy and reality.

(iv) Jo insists that the end of the story should be changed the next day. Why?

(a) Because she hates skunks.

(b) Because she thinks her father is a poor story teller.

(c) Because she wants her own mother to be punished.

(d) Because she empathises with the skunk.

Ans. (d) Because she empathises with the skunk.

(v) Why does Jack insist on his version of conclusion?

(a) He wants Jo to accept discordant notes of real life.

(b) He does not want to encourage rebellious tendencies.

(c) He is basically a strict father.

(d) He totally lacks understanding of child psychology.

Ans. (a) He wants Jo to accept discordant notes of real life.

Read the given extract to attempt questions that follow:

6. *Jo looked at him solemnly; she hadn't foreseen this. "Whenever he would go out to play," Jack continued with zest, remembering certain humiliations of his own childhood, "all of the other tiny animals would cry, "Uh-oh, here comes Roger Stinky Skunk," and they would run away, and Roger Skunk would stand there all alone, and two little round tears would fall from his eyes." The corners of Jo's mouth drooped down and her lower lip bent forward as he traced with a forefinger along the side of her nose the course of one of Roger Skunk's tears. "Won't he see the owl?" she asked in a high and faintly roughened voice.*

(i) '__________ she hadn't foreseen this.' What is the word 'this' referring to in the given context?

(a) Skunks can feel resentment

(b) Skunk's isolation from peer group

(c) That skunks smell awful

(d) That jack could be so unfair to skunks

Ans. (b) Skunk's isolation from peer group

(ii) 'Jack continued with zest, remembering certain humiliations of his own childhood.' On the base of this observation, classify the tone of Jack's story.

(a) Biographical

(b) Cynical

(c) Misogynistic

(d) Autobiographical

Ans. (d) Autobiographical

(iii) From the extract pick out expressions involving alliteration.

I. Two little round tears

II. Drooped down

III. Stinky Skunk

IV. Side of her nose

(a) I and III (b) II and IV (c) III and II (d) IV and III

Ans. (c) III and II

(iv) What is the implication of Jo asking if Roger would not consult the owl?

(a) Reflection of set pattern of the stories.

(b) She is weary of the story.

(c) She is sarcastic towards Jack.

(d) It's a caustic comment.

Ans. (a) Reflection of set pattern of the stories.

(v) The word 'zest' in the extract means enthusiastic and energetic. However, towards the last phase of the story Jack feels different. Select from the given option the best way to refer to his feeling.

(a) Incompetent but patronising.

(b) Contrite and cajoling.

(c) Angry and aggressive.

(d) Listless or enervated.

Ans. (d) Listless or enervated.

(vi) The wizard of the story becomes a bone of controversy for Jo and Jack. What is the fundamental reason for this controversy?

(a) Height of idiosyncrasy.

(b) Obstinate nature of the duo.

(c) Diversity of perception.

(d) Illogical conclusion.

Ans. (c) Diversity of perception.

7. *Jack rapped on the window sill, and under the covers Jo's tall figure clenched in an infantile thrill. "And then a tiny little old man came out, with a long white beard and a pointed blue hat, and said, "Eh? Whatzis? Whatcher want? You smell awful." The wizard's voice was one of Jack's own favourite effects; he did it by scrunching up his face and somehow whining through his eyes, which felt for the interval rheumy.*

(i) Why did Jack knock on the window sill?

(a) To wake up Jo.
(b) To make the wizard listen to him.
(c) To create the sound effect.
(d) To call his wife.

Ans. (c) To create the sound effect.

(ii) Which word in the above extract has the meaning closest to 'immature or childish'?

(a) Tiny (b) Infantile (c) Robust (d) Scrunching

Ans. (b) Infantile

(iii) How did the wizard look like?

(a) Wizard was a tiny and old creature.
(b) Wizard had a long white beard.
(c) Wizard was wearing blue pointed hat.
(d) All of these.

Ans. (d) All of these.

(iv) How did Jack show that wizard's voice was his favourite one?

(a) He said this to Jo.
(b) He did it by scrunching up his face.
(c) He had written about it in his diary.
(d) He often made sounds of wizard generally.

Ans. (b) He did it by scrunching up his face.

8. *Jo sat up, her hands dabbling in the air with genuine fright. "But Daddy, then he said about the other little animals run away!" Her hands skittered off, into the underbrush. "All right. He said, 'But Mommy, all the other little animals run away,' and she said, 'I don't care. You smelled the way a little skunk should have and I'm going to take you right back to that wizard,' and she took an umbrella and went back with Roger Skunk and hit that wizard right over the head." "No," Jo said, and put her hand out to touch his lips, yet even in her agitation did not quite dare to stop the source of truth. Inspiration came to her. "Then the wizard hit her on the head and did not change that little skunk back."*

(i) Choose the correct alternative and rewrite the statement:

Mommy went back to the wizard because

(a) She wanted to get his old smell back.
(b) Roger Skunk smelled the way a little skunk should have.
(c) She wanted to get her umbrella to him.

Ans. (a) She wanted to get his old smell back.

(ii) Give one word for :

(a) immerse and move one's feet partially in water.
(b) move quickly and hurriedly.

Ans. (a) dabble (b) skitter

(iii) Pick out from the extract, the words that mean the opposite of:

(a) artificial (b) appreciation

Ans. (a) genuine (b) agitation

(iv) Fill in the blanks appropriately :

(a) Jo could dare to stop _______.
(b) ________ came to her on its own.

Ans. (a) the source of truth (b) Inspiration

Multiple Choice Questions

1. **What part of the story did Jack himself enjoy the most?**
   (a) When mother hits the wizard.
   (b) When Roger finds pennies from the magic well.
   (c) When at the wizard's house, Roger imitates wizard's voice.
   (d) When the wizard fulfills Roger's wish.

Ans. (c) When at the wizard's house, Roger imitates wizard's voice.

2. **Why did Jack enjoy Roger's imitation of wizard's voice?**
   (a) He recalls his past.
   (b) He recalls his childhood.
   (c) He relates his own childhood experiences with it.
   (d) Her daughter enjoys it.

Ans. (c) He relates his own childhood experiences with it.

3. **What is the moral of the story?**
   (a) Parents are wise and know what is best for their children.
   (b) Parents are always right.
   (c) Mothers think about the best for her children.
   (d) Children are naive.

Ans. (a) Parents are wise and know what is best for their children.

4. **What does a 4 year old child symbolise in the story?**
   (a) Innocence (b) Smartness (c) Obstinacy (d) Stubborness

Ans. (a) Innocence

5. **What do adult people signify in the story?**
   (a) Maturity and experience (c) Cruelty
   (b) Wise words (d) Indifference

Ans. (a) Maturity and experience

6. **Pick out phrases from the following options which are closest in the meaning?**
   (i) Too enervating
   (ii) Too weary
   (iii) Too wary
   (iv) Too agitated
   (a) (i), (iii) and (iv) (b) (i) and (ii) (c) (ii) and (i) (d) (i), (ii) and (iii)

Ans. (b) (i) and (ii)

7. **According to the normal trend in Jack's story, where does the father of Roger usually come home from work?**
   (a) Kinston (b) Kensington (c) Boston (d) Wellington

Ans. (c) Boston

8. **'She hadn't foreseen this.' Based on the story, what unexpected twist came into the story as far as Jo was concerned?**
   (a) That skunk smelt badly. (c) That other animals fought with him.
   (b) That skunk refused to play with other animals. (d) That he was ostracised by other animals.

Ans. (d) That he was ostracised by other animals.

9. ***An enormous wise old owl*. In the given phrase, three adjectives are used in succession to modify the noun owl. What are they known as?**
   (a) Sequential (b) Clubbed (c) Cumulative (d) Embedded

Ans. (c) Cumulative

10. This was a new phase, just this last month, a ________ phase. Choose the appropriate option to complete the sentence.

(a) real (b) new (c) reality (d) surprising

Ans. (c) reality

11. In the phrase *'sly yet eager smile'* suggests that Jo's smile was:

(a) Clever and curious.
(b) Cunning and enthusiastic.
(c) Wicked and mocking.
(d) Genuinely interested.

Ans. (b) Cunning and enthusiastic.

12. 'Go through the dark woods, under the apple trees, into the swamp, *over the crick.*' Suggest the meaning implied by the italic words.

(a) Over the lake.
(b) Beside the stream.
(c) Up above the creak.
(d) Over the little river.

Ans. (d) Over the little river.

13. The wizard's house was dusty because he had no ________.

(a) time to look after (b) vacuum cleaner (c) cleaning lady (d) wife

Ans. (c) cleaning lady

14. Roger Skunk's mommy said, 'What's that awful smell?' In the light of what mommy says, which of the following expressions come closest to the inference?

(a) One man's meat is another man's poison.
(b) You scratch my back, I scratch your back.
(c) A good scent is a form of good manners.
(d) Smell binds a group together.

Ans. (a) One man's meat is another man's poison.

15. *"Joanne. It's Daddy's story. Shall Daddy not tell you any more stories?"* What does his imply?

(a) In reality, things do not happen according to what one wants.
(b) Jo should learn to accept realities.
(c) That the story maker should be allowed to choose the twists and turns of the story.
(d) All of the above

Ans. (d) All of the above

16. What reassurance did Jack give Jo at the end of Roger Skunk's story?

(a) Skunk submitted to the wish of his mother.
(b) Skunk was accepted by his fellow mates.
(c) Skunk was happy in his own bubble.
(d) Skunk happily got reconciled to his fate.

Ans. (b) Skunk was accepted by his fellow mates.

17. What word does Jo mispronounce as *evenshiladee*?

(a) Even as (b) Evidently (c) Evidences (d) Eventually

Ans. (d) Eventually

18. Towards the end of the story Jack feels trapped in an ugly middle position. Select from the options below the emotion he is likely to feel.

(a) Manic depression (b) Claustrophobia (c) Acrophobia (d) Autophobia

Ans. (b) Claustrophobia

19. What was the tone of Jack's voice when he chanted the magic spell to engage Jo?

(a) Brusque tone
(b) Elderly irritable voice
(c) Mellifluous
(d) Old man's harsh voice

Ans. (b) Elderly irritable voice

20. Roger Skunk's mother's ultimate victory over the wizard suggests a victory of:

(a) mother's tantrum over her son's pleadings.
(b) familial obligation over freedom to follow one's own desires.
(c) parental dominance over the demands of society.
(d) arrogance over childhood fantasy.

Ans. (b) familial obligation over freedom to follow one's own desires.

21. What do Wizard represents in the story 'Should Wizard Hit Mommy?'

(a) A sense of freedom from obligation.
(b) A will to change reality.
(c) A flippant attitude to children's desire.
(d) None of these.

Ans. (a) A sense of freedom from obligation.

22. What did Jo think about Roger's mother?

(a) A super power.
(b) A villainous figure.
(c) An interfering old woman.
(d) A comic character.

Ans. (b) A villainous figure.

23. Half old tan and half new ivory cage appearing at the end of the story is a metaphor for Jack's life. This signifies Jack is caught between:

(a) children and wife.
(b) new feminist changes and the old family structure.
(c) his childhood memories and the present life.
(d) rise and flow of life.

Ans. (b) new feminist changes and the old family structure.

24. Jack didn't like women when they took anything for granted, he liked them apprehensive, hanging on his words. Choose the options with the correct reference to the textual statement given above.

(i) Jack had a male chauvinistic streak in him.
(ii) He had patriarchal mentality.
(iii) He was a misogynist.
(iv) He felt apprehensive about his coming child.

(a) (iii) and (iv)
(b) (i) and (iii)
(c) (i) and (ii)
(d) (iv) and (ii)

Ans. (c) (i) and (ii)

25. What similarity did Jack view in Roger Skunk and himself?

(a) He had a strict upbringing.
(b) He must be alienated from peers and left alone in tears.
(c) He respected his mother's decisions.
(d) All of the above

Ans. (d) All of the above

26. 'You said Roger Fish', insisted Jo. What inference can you make out of this statement regarding Jo?

(a) She is alert and quick to point out.
(b) She is rude and critical.
(c) She is mocking and insulting.
(d) She is meticulous and demanding.

Ans. (a) She is alert and quick to point out.

27. Why does Roger's mother not want him to smell like a rose?

(a) Because she hated it.
(b) Because she is allergic to it.
(c) Because he is a skunk and he should smell like a skunk.
(d) She did not want her son to mingle with other animals.

Ans. (c) Because he is a skunk and he should smell like a skunk.

28. Jack prolongs story telling for two of the reasons mentioned below: Select the most possible reasons?

(i) Jack enjoyed the routine session of story telling.
(ii) He was savouring the autobiographical comparison with skunk.
(iii) He did not want to help or be near Clare.
(iv) He detested manual labour.

(a) (i) and (iii)
(b) (iii) and (iv)
(c) (ii) and (iii)
(d) (ii) and (iv)

Ans. (c) (ii) and (iii)

29. Considering the undercurrents in the plot development, what could be the tone of Clare when she remarked that it was a particularly long story.

(a) Sympathetic (b) Sarcastic (c) Jocular (d) Genial

Ans. (b) Sarcastic

30. Considering the patriarchal cultural climate that began to unravel in the late 90s, Jack's resentment can be a product of:

(a) unsettling of gender roles.
(b) obsession with male child.
(c) displacement from the head of family.
(d) hatred for domestic work.

Ans. (a) unsettling of gender roles.

31. Jo's demand to change the end of the story is mainly because of her:

(a) ingrained adamancy.
(b) open defiance against father.
(c) her need to belong to the peer group.
(d) her inability to conform with the norm.

Ans. (c) her need to belong to the peer group.

32. Jo had a wise noiseless grin which resembled his wife ______ pleasure at cocktail parties. Fill in with appropriate word from text.

(a) pretending (b) fabricating (c) simulating (d) feigning

Ans. (a) pretending

33. 'I don't care', says Roger's mommy. What picture of a mother could have been created in Jo's mind by this attitude?

(a) Uncaring and uncompromising
(b) Rude and insensitive
(c) Strict and unbending
(d) All of these

Ans. (a) Uncaring and uncompromising

34. What two possible implications are revealed by the title of the story?

(i) Jack may relent from his rigid attitude.
(ii) Jack could stick with his chosen stance.
(iii) Jack can leave the decision to his wife.
(iv) Jack could take the decision himself.

(a) (i) and (ii) (b) (ii) and (iii) (c) (i) and (iii) (d) (iv) and (i)

Ans. (a) (i) and (ii)

35. There is a hint of husband-wife tension revealed towards the end of the story. How can it be best expressed?

(a) Martial tension (b) Marital conflict (c) Filial placation (d) Survival instinct

Ans. (b) Marital conflict

36. What picture does the author create by referring to the full course dinner the family had after Daddy skunk came home?

(a) Rigid family atmosphere.
(b) A suppression of will under family pressure.
(c) Resolution of conflict and acceptance of parental wisdom.
(d) Underlying tension and potential conflict.

Ans. (c) Resolution of conflict and acceptance of parental wisdom.

37. 'Above him footsteps vibrated'. Pick up two options to indicate about the effect of the story on Jo?

(i) That it was too uninteresting to put the child to sleep.
(ii) That it was too agitating because of its controversial ending.
(iii) That it piqued the infantile interest of the child.
(iv) That she has grown out of her afternoon nap stage.

(a) (i) and (ii) (b) (ii) and (iii) (c) (ii) and (iv) (d) (i) and (iii)

Ans. (c) (ii) and (iv)

38. Jack's unwillingness to help Clare can be attributed to:

(a) lazy nature.
(b) his alienation with family.
(c) his resentment for his daughter.
(d) thought Clare was capable of handling work.

Ans. (b) his alienation with family.

39. How can Jack's mentality at the end of the story best described?

(a) ennui (b) crazy (c) elated (d) cranky

Ans. (a) ennui

40. When Jack says 'the poor kid', he is thinking about:

(a) his nostalgia about his childhood.

(b) that Jo may have to undergo the challenges faced by skunk.

(c) that Jo will suffer from sleep deprivation.

(d) that Jo will have to be spanked.

Ans. (b) that Jo may have to undergo the challenges faced by skunk.

41. Right from the title to certain loose ends in the story of 'Should Wizard Hit Mommy', what does the author try to convey?

(a) That life is a bed of roses.

(b) Life is complicated and all have to fit in a groove.

(c) Life often confuses us by offering choices.

(d) One has to always obey one's parents.

Ans. (c) Life often confuses us by offering choices.

42. Who is the author of the lesson?

(a) John Updike (b) John Donne (c) William Blake (d) John Williams

Ans. (a) John Updike

43. Why does Jo call Roger's mom stupid?

(a) As she doesn't listen.

(b) As she is stupid.

(c) As it is because of her action that Roger start smelling bad again.

(d) None of the above

Ans. (c) As it is because of her action that Roger start smelling bad again.

44. Why did Jo think that Roger Skunk was better with new smell off?

(a) Because she was able to bear him now.

(b) She was able to be with him now.

(c) Because of pleasant smell now people were able to be friends with him.

(d) All of the above

Ans. (c) Because of pleasant smell now people were able to be friends with him.

45. What did Roger's mother decide finally?

(a) To take him back to awful wizard and get his bad smell back.

(b) To take him with her.

(c) To get him new smell.

(d) To bathe him.

Ans. (a) To take him back to awful wizard and get his bad smell back.

46. How does Jo want the wizard to behave with Roger's mother?

(a) She wants the wizard to behave nicely with her.

(b) She wants the wizard to kill her.

(c) She wants the wizard to shout at her.

(d) She wants the wizard to hit her.

Ans. (d) She wants the wizard to hit her.

47. Why did Roger Skunk visit the owl?

(a) To be his friend.

(b) To talk to him.

(c) To learn the art of flying.

(d) To seek his advice to solve his problem.

Ans. (d) To seek his advice to solve his problem.

48. Where did the wizard suggest Roger to get rest three pennies?

(a) From a tree

(b) From a river

(c) From the ocean

(d) From a magic well

Ans. (d) From a magic well

49. Why does Jo want her father to tell her story in a different way?

(a) To give the story a sad ending.

(b) To understand the story better.

(c) To complete the story.

(d) To give the story a happy ending with an adult and mature understanding.

Ans. (d) To give the story a happy ending with an adult and mature understanding.

50. Where does Jo prefer to live?

(a) In the world of friends.

(b) In the school of swings.

(c) In her world of dreams and fantasies.

(d) In the world of wizards and magic.

Ans. (c) In her world of dreams and fantasies.

51. Why did Jack start finding story telling ritual a chore?

(a) Because it became a routine to make Jo sleep.

(b) Because it was becoming interesting day-by-day.

(c) Friends were liking it.

(d) Because he disliked it.

Ans. (a) Because it became a routine to make Jo sleep.

52. Based on the reading of the story 'Should Wizard Hit Mommy', what have you inferred about Jack's character?

(a) He is a happy go lucky person.

(b) He is torn between his wife and daughter.

(c) He no longer has will enough to fulfill his filial responsibilities.

(d) He is basically a lazy person.

Ans. (c) He no longer has will enough to fulfill his filial responsibilities.

53. Roger ultimately acquiesces to his mother's wishes because he accepts that:

(a) ultimately he has to live with his mother and it is better to make peace with her.

(b) that his smell cannot be altered because it is a part of who he is.

(c) the spell is for a short time and he will have to bear his original smell anyway.

(d) it is better to go with the flow rather than rebel.

Ans. (b) that his smell cannot be altered because it is a part of who he is.

54. Jack could have relented and ended the story the Jo way, but he did not. What could be the reason for not acquiescing with his daughter's wish?

(a) He wanted her to accept the concept of compromise and sacrifice.

(b) He wanted to teach her the futility of rebellion.

(c) He was not sensitive to his daughter's feelings.

(d) He was simply stubborn.

Ans. (a) He wanted her to accept the concept of compromise and sacrifice.

55. Jo insisting on a happy ending of the skunk retaining his rosy smell shows.

(a) Her resentment for mother figure.

(b) Her adamant nature.

(c) Innocent desire for happiness without compromise.

(d) She is sure she can manipulate her father by throwing tantrum.

Ans. (c) Innocent desire for happiness without compromise.

56. Jack tells the skunk's story is meant to convey a profound message. What is this type of literature known as?

(a) An allegory (b) An analogy (c) An anecdote (d) An antecedent

Ans. (a) An allegory

57. In the onward march of civilization, there is bound to be corresponding shift in family relationship. What is required to flow with such times?

(a) Relaxation of rigidity
(b) Attitudinal shift
(c) Acceptance of gender equality
(d) All of these

Ans. (d) All of these

58. Jack enjoys doing the role of wizard; in fact, he feels old man's role is most suitable for him. What does it convey about Jack's present mentality?

(a) Jack's body is not supporting him.
(b) Jack has a death wish.
(c) Jack is becoming weary of life.
(d) Jack is euphoric at the thought of his third child.

Ans. (c) Jack is becoming weary of life.

59. Why did Jack enjoy Roger's imitation of wizard's voice?

(a) he recalls his past
(b) he recalls his childhood
(c) he relates his own childhood experiences with it
(d) none of the above

Ans. (c) he relates his own childhood experiences with it

❑❑

6. On the Face of It–by Susan Hill

Summary :

The play depicts beautifully yet grimly, the sad world of the physically impaired. It is not the actual pain or inconvenience caused by a physical impairment that troubles a disabled man but the attitude of the people around him. Two physically impaired people, Mr. Lamb with a tin leg and Derry with a burnt face, strike a bond of friendship. Derry is described as a young boy-shy, withdrawn and defiant. People tell him inspiring stories to console him but no one has ever kissed him except his mother and that too on the other side of his face. He mentions about a woman telling that only a mother can love such a face. Mr. Lamb revives the dead feelings of Derry towards life. He motivates him to think positively about life and changes his mind set about people and things. How a man locked himself as he was scared, a picture fell off the wall and he got killed. Everything appears to be the same but is different.

Derry is inspired and promises to come back. His mother stops him but he is adamant saying if he does not go now, it would be never. When he comes back, he sees lamb lying on the ground. It is ironical that when he searches a new foothold to live happily, he finds Mr. Lamb dead. In this way the play depicts the heart-rendering life of physically-disabled people with their loneliness, aloofness and alienation. But at the same time, it is almost a true account of the people who don't let a person live happily.

Textbook Questions :

Read and find out :

Q. 1. Who is Mr. Lamb? How does Derry get into his garden?

Ans. Mr. Lamb was an old man who lived in a big house with a beautiful garden in it. He had lost one of his legs, due to a bomb explosion, which was replaced with an artificial tin-leg. He liked talking to people and making friends. He kept the gates of his garden always open for people. Derry was a fourteen-year-old boy who was down with inferiority complex due to his mutilated face due to which he liked to stay alone. He thought the garden to be empty, so he jumped over the wall to hide away from the rest of the world.

Q. 2. Do you think all this will change Derry's attitude towards Mr. Lamb?

Ans. Derry's burnt face was the only reason of his embarrassment. Although people sympathized with him, he never appreciated their sympathy which resulted in his pessimistic approach towards life. On the contrary, Mr. Lamb showed his affection towards him. He welcomed him in his garden and helped the boy to love and live life happily without any inferiority complex. Derry had initially thought the old man to be like others, but he gradually started respecting and liking him for the moral strength he got from him.

Reading with Insight :

Q. 1. What is it that draws Derry towards Mr. Lamb in spite of himself?

Ans. Derry was a young boy whose face was mutilated by acid which shattered his self confidence and therefore, he could not face the world normally. He preferred to stay in solitude resulting in ~~an~~ isolation from the society. He met Mr. Lamb, an old man, by chance who did not show any dislike or horror at his look which surprised him. Although he wanted to leave the garden but the old man's interesting and 'peculiar' conversation stopped him from leaving. He also noticed that Mr. Lamb who was crippled of one leg, never gave up and was living a happy life despite being mocked by the people. Mr. Lamb spoke words of encouragement and hope, made him aware of his physical strength and explained the importance of emotional well-being which gave him moral strength. Thus, he felt himself drawn to Mr. Lamb

Q. 2. In which section of the play does Mr. Lamb display signs of loneliness and disappointment? What are the ways in which Mr. Lamb tries to overcome these feelings?

Ans. Although the loneliness of Derry dominates the play, there are evident traces of Mr. Lamb's loneliness throughout the first scene of the play. The old man says that having heard the bees for a 'long time' he knows that they 'sing', not buzz. It not only depicts how his perception was different from others but also illustrates that he was lonely and that he did not have any one to be with. Another evidence of his loneliness is the fact that the whole day he sat in the sun and read books. This proves that books were his only true friends. He says that his 'empty house' is full of books, underlining the way in which the void of his empty life was filled in by books. By the end of this scene, it becomes even clearer that he is lonely and sad when he mutters to himself that no one comes back to him after the first meeting. Likewise, he did not expect Derry to return. He was so sure that Derry would never return so, he climbed the ladder to collect all the apples himself, although Derry had offered to help him after informing his mother. Ironically, the old man would have died unnoticed if Derry had not returned to fill the emptiness of his own life.

Q. 3. The actual pain or inconvenience caused by a physical impairment is often much less than the sense of alienation felt by the person with disabilities. What is the kind of behaviour that the person expects from others?

Ans. A person with any physical impairment can live life with respect and honour, if he is not ridiculed and ignored by the society. He expects empathy rather than sympathy. If everyone looks down at him with a pessimistic approach, he may never be able to come out of his sorrow, and consequently, retire to his own secluded world. Being under tremendous mental and emotional pressure, he expects others to be more understanding rather than reminding him of his disability. In the play, Derry and Mr. Lamb, are caught in a similar situation. Mr. Lamb, as an adult, is able to cope with such problems, but Derry, being a child, is not able to untangle this web alone. He develops a strong liking for this old man because he gets moral and emotional strength from him.

Q. 4. Will Derry get back to his old seclusion or will Mr. Lamb's brief association effect a change in the kind of life he will lead in the future?

Ans. The brief association of Derry with Mr. Lamb boosted his self-confidence and helped him respect his own self. He undergoes a remarkable change and starts to think optimistically. He defends the old man for encouraging him. He tells his mother that his looks are not important and he has learned to accept himself. He craves to become self sufficient. It is not likely that the death of Mr. Lamb would take him back to his secluded life. This big change is definitely here to stay and would not be undone due to setbacks. The entire conversation between the two is the passing of wisdom from one generation to the other.

Additional Questions

Short Answer Questions : **(30-40 words)**

Q. 1. This is a play featuring an old man and a small boy meeting in the former's garden. The old man strikes up a friendship with the boy who is very withdrawn and defiant. What is the bond that unites the two?

Ans. Derry jumped over the wall and sneaked into the garden of Mr. Lamb. He did not want to get noticed by anyone. His burnt and distorted face made him run away from the society. On the other hand, Mr. Lamb who had an artificial leg, was the subject of mockery for everyone because of his crippled leg. People came to sit in his beautiful garden, ate apples, pears and toffees but mocked him of his disability. Derry and Mr. Lamb were bound by a single cord on the grounds of their disability. The old man was able to understand the lonely boy's feelings and told him to be optimistic but the boy was not able to overcome his grief and self-contempt. After getting moral strength from Mr. Lamb, he realized a great change of living a happily life within himself and started perceiving life optimistically. That was the bond which united the two.

Q. 2. Use your imagination to suggest another ending to the above story.

Ans. This story could have had another ending where, after falling, Mr. Lamb got seriously injured and Derry called an ambulance that took him to the hospital. When Derry's mother came to know about the accident, she allowed Derry to take care of Mr. Lamb in the hospital as well as after being discharged. During his stay with the old man, he read his books, took care of his garden and made him his friend which changed his perspective towards life completely. Later, he befriended a boy whose father was a plastic surgeon, who operated on him and helped him return to his normal life.

Q. 3. What does Mr. Lamb tell about himself?

Ans. Mr. Lamb told Derry that he was an old man and had an artificial tin-leg. Children teased him by calling him 'Lamey-Lamb', but still they used to come to his garden. They were not afraid of him because he loved them. He was never bothered about his old age or artificial leg as life had many more things to offer.

Q. 4. "I'm not fond of curtains shutting things out" says Mr. Lamb. What does this reveal about his personality?

Ans. He did not allow his physical disability to crush his openness and large heartedness. He kept his house and heart open for people, he kept the gate of his garden open and anybody could enter it. He did not believe in shutting things out or disconnecting himself from the people.

Q. 5. Why does Derry's mother warn him not to go to meet Mr. Lamb?

Ans. Derry's mother had heard many things about Mr. Lamb. She was warned by the people about him. So, she asked Derry not to go there.

Q. 6. It's all relative, beauty and beast. Justify the statement.

Ans. Mr. Lamb told Derry that there are plenty of things to stare at and the people should not mind their disability because they will be soon tired of it. He further told Derry that beauty or ugliness depends upon an individual's perception. One might see beauty in a thing but to another it might be a beast.

Q. 7. How did Derry's attitude change?

Ans. Derry led a life of isolation due to his burnt face. He felt bad when people stared at him. His attitude changed when he was morally encouraged by Mr. Lamb to live life without inferiority complex. Mr. Lamb told him that he had an artificial leg but it did not stop him from making friends. He further told him that he did not mind people making mockery of his disability.

Q. 8. What do you think the play 'On the Face of It' is all about?

Ans. This play about frustration, loneliness and sadness of physically-disabled people. It is about the pain, which is caused due to criticism, by some unscrupulous people at their disabilities, which is reflected through the character of Derry. The play is also about courage and self confidence to live life in spite of disabilities.

Q. 9. What is common between Derry and Mr. Lamb?*

Ans. Derry was a boy whose face was burnt because of acid and Mr. Lamb was an old man who had a tin leg because his leg was blown off by a bomb in the war. The common thing in both of them was that they both were physically impaired but their attitude towards life was very much opposite.

Q.10. Why does Mr. Lamb leave the gate of his house always open?*

Ans. Mr. Lamb always left the gate of his house open. He lived alone and did not mind if strangers entered his house or garden. As he lived alone, he hoped that someone would come and talk to him.

Long Answer Questions : **(120-150 words)**

Q. 1. Both Derry and Mr. Lamb suffer from physical disabilities but their attitude towards life and people is totally different.

Ans. Derry has a burnt face. He had got acid all down on his face in an unfortunate accident. The acid burned it all. It ate his face up. He is always conscious of it. He thinks that people are afraid of him due to which he got alienated from the world. He became an escapist. On the other hand, Mr. Lamb doesn't allow his physical disability to come into his way. He accepted life as it came. He didn't find solace in escapism but believed in keeping up with the mainstream of life. He didn't mind children calling him 'Lamey-lamb' and instead, give them jelly and chocolates. Derry is defiant and withdrawn. He doesn't trust people and thinks that no one, except his mother, loves him. He can't stand people staring and passing unpleasant remarks at him, whereas Mr. Lamb is open-hearted and open minded, he welcomes everybody in his garden and always keep the gate open. He shows Derry, the way of dealing with people and things.

Q. 2. Physically challenged people don't want sympathy, they just need acceptance. Comment with illustrations from '*On the face of it*'.

Ans. The actual pain caused by a physical impairment was much less than the mental agony caused by it. Any physical disability creates a deep inferiority complex. The affected person starts thinking of oneself as an incomplete, incompetent and impaired person. Such feelings give birth to a sense of alienation in them. There is a need for acceptance by fellow beings around such people. They are constantly bearing the pain of being ignored. They don't want to be reminded of their disabilities time and again. As most of them have grown up listening to the uncharitable remarks of the world, they become like an open wound i.e. touchy and hypersensitive. The emotional scars are much deeper than the physical ones. Pity and sympathy weakens them. They need to be inspired and encouraged.

Q. 3. *Derry is a victim of his own complex. He develops negative attitude towards life and people.* Do you find some change in him in the end ?

Ans. Derry was a victim of inferiority complex which was born out of a distorted understanding of himself and the world. One side of his face was burnt by acid and he took it to be the ugliest thing in the world. He got scared of himself whenever he saw his face in the mirror. He doesn't find himself fitting anywhere. He became withdrawn and defiant. His complexed him to total alienation. He made himself pitiable and miserable. Cruel remarks by people, made him upset. All this resulted in making him think negative towards life. But we find the change in him towards the end. Mr. Lamb's ideas left their imprints on his mind and soul. He is free from that diseased complex now. He doesn't care about his burnt face and it is no more important for him.

Q. 4. What is the significance of Derry's words,' I thought it was an empty house' in the play?

Ans. Derry said these words to Mr. Lamb when the latter sees Derry entering into his garden by climbing over the boundary wall. Mr. Lamb was not surprised as he was used to children coming into his garden to pick and eat apples. But, Derry has ventured into it out of curiosity, supposing to be empty. So, when Mr. Lamb accosts him, Derry was embarrassed and wanted to go back, but, not before explaining that he has not stolen any apples. His words point out to his terrible sense of frustration, loneliness and isolation on account of his

* are board exam questions from previous years

burnt face. At the same time his words also prompt Mr. Lamb to spill out his loneliness too, towards the end of the first scene. They go a long way in Mr. Lamb's (and the reader's) understanding of Derry's character and Mr. Lamb's subsequent efforts in helping him come out of his inferiority complex, poor self-regard and self-rejection. These words were a reminder of the bitterness that had crept into Derek's mind due to other people's dislike and hatred for his ugly face. These words were a desperate cry of a fourteen year old for love and acceptance.

Q. 5. Why do you think Mr. Lamb attaches no importance to Derry's deformity? Why does Mr. Lamb change the topic when Derry speaks about his ugliness?

Ans. Mr. Lamb does not pay any importance to Derry's outburst on his deformity because he knows that Derry is drowned in self-pity and self-rejection and was paying unwanted and undue attention to his deformity. He does not want Derry to dwell deep and unduly on the issue of his ugly looks, so, he changes his topic. He wanted to tell Derry that one must accept one's self. Life affords so many bounties that need appreciation. Mr. Lamb's special mention of apples, pears and jelly he give out to children is his indirect comment on the sweetness of life. His indifference to Derek's outburst aims at helping Derek to learn the lesson of positivity in life.

Q. 6. Do you find any wisdom in the statement, 'blind people ought to be with other blind people'?

Ans. These words were uttered by a woman in the hospital where Derry was admitted. They express her views on how a society ought to deal with handicaps and impairment of individuals. I strongly condemn this attitude and call it grossly inhuman. Obviously the woman was insensitive towards handicaps and impairments. It was her own repulsion and fear of having to look at other people's sufferings. She seemed to firmly believe that if people with similar handicaps lived together, they would be less upset with their disabilities. I agree with Mr. Lamb that such a world would be weird, inhuman and an unnatural the to live in. Identically, handicapped people living together will always remind each other of their impairment and that will act as a detriment in the interest of everyone. Handicapped people can and should live with normal people, who, should not remind the former that they are missing out on some thing in life or that they are unfortunate in some way or the other. They should allow the handicaps to live life fully as much as possible. On the other hand these handicaps should remind others that accidents can happen to anyone and sufferings can befall anyone and at anytime. We need a cohesive world of mutual understanding and co-existence based on love, compassion, kindness, concern and fellow feeling.

Q. 7. What is the significance of Derry's words regarding Mr. Lamb's falling down and breaking his neck?

Ans. This was an inadvertent comment on Derry's part, which however, without his knowing it at the time of making, becomes prophetic. Mr. Lamb dies exactly in the manner described in the statement. They are significant on two scores. Firstly, it was destined that Mr. Lamb will die exactly in the manner described by Derry and that his first coincidental meeting with Mr. Lamb will also become his last. Secondly, the author wants to suggest that Mr. Lamb is an old man now and needs a successor to carry on his noble deeds. So, an angel meets a rough ashlar, chisels it to perfect smoothness, raises it up to the required moral and social standard and departs.

Q. 8. The play 'On the Face of It' depicts the unusual behaviour of the people towards the physically disabled which makes them lonely. Comment.*

Ans. The play 'On the Face of it' aptly depicts the loneliness and sense of alienation experienced by Derry and Mr. Lamb on account of disability. The actual pain and inconvenience caused by the disabilities is often much less than the sense of alienation felt by the disabled person. Derry suffered from severe negative complexes because of his burnt face. He became a pessimistic loner who indulged in self-pity and was always suspicious of the intention of others. His anger and frustration made him an introvert. Mr. Lamb, on the other hand, was inwardly a loner who craved company and acceptance. Though outwardly he was always jovial, outgoing, and optimistic but from inside, he was an extremely sensitive person. Derry and Mr. Lamb's physical disabilities caused pain and suffering not only to their bodies but also to their minds and souls.

Previous Years' Questions :

Q. 1. Why does Derry's mother not want him to go back to visit Mr. Lamb ?

Ans. Derry's mother did not want him to go back to visit Mr. Lamb because she did not want her child Derry to wander around and get influenced by others who may even laugh at him.

She wanted him to think it out on his own. She is selfish and realizes that Mr. Lamb has played a more important role in Derry's life.

---

* are board exam questions from previous years

Q. 2. How does Mr. Lamb react when Derry enters his garden ?

Ans. Derry enters Mr. Lamb's garden by climbing over the wall. When Mr. Lamb saw him entering his garden, he was startled. Derry tried to explain that he didn't intend to steal anything, but Mr. Lamb tried to comfort him instead of blaming and asked him to pick up the apples lying in the long grass.

Q. 3. What kind of garden does Mr. Lamb have ? Why does he like it ?

Ans. Mr. Lamb's garden is a place where there is an occasional round of birdsongs and of tree leaves rustling. There are apple trees and Mr. Lamb shares the produce with the children coming to his garden. His philosophy is to love all the creatures of God so he likes his garden as it gives him a chance to be in contact with the nature and to hear the voice of God. He says, 'There's nothing God made that doesn't interest me.'

Q. 4. Both Derry and Lamb are victims of physical impairment, but much more painful for them is the feeling of loneliness. Comment.

Ans. A disabled or a handicapped person is considered to be an outcaste. People sympathize with them but do not accompany them. They are excluded from the society. The feeling of loneliness and alienation is much more troublesome than the pain which disabled people experience due to their physical impairment. This is very well revealed in the story, 'On the face of it', where the character, Derry has a burnt face and people often sympathized with him but it was not a heart felt one. This resulted in his pessimistic approach towards life. Derry had no association with the outer world till he met Mr. Lamb. Mr. Lamb's attitude and outlook towards people and life uplifted him. He learnt to live a respectful life. Mr. Lamb inspired him to face the world in spite of his disability. Mr. Lamb successfully infused in him, courage and self-determination. He advised him to ignore the comments made by people on his physical impairment and enjoy the beauty of life and nature. Although the loneliness of Derry dominates the play, there are evident traces of Mr. Lamb's loneliness also. The old man had no one to be with. He spent his day in the sun, reading books. By the end of the first scene, it becomes clearer that he is lonely when he mutters that no one comes back to him after meeting him for the first time.

Q. 5. Derry sneaked into Mr. Lamb's garden and it became a turning point in his life. Comment.

Ans. Derry sneaked into Mr. Lamb's garden and it became a turning point in his life. Before that Derry used to live an isolated life. He did not like meeting people or socializing. The reason was his burnt face, seeing which people often get terrified. He began leading a secluded life.

Meeting Mr. Lamb brought a change in his life. His attitude towards life was completely changed. Mr. Lamb gave him confidence and supported him morally as he was physically impaired like him. He had a tin leg because the original one was blown off in the war. He told Derry that he was not affected by people's sarcastic remarks. He motivated Derry to face the challenges of life and not to lament over his burnt face. According to him, he was lucky to have two arms, two legs, ears, eyes and tongue. He could do far better than others.

All these preachings left an impression on Derry and now he started looking at things and the world differently. He began to help Mr. Lamb with crab apples and developed a positive attitude towards life.

Q. 6. Both Derry and Lamb are physically impaired and lonely. It is the responsibility of society to understand and support people with infirmities so that they do not suffer from a sense of alienation. As a responsible citizen, write in about 100 words what you would do to bring about a change in the lives of such people.

Ans. In the story, both Derry and Lamb are physically impaired and lonely. Such people can only live their lives with respect and honour, if they are not ridiculed and punished with heartless pity. These people expect empathy, rather than sympathy, from others. If everyone looks down at them with a pessimistic approach, they may never be able to come out of their sorrow; consequently, they may recline to their own secluded worlds. As responsible citizens, we should understand the tremendous mental and emotional pressure these people go through. Instead of reminding them of their disabilities, we should give them the chance to live a normal life.

Q. 7. What benefits did Derry reap from his association with Mr. Lamb?

Ans. Derry had no association with the outer world till he met Mr. Lamb. His meeting with Mr. Lamb was a turning point in his life. He learnt to live a respectful life and also appreciated Mr. Lamb's attitude and outlook towards people and life. He realised his true worth. Mr. Lamb inspired him to face the world in spite of his disability. Derry's thinking towards people and life completely changed and he became self-confident. Mr. Lamb successfully infused in him courage and self-determination. He advised him to ignore the comments made by people on his physical impairment and enjoy beauty of life and nature. That was why Derry went back to Mr. Lamb's garden in spite of his mother's refusal. Now, Derry had understood the importance and true meaning of life and understanding himself better than before.

Q. 8. What is the bond that unites the two-the old Mr. Lamb and Derry, the small boy ? How does the old man inspire the small boy ?

Ans. Derry and Mr. Lamb had the same sense of loneliness and they both lived, a secluded life due to their physical inability. Derry experienced Mr. Lamb to be a peculiar person saying strange things which he was not able to understand, still he felt some kind of attraction towards him. He was differently-abled but was calm and maintained peace with people around him. He was not irritated by the children who called him 'Lamey-Lamb'. Before coming in contact with Mr. Lamb, Derry felt lonely due to the behaviour of people but lamb inspired him and filled him with self-confidence and determination. He taught him to live life to the fullest without brooding over his burnt face. He told him to move ahead in life as his brain and senses were working completely. He imbibed positive thinking in him and showed him the way to live life in spite of his inability because he could do much better than others. This was the bond that united both and Derry wept over Mr. Lamb's death.

Reference to Context :

Read the given extract to attempt questions that follow:

1. *MR LAMB: You're a boy who came into the garden. Plenty do. I'm interested in anybody. Anything. There's nothing God made that doesn't interest me. Look over there....over beside the far wall. What can you see?*

DERRY: Rubbish.

MR LAMB: Rubbish ? Look, boy, look....what do you see?

DERRY: Just....grass and stuff. Weeds.

MR LAMB: Some call them weeds. If you like, then....a weed garden, that. There's fruit and there are flowers, and trees and herbs. All sorts. But over there....weeds. I grow weeds there. Why is one green, growing plant called a weed and another 'flower'? Where's the difference. It's all life.... growing. Same as you and me.

(i) According to the extract, what two combinations of analogy can be applied as regard to the attitude of the boy and the old man?

I. Glass is half full

II. Bees buzz

III. Glass is half empty

IV. Bees sing

(a) I and II (b) II and III (c) II and IV (d) I and III

Ans. (c) II and IV

(ii) ***"It's all life.... growing. Same as you and me.'*** **Choose from the following options to denote the right word or phrase that can correctly capture the essence of the sentence.**

(a) Divisive mentality (c) Discrimination

(b) Prejudice (d) All inclusive

Ans. (d) All inclusive

(iii) ***'There's nothing God made that doesn't interest me.'*** **What does this speech say about the mentality of Lamb?**

(a) Gregarious (b) Avid (c) Garrulous (d) Cantankerous

Ans. (b) Avid

(iv) ***'Just....grass and stuff. Weeds.'*** **What expression would the character of the boy sport on stage, at this point of the play?**

(a) Ferocious (b) Surly (c) Sarcastic (d) Arrogant

Ans. (b) Surly

(v) What word given below would best describe the disposition of the old man in the story?

(a) Kind and condescending. (c) Deriding and sermonising.

(b) Critical and censuring. (d) Understanding and empathetic.

Ans. (d) Understanding and empathetic.

Read the given extract to attempt questions that follow:

2. *What do you do all day?*

MR LAMB: Sit in the sun. Read books. Ah, you thought it was an empty house, but inside, it's full. Books and other things. Full.

DERRY: But there aren't any curtains at the windows.

MR LAMB: I'm not fond of curtains. Shutting things out, shutting things in. I like the light and the darkness, and the windows open, to hear the wind.

DERRY: Yes. I like that. When it's raining, I like to hear it on the roof.

MR LAMB: So you're not. are you? Not altogether? You do hear things. You listen.

(i) Mr. Lamb's dislike for curtain stems from his __________. Select the best option to complete the sentence.

(a) desire to break away from tradition
(b) need to keep away humidity
(c) penchant for freedom
(d) none of these

Ans. (c) penchant for freedom

(ii) *"So you're not lost, are you? Not altogether?"* The connotation of the word 'lost' in the context suggests that Derry ___________.

(a) is trying not to withdraw into his shell
(b) is not totally impervious to the outside world
(c) not fully lost his mental faculty
(d) has not fully turned deaf to suggestions

Ans. (b) is not totally impervious to the outside world

(iii) Soon after this dialogue Derry refers to something else he hears. What is it?

(a) His mother's sympathetic words.
(b) People directly commiserating with him.
(c) People whispering behind his back.
(d) Tongues lashing at him.

Ans. (c) People whispering behind his back.

(iv) Mr. Lamb tries to make Derry realize through analogies/stories that shutting oneself in is not a solution to any problem. Which one do you think it is?

(a) An analogy of buzzing bees.
(b) A story of beauty and beast.
(c) A story of falling picture .
(d) All of these.

Ans. (c) A story of falling picture.

(v) Derry seems to be suffering from a psychological malaise after the acid attack. Select the term that most suits his condition.

(a) Paranoia
(b) Psychic withdrawal
(c) Dementia
(d) Bipolar syndrome

Ans. (a) Paranoia

Read the given extract to attempt questions that follow:

3. *You think I don't know about him, you think. I haven't heard things?*

DERRY: You shouldn't believe all you hear.

MOTHER: Been told. Warned. We've not lived here three months, but I know what there is to know and you're not to go back there.

DERRY: What are you afraid of? What do you think he is? An old man with a tin leg and he lives in a huge house without curtains and has a garden. And I want to be there, and sit and....listen to things. Listen and look.

MOTHER: Listen to what?

DERRY: Bees singing. Him talking.

MOTHER: And what's he got to say to you?

DERRY: Things that matter. Things nobody else has ever said. Things I want to think about.

(i) *'You shouldn't believe all you hear'*, indirectly echoes the title of the play On the Face of It? Select the option that does not support the meaning.

(a) People are prisoners of their thoughts.
(b) Prejudices blind judgement.
(c) Appearances are deceptive.
(d) Hearsay matters.

Ans. (d) Hearsay matters

(ii) The mother insists that Derry had better stay in the house because she is:

(a) callous.
(b) over protective about her son.
(c) Lamb's house is far away.
(d) there are brambles and bees in Lamb's garden.

Ans. (b) over protective about her son.

(iii) At the end of this scene, Derry runs away without permission. How would you describe this action?

(a) Outright rebellion.
(b) Sheer disobedience.
(c) An act of survival.
(d) He hardly bothers about his mother's wish.

Ans. (c) An act of survival.

(iv) Derry says he wants to go to Lamb's house; otherwise, he will never go anywhere in the world. Select the best phrase that explains the statement.

(a) It is the only place that can afford a direction to his life.
(b) Place offers a calm life in isolation.
(c) There he can escape from the rest of the world.
(d) Lamb will feel bad if he does not keep his promise of going back.

Ans. (a) It is the only place that can afford a direction to his life.

(v) Why does the author end the play on a tragic note?

(a) To show unexpected things can happen in life
(b) To point out that physically challenged people should not attempt risky actions.
(c) Just to derive a sadistic pleasure by shocking the reader with an unexpected twist.
(d) To reinforce Derry's change of attitude by never letting him forget what he has learned.

Ans. (d) To reinforce Derry's change of attitude by never letting him forget what he has learned.

Read the given extract to attempt questions that follow:

4. *MR LAMB: So you believe everything you hear, then?*

DERRY: It was cruel.

MR LAMB: Maybe not meant as such. Just something said between them.

DERRY: Only I heard it. I heard.

MR LAMB: And is that the only thing you ever heard anyone say, in your life?

DERRY: Oh no! I've heard a lot of things.

MR LAMB: So now you keep your ears shut.

DERRY: You're....peculiar. You say peculiar things. You ask questions I don't understand.

MR LAMB: I like to talk. Have company. You don't have to answer questions. You don't have to stop here at all. The gate's open.

(i) Select the option that lists the feelings and attitudes corresponding to the given dialogue:

(i) Lamb says, 'Maybe not meant as such. Just something said between them.'
(ii) Derry replies, 'It was cruel'

(a) 1. Part sympathetic: part hurtful
2. Self-pitying
(b) 1. Part generous: part rational
2. Unforgiving
(c) 1. Part empathising: part critical
2. Hurt
(d) 1. Part understanding: part intolerant
2. Unrelenting

Ans. (b) 1. Part generous: part rational
2. Unforgiving

(ii) 'You ask questions I don't understand.' Why does Derry not understand what Lamb is saying?

(a) Because he is deliberately confusing the boy.
(b) Because Lamb is invite introspection.
(c) Because Lamb preaches philosophy.
(d) Lamb wants to discourage soul searching.

Ans. (b) Because Lamb's questions invite introspection.

(iii) Lamb and the boy at the moment are poles apart in their attitude. Select the best juxtapositions that bring out this diversity.

I. Extroversion
II. Motivation
III. Introversion
IV. Reservation

(a) II and IV
(b) I and II
(c) III and IV
(d) I and III

Ans. (d) I and III

(iv) Only once does Derry laugh in the story. What makes him do that?

(a) The example of bees.
(b) The story of the Beast.
(c) The story of a man withdrawing into his shell.
(d) The story of recovering after amputation.

Ans. (c) The story of a man withdrawing into his shell.

(v) Select the phrase that best emphasises the moral of the story.

(a) Beauty is power.
(b) What you think, and how you look is not in your hands.
(c) Face is the mirror of personality.
(d) Handsome is as handsome does.

Ans. (d) Handsome is as handsome does.

5. *MR. LAMB: Not on my account. I don't mind who comes into the garden. The gate's always open. Only you climbed the garden wall.*

DERRY: [Angry] You were watching me.

MR. LAMB: I saw you. But the gate's open. All welcome. You're welcome. I sit here. I like sitting.

DERRY: I'd not come to steal anything.

MR. LAMB: No, no. The young lads steal....scrump the apples. You're not so young.

(i) What does Mr. Lamb meant by 'Not on my account'?

(a) Not because of him.
(b) Not in his account.
(c) Not according to him.
(d) Not along with him.

Ans. (a) Not because of him.

(ii) Pick the option which correctly states Derry's mental situation when he got angry on being watched by Mr. Lamb.

(a) perturbed
(b) cognitive
(c) snobby
(d) hostile

Ans. (a) perturbed

(iii) Why did Derry get angry?

(a) Mr. Lamb's tone was sarcastic.
(b) Mr. Lamb scolded him.
(c) For being pointed out.
(d) For wanting to get inside unnoticed.

Ans. (c) For being pointed out.

(iv) What clarification did Derry give to Mr. Lamb?

(a) That he had come to ask his well being.
(b) That he hadn't come to steal anything from there.
(c) That he had been asked by his friends to come.
(d) That he had come to his house mistakenly.

Ans. (b) That he hadn't come to steal anything from there.

6. *MR LAMB: Waiting. Watching. Listening. Sitting here or going there. I'll have to see to the bees.*

DERRY: Those other people who come here....do they talk to you? Ask you things?

MR LAMB: Some do, some don't. I ask them. I like to learn.

DERRY: I don't believe in them. I don't think anybody ever comes. You're here all by yourself and miserable and no one would know if you were alive or dead and nobody cares.

MR LAMB: You think what you please.

DERRY: All right then, tell me some of their names.

MR LAMB: What are names? Tom, Dick or Harry.

(i) Fill in the blanks with suitable words:

(a) Mr Lamb's tasks were ______, _______, and _______ .

Ans. waiting, watching, listening to the bees.

(ii) Write words having similar meanings :

(a) despondent (b) bothers

Ans. (a) miserable (b) cares

(iii) Say whether the statement is true or false:

(a) Everybody loved talking with Mr Lamb.

(b) Derry felt that nobody came to Mr Lamb.

Ans. (a) False (b) True

(iv) Find the phrase from the extract that means :

(a) Any random person/names.

Ans. (a) Tom, Dick or Harry.

Multiple Choice Questions

1. Who has written "On The Face of It"?

(a) Susan Hill (b) William Sydne (c) Salman Rushdie (d) Chetan Bhagat

Ans. (a) Susan Hill

2. What is this play featuring?

(a) An old man and a small boy meeting in old man's garden.

(b) Gossip of old man in his garden.

(c) Old man's woes of past.

(d) Brave acts of a small boy.

Ans. (a) An old man and a small boy meeting in old man's garden.

3. What were Derry and Mr. Lamb victims of?

(a) Vision impairment

(b) Physical impairment

(c) War

(d) Mental impairment

Ans. (b) Physical impairment

4. Why did Mr. Lamb help Derry?

(a) Because both were victims of war.

(b) Both were sad.

(c) Both were victims of physical impairment.

(d) Because he wanted Derry to change his view of life.

Ans. (d) Because he wanted Derry to change his view of life.

5. Who is Derry?

(a) Derek-a boy of 14 and has acid burnt on his face.

(b) A small boy with a tin leg.

(c) A boy with mental impairment.

(d) A young boy who lives his life to the fullest.

Ans. (a) Derek-a boy of 14 and has acid burnt on his face.

6. How does Mr. Lamb keep himself busy?

(a) By reading books.

(b) By chatting with people.

(c) By pulling down the ripe crab apples of his garden.

(d) All of the above.

Ans. (d) All of the above.

7. How did Derry enter the garden?

(a) From the front gate.

(b) By climbing the back.

(c) By climbing the front gate.

(d) By climbing the garden wall.

Ans. (d) By climbing the garden wall.

8. Why did Mr. Lamb keep the door of his garden open?

(a) To keep an eye over his garden.

(b) To be safe.

(c) To chat with the people and the children who come there to take fruit.

(d) To make friends.

Ans. (c) To chat with the people and the children who come there to take fruit.

9. Why did children call Mr. Lamb "Lamey Lamb"?

(a) Because he stopped them from taking apples.
(b) He spoke rudely.
(c) They didn't like him.
(d) Because of his broken leg.

Ans. (d) Because of his broken leg.

10. Why didn't Mr. Lamb feel hurt by children's comments?

(a) Because he thought that it suits him.
(b) He loves children.
(c) He likes them.
(d) He want them to play in his garden.

Ans. (a) Because he thought that it suits him.

11. How did Mr. Lamb pick apples?

(a) Bending down.
(b) With the help of his servant.
(c) With the help of children.
(d) Using a ladder and a stick.

Ans. (d) Using a ladder and a stick.

12. Why did Derry go to Mr. Lamb at the end?

(a) Because of his wish to live a free life.
(b) Because he wanted apples.
(c) Because he wanted to play in the garden.
(d) Because he wanted to get rid of never-ending distress.

Ans. (a) Because of his wish to live a free life.

13. Why did Derry's mother stop him to stay with Mr. Lamb?

(a) Because he was physically impaired.
(b) Because he would change him.
(c) Because he talked too much.
(d) Because she didn't want him to stay with a stranger.

Ans. (d) Because she didn't want him to stay with a stranger.

14. How did Mr. Lamb help Derry?

(a) By giving him apples.
(b) By talking to him about his own impairment.
(c) By helping his mother.
(d) By giving him a positive outlook towards life.

Ans. (d) By giving him a positive outlook towards life.

15. Why did Mr. Lamb call Derry blessed?

(a) Because he was young and capable of achieving all his dreams.
(b) Because he had a mother who used to love her.
(c) Because he had friends who loved him.
(d) Because except a burnt face he had a perfectly healthy body.

Ans. (d) Because except a burnt face he had a perfectly healthy body.

16. Which story did Mr. Lamb narrate to Derry?

(a) Cindrella
(b) The Beauty and the Beast
(c) The Dwarfman
(d) The Snowman

Ans. (b) The Beauty and the Beast

17. Why even inspite of physical disability Mr. Lamb did not feel lonely?

(a) Because he was busy in reading books.
(b) Because he had a garden to look after.
(c) Because he had servants who were friendly and sweet.
(d) Because he hever let himself to be alone and keep himself busy.

Ans. (d) Because he hever let himself to be alone and keep himself busy.

18. How the meeting with Mr. Lamb became a turning point for Derry?

(a) He encouraged Derry to be friends with everyone and not to be bothered by their comments.
(b) He taught him to look at everything positively.
(c) He taught him to admire everything.
(d) All of the above.

Ans. (d) All of the above.

19. Why was Derry startled on entering the garden?

(a) Because of the beauty of the garden.

(b) Because of Mr. Lamb's tin leg.

(c) Because he expected no one else but saw Mr. Lamb.

(d) Because he was all alone in the garden.

Ans. (c) Because he expected no one else but saw Mr. Lamb

20. What complex does Derry suffer from?

(a) Superiority (b) Oedipus (c) Inferiority (d) All of these

Ans. (c) Inferiority

21. In 'On the Face of It' the author does not want to convey a message of:

(a) Self-esteem (b) Defeatism (c) Humanism (d) Positivism

Ans. (b) Defeatism

22. Lamb does not have window curtains because:

(i) he cannot afford them.

(ii) he will be able to see trespassers.

(iii) he is open minded.

(iv) he loves outdoors.

(a) (i) is true (ii) is false

(b) (iii) is false (i) is true

(c) (iii) and (iv) are true

(d) (ii) and (iii) are true

Ans. (c) (iii) and (iv) are true

23. Select the options that list the qualities of Mr Lamb:

(i) Affable (ii) Optimistic

(iii) Arrogant (iv) Obstinate

(v) Kind hearted (vi) Altruistic

(a) (i), (ii), (iv) and (v)

(b) (iii), (v) and (vi)

(c) (i), (ii), (v) and (vi)

(d) (i), (ii), (iii) and (vi)

Ans. (c) (i), (ii), (v) and (vi)

24. Lamb's words make an indelible impression on the mind of Derry. Because:

Select the option that verifies this statement.

(a) Lamb told him to defy his parents.

(b) Lamb gave him a new lease of life by changing his perception.

(c) Lamb told him to underestimate his looks.

(d) Lamb said his tin legs do not pain.

Ans. (b) Lamb gave him a new lease of life by changing his perception.

25. Identify the tone of Lamb in the following line 'You don't have to answer questions. You don't have to stop here at all. The gate's open.'

(a) Rude (b) Angry (c) Contemptuous (d) Matter of fact

Ans. (d) Matter of fact

26. Derry says 'weeds' while referring to Lamb's garden. In the light of the circumstances we can say that it was a matter of:

(a) Arrogance (b) Derogatory (c) Frustration (d) Malice

Ans. (c) Frustration

27. Sound echoing the sense is called Onomatopoeia. Which words have the author used to echo the fall of the ladder and the man.

(a) Crash and swish

(b) Creaks and falls

(c) Crash, creaks and thump

(d) Swish, cracks and thump

Ans. (c) Crash, creaks and thump

28. Shutting <u>things out</u>, shutting <u>things in</u>. The underlined phrase suggests that Lamb was:

(a) in two minds.
(b) caught between two worlds.
(c) afraid of thieves.
(d) open to all experiences.

Ans. (d) open to all experiences.

29. "You could give me a hand." What does the sentence imply?

(a) Derry should hand him the ladder.
(b) Derry should climb the tree.
(c) Derry should help in apple picking.
(d) Derry should help in jelly making.

Ans. (c) Derry should help in apple picking.

30. Mr. LAMB: In that way? No, you won't. Bring out the implication of 'in that way'.

(a) In attitude (b) In appearance (c) In mood (d) Disposition

Ans. (b) In appearance

31. 'That's a face only a mother could love." Select the option that brings out the underlying universal truth.

(a) A mother's love is unconditional.
(b) Mothers tolerate everything.
(c) Mothers are obliged to love their children.
(d) Mothers are oblivious to children's faults.

Ans. (a) A mother's love is unconditional.

32. Pick out two figures of speech involved in 'bees buzz'.

(a) Personification and alliteration.
(b) Metaphor and simile.
(c) Alliteration and onomatopoeia.
(d) Onomatopoeia and dramatic irony.

Ans. (c) Alliteration and onomatopoeia.

33. Classify (1) to (4) as fact (F) or opinion (O), based on your reading of 'On the Face of It.'

(1) It's all life.... growing. Same as you and me.
(2) Lord, boy, you've got two arms, two legs and eyes and ears, you've got a tongue and a brain.
(3) The world's got a whole face, and the world's there to be looked at.
(4) Some call them weeds. If you like, then....a weed garden, that.

Ans. (1) F, (2) F, (3) O, (4) O

34. A picture fell off the wall on to his head and killed him. Life is full of different shades of irony. What sort of irony is reflected in this line?

(a) Verbal (b) Situational (c) Comic (d) Poetic

Ans. (b) Situational

35. Two sounds are mentioned at the opening of the play while describing the garden. Pick up the sounds from the list below:

(i) Chirping (ii) Rustling
(iii) Whistling (iv) Howling

(a) (i) and (iv) (b) (iii) and (ii) (c) (iii) and (i) (d) (i) and (ii)

Ans. (d) (i) and (ii)

36. Derry-But I'm not a friend.

"Mr. LAMB: Certainly you are. So far as I'm concerned." In what respect does Lamb consider Derry as a friend?

(a) On humanitarian ground
(b) A fellow victim
(c) On compassionate grounds
(d) A helper

Ans. (a) On humanitarian ground

37. "According to Lamb, something is worse than acid attack." Which option from the list that alludes to what he mentions?

(a) Pity for self
(b) Hatred for others
(c) Cursing fate
(d) Submitting to fate

Ans. (b) Hatred for others

38. Why does Lamb warn Derry to be careful about long grass?

(a) Because he wants to discourage Derry from entering his garden.
(b) Because he may get tangled in the grass.

(c) Because he may trip.

(d) Because he may crush the apples lying in the grass.

Ans. (c) Because he may trip.

39. "Why have you got a tin leg? Mr. Lamb: Real one got blown ________, years back." Complete the phrasal verb as given in the text.

(a) down (b) away (c) up (d) off

Ans. (d) off

40. "Mr. Lamb: It's all relative. Beauty and the beast."

Apart from the reference to the fairy tale, Lamb uses another analogy to show that all things are relative. Select from the list below:

(a) story of a recluse.

(b) war time story.

(c) bees in his garden.

(d) crab apple picking.

Ans. (c) bees in his garden.

41. "It ate my face up. It ate me up." Derry repeats the words ate up in his agitation. The dramatic effect is achieved through devices of:

(i) repetition (ii) resonance

(iii) personification (iv) metaphor

(a) (i) and (ii) (b) (iii) and (iv) (c) (iii) and (i) (d) (ii) and (iv)

Ans. (c) (iii) and (i)

42. In the light of the play, the objective of the playwright is to reveal that ________ more hurtful to the physically challenged.

(a) the physical pain and discomfort

(b) alienation

(c) sympathy

(d) indifference

Ans. (b) alienation

43. "When I'm here. Not the only one. But the world, as much as anywhere." Identify the tone of the character in the given line.

(a) With confidence and conviction.

(b) Confidential and confessing.

(c) Humorous and ironical.

(d) Cantankerous and critical.

Ans. (a) With confidence and conviction.

44. "There's nothing God made that doesn't interest me." In the perspective of the writer, what sort of disposition does Lamb have? Choose from the phrases given below:

(a) Filled with zest for life.

(b) Attention seeking.

(c) Highly imaginative.

(d) Unduly inquisitive.

Ans. (a) Filled with zest for life.

45. "You do hear things. You listen." To what comment of Derry does Lamb respond in this manner?

(a) That he hears people talking.

(b) That he listens to mother's advice.

(c) That he hears the rain on the roof.

(d) That he can listen to the bees buzzing.

Ans. (c) That he hears the rain on the roof.

46. Why does Lamb say he likes his nick name Lamey Lamb?

(a) Because it fits him.

(b) Because it is a kind of poetic expression.

(c) Because it is descriptive.

(d) Because it is classy.

Ans. (a) Because it fits him.

47. Based on your understanding of the play, what quality of human being can see him through the adversities of life?

(a) Escapism (b) Resistance (c) Resilience (d) Rejection

Ans. (c) Resilience

48. What specific things about Mr. Lamb impressed the teen?

(a) Acceptance of his condition.

(b) His jovial nature.

(c) His no nonsense attitude.

(d) All of these

Ans. (d) All of these

49. "Mr. Lamb preserved his happy nature in spite of his disability." What do you think are the ingredients that contributed to this disposition?

(i) His capacity to see silver things.
(ii) Maturity of thought.
(iii) Lack of bitterness.
(iv) Careless nature.

(a) (iii), (ii) and (i) (b) (ii), (iii) and (iv) (c) (i) and (ii) (d) (i), (ii) and (iii)

Ans. (d) (i), (ii) and (iii)

50. "Why is one green growing plant called a ______ and another a flower?" Is a thought provoking question from Lamb. Insert the right word from the text.

(a) thorn (b) grass (c) twig (d) weed

Ans. (d) weed

51. Mr. Lamb says, It's all _______. Complete the given sentence in reference to 'Beauty and the Beast.'

(a) relative (b) a myth (c) imagination (d) interconnected

Ans. (a) relative

52. If Derry hadn't gone back, he would have been accused of ________.

(a) breach of promise
(b) cowardice
(c) frivolous attitude
(d) negligence of duty

Ans. (a) breach of promise

53. The play "On the Face of It" alludes to the idea that:

(a) still waters run deep.
(b) appearances are deceptive.
(c) out of sight out of mind.
(d) strike while the iron is hot.

Ans. (b) appearances are deceptive.

54. On the basis of your understanding of character, identify the most appropriate description of Mr. Lamb from the given options.

(a) A man of few words.
(b) A glib talker.
(c) A life skill counselor.
(d) A garrulous person.

Ans. (c) A life skill counselor.

❑❑

7. Evans Tries an O-Level–By Colin Dexter

Summary :

James Roderick Evans, a kleptomaniac, was imprisoned thrice and every time he escaped from the prison. Now he was in prison for the fourth time and all of a sudden developed a curiosity to appear in O-level German Examination which also was an effort to break the prison. The Governor takes utmost care to see that he is not fooled. Every care was taken to make Evans prepare for the exam. He was tutored by a German tutor for 6 months. The day before the exam, the tutor wished him good luck but made it clear that he had hardly any 'chance of getting through it.' But Evans gave an ironical twist to the tutor's observation by saying 'I may surprise everybody.' On the day of the exam Jackson and Stephens visited Evans' cell. Evans was insisted to take away the hat but he refused saying that it was his lucky charm. Evans cell was bugged so that the Governor could himself listen to each and every conversation in the cell. The invigilator, Rev. S. McLeery, too was searched and then left to complete the task. Stephen sat outside the cell and every now and then, peeped into the cell. The exam went on smoothly. Stephen escorted the invigilator to the main gate and returned back to take a look into Evans' cell and found the invigilator (who looked like Evans sitting in his chair) wounded. He informed the Governor. The invigilator was to be hospitalized but he said that he was alright and asked them to follow Evans. Thus he too escaped the prison. When the invigilator was not found in the hospital, they went to residence of Rev. S. McLeery the invigilator, only to find him 'bound and gagged in his study in Broad Street'. He has been there, since 8.15 a.m which meant that the invigilator in the prison was fake. Then, everything was clear to the Governor. Evans escaped the prison again. But by taking the hint from the question paper, the Governor reached the hotel where Evans was and captured him and came to know how he planned his escape now. Evans surrendered himself to the Governor. The Governor tells Evan they would meet soon. The moment they got rid of the Governor, the so called 'prison officer'-a friend of Evans-unlocked the handcuffs and asked the driver to move fast. Evans tells him to turn to Newbury. Thus, had the last laugh.

Text Book Questions :

Read and find out :

Q. 1. What kind of a person was Evans?

Ans. Evans was a congenital kleptomaniac who was imprisoned in the Oxford Prison. He urged the prison authority to allow him to take the examination for O-level in German as it would help him gain some educational qualification. He was a person with a pleasant personality with no record of violence and had managed to escape thrice from the prison. His intelligent and conspiring mind was the focus of the story. He managed to dodge everyone with his foolproof plans. Even the Governor could not help appreciating his shrewd mind.

Q. 2. What were the precautions taken for the smooth conduct of the examination?

Ans. The Governor was suspicious of the true intentions of Evans in wanting to take the examination. Fearing his fourth escape, the examination was ordered to be conducted inside the prison cell which was installed with a microphone, to keep a check on this intelligent prisoner. His cell was properly scrutinized by the prison staff who took away everything which could pose a threat in the smooth conduct of the examination. On the day of examination, the prison staff was put on a high alert and a special care was promptly taken by locking all doors and gates. Stephens was ordered to keep an eye on the exam proceedings. Even the invigilator, a parson, was frisked thoroughly before the examination.

Q. 3. Did the exam go as scheduled?

Ans. Everything was in order for the examination to start on its scheduled time. The Governor, who was still apprehensive, ordered a last minute change in plan. As a precautionary measure, he ordered frisking of the invigilator before allowing him to carry out his assigned job. The examination started at 9:25 am, ten minutes after than the scheduled time.

Q. 4. Did the Governor and his staff finally heave a sigh of relief?

Ans. Evans was a shrewd man who allowed only a momentary sigh of relief to the Governor and his staff. The examination was supposed to have ended peacefully, but when Stephens rechecked Evans's cell, he was stunned to see a profusely bleeding McLeery still in the cell. He concluded that the man he had escorted to the gate was actually Evans. Measures were taken to recapture Evans with the help of the bleeding McLeery, who was later sent off to a hospital for treatment. However, soon it was exposed that this 'bleeding McLeery' was the real Evans. Finally, when the Governor traced Evans and ordered him to be taken back to the prison with a prison officer in the official van, another conspiracy unfolded. Evans fled again, as the prison officer and the van were a part of his back-up plan. His flawless plans left everyone perplexed and troubled.

Q. 5. Was the injured McLeery able to help the prison officers track Evans?

Ans. The injured McLeery, showcasing his knowledge of German, revealed the supposed plan of Evans through the superimposed question paper. He proposed to guide the officials to the whereabouts of Evans. However, that was later revealed to be a part of the Evans plan to flee to safety, as it was Evans himself who was disguised as the injured McLeery. It could be, thus, noticed that the disguised McLeery's help to the officials was fake as it was just a part of Evan's escape plan.

Q. 6. Did the clues left behind on the question paper; put Evans back in prison again?

Ans. Evans escaped from the prison with the help of a clever, infallible plan. Certain clues were left behind by the shrewd fugitive, which was a 'careless' act according to the Governor. There was a superimposed question paper with directions to the supposed plan. However, it was soon discovered that all of it was fake and a part of the plan to misguide the officials. But the little German that the Governor knew and the 'correction slip', helped them to track him down.

Q. 7. Where did Evans go?

Ans. After deceiving the police intelligently, Evans went to the hotel Golden Lion located in Chipping Norton.

Reading with Insight :

Q. 1. Reflecting on the story, what did you feel about Evans having the last laugh?

Ans. Evans smartly devised and executed the plan of his escape. He managed to fool everyone till the end of the story. He left fake clues to misguide the officials chasing him. Even as the Governor heaved a sigh of relief after nabbing him in the Golden Lion Hotel, Evans was secretly executing another path of his escape. The prison officer and the van used by the Governor for transferring Evans back to the prison were forged. The Governor was happy that ultimately he was able to track him down using his intelligence and knowledge of German language. However, Evans had planned a step ahead. With his successful escape, Evans definitely had a well earned last laugh.

Q. 2. When Stephens comes back to the cell he jumps to a conclusion and the whole machinery blindly goes by his assumption without even checking the identity of the injured 'McLeery'. Does this show how hasty conjectures can prevent one from the obvious? How is the criminal able to predict such negligence?

Ans. On his return, Stephen saw McLerry bleeding profusely in the cell. Presuming the man he had escorted to the gate to be Evans and not McLeery, he raised an alarm. None of the official staff tried to verify whether that person was McLeery. As the bleeding McLeery offered to help the police to track Evans, nobody questioned how he knew the plan. Later, when the Governor nabbed Evans and sent him back to jail with the prison officers, he did not notice that this officer was unknown to him. It was soon unearthed that the officers were Evan's own men who helped him escape again. Thus, it was definite that the gullible officials made speculations which resulted in their negligence. On the contrary, a plotting criminal makes a foolproof plan taking care of the intricacies and does not make hasty assumptions. He made back-up plans. Also, a criminal's mind is observant enough to predict any possible negligence on the part of the officials. Evans too must have easily observed these during his stay in the prison, and planned accordingly.

Q. 3. What could the Governor have done to securely bring back Evans to the prison when he caught him at the Golden Lion? Does that final act of foolishness really prove that 'he was just another good-for-a-giggle, gullible governor, that was all'?

Ans. At the Golden Lion, when the Governor arrested Evans, he should have been extra cautious in sending him back to jail. If he knew the whereabouts of Evan, he should have taken along more police officials. Also, considering the fact that Evans had successfully fooled them many times earlier, he should not have taken chances by sending him in a van with just a couple of police officers whom, apparently, he did not even know. As a result, Evans easily escaped once again. Ideally, the Governor should have escorted Evans himself. Thus, this final act of foolishness really proved that 'he was just another good-for-a-giggle, gullible governor, that was all'.

Q. 4. While we condemn the crime, we are sympathetic to the criminal. Is this the reason why prison staff often develops a soft corner for those in custody?

Ans. 'Crime' and 'criminals' are usually considered synonymous. However, our perception changes when we see a criminal suffering or serving his punishment. This is what happens with the prison staff. Seeing a criminal suffer in the prison, they unwittingly develop a soft corner for him in their hearts. They look at him as a human being and not as a mere criminal. They start appreciating his mental capabilities rather than just remembering his crime. In the story, Jackson lets Evans keep his hat after knowing that he considered it to be his lucky charm. Evans knew the emotional side of Jackson and so hit it directly through his talk about 'lucky charm', and managed to fool the stern and practical officer. Even the Governor could not help noticing his intelligence when he caught him in the hotel. Thus, he was not cruel or stern with Evans, and regrettably, treated him leniently.

Q. 5. Do you agree that between crime and punishment it is mainly a battle of wits?

Ans. In every battle the stronger side wins; and this strength could be physical or mental. However, after reading the story we can conclude that between crime and punishment, it is mainly a battle of wits. It is not always that a criminal gets punished. In the given story, the well trained police officials were easily fooled by the clever Evans, who managed to escape from right under their nose.

Additional Questions :

Short Answer Questions : **(30-40 words)**

Q. 1. Who was James Roderick Evans? Why was he put in the Oxford Prison?

Ans. Evans was a smart young man who was notorious for breaking out of prison. He had a gang of friends who used to make money by imitating other people. He was sent to the Oxford prison because it was thought to be the most secured prison in England.

Q. 2. How was Evan's presence in the prison felt by the authorities?

Ans. Although Evans was a prisoner he was loved by prison authorities. He was smart, tricky, intelligent and the most popular inmate of the prison. Even the prison authorities admired his skills and at times he was also praised by the Governor. His notorious nature of escaping from the prison was always a point of concern for the prison authorities.

Q. 3. Do you think Evan's statement, 'I may surprise everybody,' has some special significance?

Ans. Evans seemed to be telling his teacher that he might surprise everybody by doing well in the examination but in reality, it was a warning that he was going to jolt everybody by escaping from the prison which he had planned.

Q. 4. Why did the Governor apply for an examination for Evans?

Ans. Evans was a prisoner in the Oxford Prison. He had convinced the authorities that he was genuinely interested in learning German so he was tutored for a while. When the tutor announced that Evans was prepared for an 'O' Level exam, the Governor of the prison applied to the Examination Board for his examination.

Q. 5. Who was McLeery? What is his role in the story?

Ans. Rev. McLeery was a parson at St. Mary Mags, a monastery. He was supposed to invigilate Evan's examination at the Oxford Prison. He was about to leave his residence for the prison when two of Evans' friends entered his room, tied and gagged him until Evans had escaped from the prison.

Q. 6. Why was Evans particular about keeping his hat on his head during his exam?

Ans. Evans wore a bobble hat at the time of his examination. When he was asked to remove that, he pleaded not to let it off because he believed it to be his lucky charm. In fact he had hidden some of the makeup materials in his hat which was the reason he didn't want to remove it.

Q. 7. Why did the Governor think of frisking McLeery?

Ans. McLeery was the invigilator of the examination and he was to sit inside Evan's cell while the latter wrote the exam. The Governor had ensured that Evans was thoroughly frisked and there was nothing to fear about anything threatful. When he thought about the possibility of McLeery carrying a paper-knife, he feared that Evans would misuse that and escape by making the parson his hostage.

Q. 8. Why did McLeery's expressions change when he was frisked?

Ans. While frisking Mc Leery, the prison officers found out a semi-inflated rubber tube in his bag. When he was asked about that, McLeery's amiable appearance suddenly changed and he turned shy and embarrassed for having made to admit that he was suffering from piles. In fact that was only an excuse to stop the authorities from asking further questions and to allow him to carry the rubber tube that had some blood inside for the escape drama.

Q. 9. What was the intention behind the call from the Examinations Board?

Ans. It was one of Evans' friends who made the call from the Examination Board. This call was primarily meant for confirming the time of the commencement of examination in order to calculate the end of the examination. The equally important reason behind this call was to misguide the Governor into Hotel Golden Lion to arrest Evans from there and thereby to make the escape safer altogether.

Q.10. The Governor's pride in his little knowledge in German was of great help for Evans to escape. Explain.

Ans. The Governor had acquired a little bit of German earlier and was proud of that. On seeing the correction sheet and faintly recognizing the hidden message that would help him to trace the escaped Evans, he became over-enthusiastic and decided to track the prisoner with the assistance of another officer. Later, when he trapped Evans so 'smartly,' the Governor forgot all the cautions and went blind with pride. This gave Evans a great opportunity to escape.

Q.11. What had 'McLeery' brought with him to the prison to help Evans' escape?

Ans. Evans' friend dressed up like McLeery had brought some very useful articles for Evans' escape. He had worn an extra clerical collar and a clerical front. In his bag, he had carried a semi inflated rubber tube filled with blood. He had also carried a pair of paper scissors which was frisked by the prison authorities.

Q.12. Why did Evans ask for a blanket while writing the exam?

Ans. As a part of his escape plan, Evans had to dress up to look like McLeery, the invigilator. For that he wanted a hiding. Moreover, he had hidden the invigilator's costume under the blanket.

Q.13. How did Stephens feel when he was asked to accompany McLeery out of the prison?

Ans. Stephens was a new officer at the Oxford Prison and was naturally apprehensive about his duties. He was glad that he was in charge of the invigilator and the exam. When he was asked by the Governor to accompany the invigilator out of the prison, Stephens felt greatly flattered and proud of himself.

Q.14. When did the Governor realize that the invigilator was fake?

Ans. The Governor had initially assumed that it was Evans who had run out of the prison after hitting the invigilator. But later, when he made a call to the Radcliffe Hospital, was informed that the hospital had not admitted the invigilator. In the state of confusion, the Governor searched for the parson at Mary Mags, his residence and confirmed that the parson who was the actual invigilator was tied and gagged in his room and the one who came as the invigilator was Evan's accomplice.

Q.15. Why did Evans want the Governor to arrest him at Hotel Golden Lion?

Ans. Evans' masterminded plan was intelligently crafted. He wanted to ensure that his plan was to take everyone by surprise. To do that, he wanted the Governor to get him arrested and feel elated, proud, over-confident and consequently less careful about keeping Evans under high security.

Q.16. Evans was 'visibly shaken' when he saw the Governor in his room in the hotel. Why was he shaken?

Ans. It was a part of the escape plan that the Governor had to come to the Golden Lion Hotel to arrest Evans from there and take him to the prison. The purpose was to make the Governor believe that he was really intelligent and efficient and thereby become careless. It was because of Evans who pretended to be really caught.

Q. 17. Should criminals in the prison be given the opportunity of learning and education?

Ans. No one should be denied the right to education. If the criminals in prison are provided with education and work-skills, their life can turn towards a bright and crime-free future. Education can help them become responsible citizens, therefore, efforts should be put in to provide opportunity of learning and education even to the criminals in prisons.

Q. 18. Why is the Governor called a 'good for a giggle Governor?'

Ans. The Governor was an intelligent and smart man. He was successful in tracing Evans in the Hotel Golden Lion and arresting him, but he did not realize that it was Evans who wanted the Governor to arrest him. When he caught Evans, the Governor thought that he was the most intelligent prison governor in the world and drove to the prison dreaming of the praises and promotion he would be given for that arrest. In the prison, he came to know that he was fooled by Evans and the world would only giggle at him.

Q. 19. How did Evans escape from Detective Carter?

Ans. Disguised as an invigilator, Evans misguided detective Carter in the pretext of helping the officer to find the escaped Evans. When they reached Radcliff Hospital, Evans pretended to be the most critical and told the detective to admit him in the hospital. Carter wanted to drive the wounded invigilator into the hospital but Evans advised him to call the ambulance and drop him on the roadside to be picked by the ambulance so that the detective could continue his chase.

Q. 20. Can you imagine what had happened when the Governor reached the prison?

Ans. While driving to the prison the Governor thought that he was the most efficient and intelligent prison governor in the world. He got so confident and overwhelmed that he became careless. When he reached the prison he was shocked to find that Evans and his friends had escaped by fooling and disgracing him. He realized that he too was one among the idiots like Stephens and Jackson.

Q. 21. Why was Evans not ready to remove his hat ?*

Ans. When Evans was asked by the prison officer, Mr. Jackson, to take off his hat and he denied doing that. He was asked by the officer to smarten himself in half an hour. After half an hour, he was seen with his hat and was ordered to take it off. In reply, he said that the hat was a symbol of good luck for him and he won't take it off.

Q. 22. Why did the prison officers call Evans, 'Evans the Break'?

Ans. The prison officers called Evans, 'Evans the Break' because he was a habitual jail breaker. Before being shifted to the Oxford Prison, he had tried breaking out of the previous prison thrice.

Long Answer Questions : (120-150 words)

Q. 1. Do you think that the Governor was really intelligent? Support your answer with instances.

Ans. The Governor was a very intelligent officer but his over-confidence was his weak point. The instances of his intelligence could be seen at various places in the story. He didn't believe that Evans was genuinely interested in learning German when he noticed that Evans didn't understand the basic German expression, 'Gutten Gluck.' He was doubtful when the call came from the Examination Board and he made a return call to confirm if the call really came from the Board. It was his intelligence to frisk the invigilator and find the rubber tube. It was he who discovered the secret message regarding the assault on the invigilator superimposed at the back of the question paper. Soon he found out that the real McLeery had never come to the prison and that it was Evans who had escaped from the prison as the injured invigilator. The Governor deserved praises for tracing Evans to Hotel Golden Lion at Chipping Norton and arresting him.

Q. 2. How far was Stephens helpful for Evans' escape?

Ans. Stephens was a newly-recruited officer in the prison. He was very particular about showing his efficiency in front of the higher authorities and was glad to be incharge of Evans' examination which was a risky job indeed. Evans complained of Stephens' breathing and got him naturally out of the cell. Once out of the cell, Stephens kept peeping into the cell but soon found it childish. To show that he was very confident and efficient, he left the cell door and came after short intervals. The short intervals soon became longer giving time for Evans to dress himself up inside the cell. Stephens was taken to the highest joy when he received the fake call from the Governor to take the invigilator out of the prison. He in his pride took the invigilator out of the prison and made way for Evans' escape in a wonderful way.

Q. 3. What were the precautions taken for the smooth conduct of the examination?

Ans. Since Evans had already escaped from the jail on three earlier occasions, there was always a constant fear that he might make another attempt to escape. Therefore, all the possible precautions were taken to see that the O'level German examination arranged in the prison did not provide any means of escape. The Governor personally monitored all security arrangements and heavily guarded the Recreation Block from where he expected the prisoner to make another break. Evans cell was thoroughly checked by Jackson to score off the possibility of the presence of an incriminating material which might hamper the smooth conduct of the examination. His nail scissors, nail-file and razor were taken away; and to keep a strict watch on the activities of the cell during the examination, the Governor got it bugged. A police officer named Stephen was posted to keep a constant vigil on his activities. The invigilator, too was frisked to make sure that he carried no objectionable material with him.

Previous Years Questions :

Q. 1. Which article in McLeery's suitcase played perhaps the most significant role in Evans' escape and how?

Ans. The semi-inflated rubber ring played the most significant role in Evans' escape. It was filled with pig's blood from the slaughterhouse in Kidlington. It was mixed with actual blood with 1/10th of its own volume of 3.8 per cent trisodium citrate. Evan covered his head and face with this blood and thus was able to hide his identify from the eyes of the prison officer.

Q. 2. How did the Governor, Oxford Prison describe Evans to the Secretary, Examination Board ?

Ans. The Governor of the Oxford Prison made a call to the Secretary of Examination Board telling him that a prisoner named Evans wanted to take the 0-level examination in German. The Governor then requested the Secretary to see whether the arrangements could be made in the prison itself.

Q. 3. What was his German teacher's opinion of Evans' proficiency in German ?

Ans. Evans' German tutor started giving him tuitions for six months in night classes in the prison itself. Evans wanted to take the (O)level examination in German. When he was permitted by the Governor and the Board

---

* are board exam questions from previous years

to take the examination, his tutor came to meet him the day before. He wished him good luck but said that he hardly had any 'chance of getting through'. But Evans gave an ironical twist by saying that he would surprise everybody.

Q. 4. What could the Governor have done to securely bring Evans back to the prison from the 'Golden Lion' ?

Ans. The Governor was extra careful at every place except in the end. He took all the steps and precautions for not letting Evans escape anyway. He got success also to bring Evans back to the prison from Golden Lion but in the end acted foolishly. He could not judge Evans' cleverness. He should understand that Evans could not go out of the cell in Mcleery's disguise. McLeery was found injured and covered with blood in the cell. No one took the pain to check the identity of the injured. It was Evans himself. Further, when Evans was arrested and handcuffed, he was made to sit in the police van. But the van and driver's identification was not done and Evans was able to escape.

Q. 5. Describe the precautions taken by the prison officers to prevent Evans from escaping.

Ans. Special precautions were taken by the prison staff to prevent Evans from escaping during his O-level German test. The test was to be taken where he was kept. A parson from St. Mary Mags was called to invigilate and to keep the prisoner incommunicado during the exam. Evans was kept in the heavily guarded Recreational Block. There were two locked doors between his cell and the yard, which boasted of a high wall. All the prison officers were also on high alert. The Governor got a microphone installed in Evans' cell, while Stephens kept, a hawk's eye on Evans. Two prison officers, Mr. Jackson and Mr. Stephens, thoroughly checked his cell for any sign of a possible escape. Even his razor, nail filer and mail scissors were taken away.

Q. 6. Give a character-sketch of the Governor of Oxford Prison based on your understanding of the story 'Evans Tries an O-level'.

Ans. The Governor of Oxford Prison was a generous man who allowed Evans to appear for the exam. Evans was a criminal and had escaped from jail twice, so the Governor took all the possible precautions for the smooth conduct of the examination. The examination had been arranged in the cell itself. The door was locked one day before and the security was made very tight. Everything was checked thoroughly to ensure that there was no way that could help him escape. This shows that he was very wise and on the other, hand he was so simple that he couldn't understand the cunningness of Evans.

Reference to Context :

Read the given extract to attempt questions that follow:

1. *"Just one thing, Governor. He's not a violent sort of fellow, is he? I don't want to know his criminal record or anything like that, but — "*

"No. There's no record of violence. Quite a pleasant sort of chap, they tell me. Bit of a card, really. One of the stars at the Christmas concert. Imitations, you know the sort of thing: Mike Yarwood stuff.

No, he's just a congenital kleptomaniac, that's all." The Governor was tempted to add something else, but he thought better of it. He'd look after that particular side of things himself.

(i) The Secretary's breaking his sentence with 'but' - suggests he is:

(a) Sceptical (b) Disapproving (c) Aghast (d) Cynical

Ans. (a) Sceptical

(ii) Of the four meanings of 'Bit of a card', select the option that matches in meaning with its usage in the extract.

(a) Somewhat stupid.
(b) A witty or eccentric person.
(c) Totally mad.
(d) A dangerous individual.

Ans. (b) A witty or eccentric person.

(iii) The fact that Evans was good at imitation _______ his impersonation as McLeery.

(a) paradox (b) double entendres (c) foreshadows (d) flashbacks

Ans. (c) foreshadows

(iv) Select the option that reveals the feelings towards Evans corresponding to the 'Mike Yarwood stuff.'

(a) Sarcastic and bitter.
(b) Ironical and derogatory.
(c) Jocular and condescending.
(d) Appreciative.

Ans. (c) Jocular and condescending.

(v) Select the option that lists reasons why Evans has been called 'a congenital kleptomaniac'.

(a) He is a liar.
(b) He is a ruthless character.
(c) He is a compulsive law breaker.
(d) He is a born thief.

Ans. (d) He is a born thief.

Read the given extract to attempt questions that follow:

2. *At 8.30 the following morning, Evans had a visitor. Two visitors, in fact. He tucked his grubby string-vest into his equally grubby trousers, and stood up from his bunk, smiling cheerfully. "Mornin", Mr Jackson. This is indeed an honour."*

Jackson was the senior prison officer on D Wing, and he and Evans had already become warm enemies. At Jackson's side stood Officer Stephens, a burly, surly-looking man, only recently recruited to the profession.

Jackson nodded curtly. "And how's our little Einstein this morning, then?"

"Wasn't 'e a mathematician, Mr Jackson?"

"I think 'e was a Jew, Mr. Jackson."

Evans's face was unshaven, and he wore a filthy-looking red-and-white bobble hat upon his head. "Give me a chance, Mr Jackson. I was just goin' to shave when you bust in."

(i) ***At 8.30 the following morning, Evans had a visitor. Two visitors, in fact.*** **Who was the other visitor?**

(a) McLeery
(b) Stephens
(c) Senior prison officer
(d) A friend

Ans. (b) Stephens

(ii) Name the literary device used in the expression 'warm enemies'.

(a) idiom (b) oxymoron (c) personification (d) irony

Ans. (b) oxymoron

(iii) Jackson calls Evans little Einstein because he ___________. Choose a description that can fill the blank.

(a) admires his intellect
(b) appreciates his writing O-Level
(c) is poking fun at Evan's ambition
(d) critical of Evan's attempt

Ans. (c) is poking fun at Evan's ambition

(iv) Stephens is described as a 'burly, surly- looking man'. How would you interpret this?

(a) Huge and unfriendly.
(b) Big built and strong.
(c) Heavily built and bad tempered.
(d) Muscular and sinewy.

Ans. (c) Heavily built and bad tempered.

(v) How would you describe Evan's behaviour from this interlude?

(a) Bold and defiant.
(b) Diffident and cautious.
(c) Affable and nonchalant.
(d) Respectful and humble.

Ans. (c) Affable and nonchalant.

Read the given extract to attempt questions that follow:

3. *Stephens felt pleased that the Governor had asked him, and not Jackson, to see McLeery off the premises, and all in all the morning had gone pretty well. But something stopped him from making his way directly to the canteen for a belated cup of coffee. He wanted to take just one last look at Evans. It was like a programme he'd seen on TV — about a woman who could never really convince herself that she'd locked the front door when she'd gone to bed: often she'd got up twelve, fifteen, sometimes twenty times to check the bolts.*

(i) What term is given to the condition of the woman mentioned here?

(a) Obsessive compulsive disorder.
(b) Restless uncontrolled response.
(c) Habitual anxiety syndrome.
(d) Insomnia.

Ans. (a) Obsessive compulsive disorder.

(ii) What was the first thing Stephens did when he realize McLeery is wounded?

(a) He called a doctor.
(b) He shouted for Jackson.
(c) He called the police.
(d) He rang for ambulance.

Ans. (b) He shouted for Jackson.

(iii) What tell-tale signs of the person he escorted out should have warned Stephens?

1. His long coat.
2. His dialect and gait.
3. His slim frame.
4. Accentuated Scottish accent.

(a) 1 and 2 (b) 2 and 4 (c) 2 and 3 (d) 3 and 4

Ans. (d) 3 and 4

(iv) Mention the things Evans had somehow concealed.

(a) False beard and moustache
(b) A pair of glasses and pocket watch
(c) A dog collar and a weapon and spray
(d) Glasses, beard and a dog collar

Ans. (d) Glasses, beard and a dog collar

(v) Evans has been nicknamed 'The Break' for his record of breaking prison. Choose the apt word that is synonymous with nick name.

(a) Sobriquet (b) Pseudonym (c) Pen name (d) Alter name

Ans. (a) Sobriquet

Read the given extract to attempt questions that follow:

4. *He unlocked his bedroom door and closed it quietly behind him — and then stood frozen to the spot, like a man who has just caught a glimpse of the Gorgon. Sitting on the narrow bed was the very last man in the world that Evans had expected — or wanted — to see. "It's not worth trying anything," said the Governor quietly, as Evans's eyes darted desperately around the room. "I've got men all round the place." .) He let the words sink in. "Women, too. Didn't you think the blonde girl in reception was rather sweet?" Evans was visibly shaken. He sat down slowly in the only chair the small room could offer, and held his head between his hands. For several minutes there was utter silence.*

(i) A Gorgon has the power to turn onlookers to stone. Choose from the list the best word that suits the expression.

(a) Petrified (b) Frozen (c) Solidified (d) Immobilized

Ans. (a) Petrified

(ii) In which place is Evans now?

(a) In the foyer of Golden Mane.
(b) In a hotel room in the centre of Chipping Norton.
(c) In a room in Golden Lion.
(d) In the reception room of Broad Street Hotel.

Ans. (c) In a room in Golden Lion.

(iii) *"I've got men all round the place."* How many men had the Governor placed around the place?

(a) A staggering number.
(b) A couple of men.
(c) Five to ten.
(d) None.

Ans. (d) None.

(iv) How would you describe the protagonist of *Evans Tries an O Level?*

(a) Ingenious (b) Indigenous (c) Impetuous (d) Indolent

Ans. (a) Ingenious

(v) How can you best describe the end of the story?

(a) An anti-climax (b) A twist in the tale (c) Ambiguous (d) A tragicomedy

Ans. (b) A twist in the tale

Read the given extract to attempt questions that follow:

5. *All right, so far. But one of the objects in McLeery's suitcase was puzzling him sorely. "Do you mind telling me why you've brought this, sir?" He held up a smallish semi-inflated rubber ring, such as a young child with a waist of about twelve inches might have struggled into. "You thinking of going for a swim, sir?" McLeery's hitherto amiable demeanour was slightly ruffled by this tasteless little pleasantry, and he answered Jackson somewhat sourly. "If ye must know, I suffer from haemorrhoids, and when I'm sitting down for any length o' time —" "Very sorry, sir. I didn't mean to, er..." The embarrassment was still reddening Jackson's cheeks when he found the paper-knife at the bottom of the case. "I think I'd better keep this though, if you don't mind, that is, sir."*

(i) One of the objects in McLeery's suitcase was puzzling him sorely. Why was it puzzling?

(a) Because it was too small.
(b) It was incongruous.
(c) It was crudely made.
(d) It had a funny shape.

Ans. (b) It was incongruous.

(ii) 'hitherto amiable demeanour' – the expression means Mcleery had __________so far. Fill in the blank with the right phrase from the list.

(a) a composed expression
(b) a funny expression
(c) pleasant bearing
(d) nonchalant attitude

Ans. (c) pleasant bearing

(iii) Pick up a word from the extract which is the antonym of pleasantly?

(a) sorely (b) sourly (c) ruffled (d) tasteless

Ans. (b) sourly

(iv) What is the common name for haemorrhoids?

(a) Cyst (b) Thrombosis (c) Boil (d) Piles

Ans. (d) Piles

(v) Whose presence in the cell did Evans object to?

(a) The Secretary of the Examinations Board.
(b) The senior prison officer.
(c) The newly appointed prison officer.
(d) Detective Superintendent.

Ans. (c) The newly appointed prison officer.

Read the given extract to attempt questions that follow:

6. *"Nah! Course I couldn't. I knew roughly what it was all about, but we just 'oped it'd throw a few spanners in the works — you know, sort of muddle everybody a bit.' The Governor stood up. "Tell me one thing before we go. How on earth did you get all that blood to pour over your head? Evans suddenly looked a little happier. "Clever, sir. Very clever, that was — 'ow to get a couple o' pints of blood into a cell, eh? When there's none there to start off with, and when, er, and when the "invigilator", shall we say, gets, searched before 'e comes in. Yes, sir. ..... Evans grinned feebly. "Clever, though, wasn't it? "Must have been a tricky job sticking a couple of pints "Nah! You've got it wrong, sir. No problem about that."*

(i) Select the option that lists reasons why Evans is considered clever by Jackson?

I. Shrewd judgement of characters.
II. Indulging in jokes.
III. Meticulous way of answering the paper.
IV. Proactive planning.

(a) II and III (b) IV and II (c) I and IV (d) IV and II

Ans. (c) I and IV

(ii) "Throw a few spanners in the works." Which option given below fits the idiom best in the context ?

(a) Cause delay in decision making.
(b) Cause obstacle in some plan.
(c) To add some extra fittings to the arrangement.
(d) To muddle a fool proof plan.

Ans. (b) Cause obstacle in some plan.

(iii) "Must have been a tricky job sticking a couple of pints." What was brought, in pints?

(a) Red port wine (b) Pig marrow (c) Swine's blood (d) Human blood

Ans. (c) Swine's blood

(iv) "Nah! You've got it wrong, sir. No problem about that." What was the problem?

(a) To hide the blood from officers.
(b) To stick a couple of pints into a cell.
(c) To keep the blood in a flowing form.
(d) To pour blood on self.

Ans. (c) To keep the blood in a flowing form.

(v) Human blood was required to prevent_______Complete the sentence with the most appropriate option from the list.

(a) congealing (b) bleeding (c) clotting (d) thickening

Ans. (c) clotting

Read the given extract to attempt questions that follow:

7. *"We'll get him, sir," said Bell. "We'll get him, with a bit o'luck." The Governor sat back, and lit a cigarette. Ye gods! What a beautifully laid plan it had all been! What a clever fellow Evans was! Careless leaving that question paper behind; but then, they all made their mistakes somewhere along the line. Well, almost all of them. And that's why very very shortly Mr clever-clever Evans would be back inside doing his once more.*

(i) Clue intended to be misleading is called a red herring. Which of the following served as the red herring in the beautifully laid plan of Evans?

(a) Evan's conversation just before exam.
(b) Ordnance Survey Map for Oxfordshire.
(c) Instructions given before the start of the test.
(d) The paperknife which McLeery brought.

Ans. (b) Ordnance Survey Map for Oxfordshire.

(ii) On the hindsight we learn the injured McLeery leaves the prison in police car as a________.

(a) as a prisoner (b) as a police officer (c) as a witness (d) as a convict

Ans. (c) as a witness

(iii) Where had Evans procured the props to impersonate as the parson?

(a) From the prison house.
(b) An officer smuggled them in.
(c) In the suitcase brought by the invigilator.
(d) Peeled off from the invigilator.

Ans. (d) Peeled off from the invigilator.

(iv) But then, they all made their mistakes somewhere along the line–so thinks the Governor at this juncture; but later, we come to know he himself made the biggest blunder. What, in literary term, does this situation prove to be?

(a) Ironical (b) Ridiculous (c) Mirthful (d) Identical

Ans. (a) Ironical

(v) "Ye Gods, what a beautifully made plan it had been "Select the option that lists the feelings and attitudes corresponding to the Governor's thoughts on Evans towards the end of the story:

(a) Grudgingly admiring.
(b) Satirical.
(c) Scathing and critical.
(d) Half fun and half derogatory.

Ans. (a) Grudgingly admiring.

8. *"Evans the Break" as the prison officers called him. Thrice he'd escaped from prison, and but for the recent wave of unrest in the maximum-security establishments up north, he wouldn't now be gracing the Governor's premises in Oxford; and the Governor was going to make absolutely certain that he wouldn't be disgracing them. Not that Evans was a real burden: just a persistent, nagging presence. He'd be all right in Oxford, though: the Governor would see to that — would see to it personally. And besides, there was just a possibility that Evans was genuinely interested in O-level German. Just a slight possibility. Just a very slight possibility.*

(i) Complete the following statement :

(a) The prison officers called him ____________.
(b) Evans was gracing the _________________.

Ans. (a) Evans the Break (b) Governor's premises in Oxford

(ii) Pick out the antonyms of the given words :

(a) calm (b) honouring

Ans. (a) unrest (b) disgracing

(iii) Name the following :

(a) an educational institution
(b) a European language

Ans. (a) Oxford (b) German

(iv) Find the words from the extract that mean :

(a) chance (b) sincerely

Ans. (a) possibility (b) genuinely

9. *At 8.45 the same morning the Reverend Stuart McLeery left his bachelor flat in Broad Street and stepped out briskly towards Carfax. The weatherman reported temperatures considerably below the normal for early June, and a long black overcoat and a shallow-crowned clerical hat provided welcome protection from the steady drizzle which had set in half an hour earlier and which now spattered the thick lenses of his spectacles. In his right hand he was carrying a small brown suitcase, which contained all that he would need for his morning duties, including a sealed question paper envelope, a yellow invigilation form, a special "authentication" card from the Examinations Board.*

(i) Write down the names of any two professions mentioned in the extract.

Ans. Reverend/ priest, weatherman

(ii) Pick out words from the extract that are synonymous with :

(a) shelter (b) priestly

Ans. (a) protection (b) clerical

(iii) List the things the Reverend was carrying in his suitcase:

Ans. (a) a sealed question paper envelope.

(b) a yellow invigilation form.

(c) a special authentication card from the Examinations Board.

(iv) Fill in the blanks with suitable words:

(a) The Reverend lived in a flat in ______.

(b) The weatherman reported normal temperature for early _______.

Ans. (a) Broad Street (b) June

Multiple Choice Questions

1. Who ordered Evans to take off his hat?

(a) Jackson (b) Stephens (c) The Governor (d) The invigilator

Ans. (a) Jackson

2. Who checked the cell thoroughly?

(a) Stephens
(b) The Governor
(c) Jackson and Stephens
(d) Jackson

Ans. (d) Jackson

3. Who arrived first on the scene after Stephen found McLeery?

(a) Jackson
(b) Stephens
(c) Detective Superintendent Carter
(d) Governor

Ans. (c) Detective Superintendent Carter

4. What did the Governor want Carter to do?

(a) He wanted him to find Evans.
(b) He wanted him to go with Evans.
(c) He wanted him to accompany Evans.
(d) He wanted him to accompany injured McLerry.

Ans. (d) He wanted him to accompany injured McLerry.

5. Why did Evans want to write exam?

(a) To pursue higher studies.
(b) To impress others.
(c) To hoodwink authorities.
(d) For self-satisfaction.

Ans. (c) To hoodwink authorities.

6. Visual impact like blood pouring out of a wounded man's body often overrides our rationality making us jump to conclusion. Based on what happens in the story, 'Evans Tries an O-Level', select the best saying that matches the situation.

(a) Seeing is believing
(b) You only see what your eyes want to see
(c) Out of sight, out of mind
(d) The mind is for seeing, the heart is for hearing

Ans. (b) You only see what your eyes want to see

7. The clues given in the fake sheet were written to lead the Governor on:

(a) a wild goose chase
(b) a primrose path
(c) hoodwink
(d) all of these

Ans. (a) a wild goose chase

8. What is your perception of Evans the Break in the story 'Evans Tries an O-Level'.

(a) He is an erudite person.
(b) He is an intellectual giant.
(c) He is a timid character.
(d) He is sharp witted and astute.

Ans. (d) He is sharp witted and astute.

9. The Governor was proud and overjoyed at finally nabbing the culprit. What was the main reason for him being fooled by Evans?

(a) His animosity towards Evans.
(b) His elation at finding Evans.
(c) His generosity.
(d) His admiration for Evans' intelligence.

Ans. (b) His elation at finding Evans.

10. What is the irony of the title Evans Tries an O-Level?

(a) Evans excels in language; so hopes to get O-Level despite being a prisoner.

(b) Evans is ambitious; so tries an O-Level to be academically qualified.

(c) Evans gets an O-Level; but in outwitting jail authorities.
(d) Evans creates history by failing in the exam.

Ans. (c) Evans gets an O-Level; but in out witting jail authorities.

11. Evans was only _______ for the jailors. Select the best option to fill in the blank.

(a) an unpleasant inmate
(b) a hooligan
(c) a heinous criminal
(d) a nagging irritation

Ans. (d) a nagging irritation

12. Based on the reading of the story of Evans, what message is projected by the author?

(a) Never be kind to prisoners.
(b) Never ever underestimate the chicanery of a criminal.
(c) Catch a thief and there ends the story.
(d) All prisoners should be handcuffed.

Ans. (b) Never ever underestimate the chicanery of a criminal.

13. The jail break was meticulously planned. Enumerate the various steps of this elaborate planning in the order of its happening.

(i) Getting a tutor to teach German.
(ii) Escaping in the police van.
(iii) Impersonating as parson.
(iv) Inviting invigilator from the parsonage.
(v) Requesting permission to write O-Level.

(a) (i), (v), (iv), (iii), (ii)
(b) (ii), (iv), (i), (iii), (v)
(c) (i), (ii), (iii), (iv), (v)
(d) (i), (iii), (ii), (v), (iv)

Ans. (a) (i), (v), (iv), (iii), (ii)

14. The blanket was used by Evans to:

(a) throw at McLeery and overpower him.
(b) puzzle Stephens.
(c) change his get up under its cover.
(d) he liked the smell and feel of it.

Ans. (c) change his get up under its cover.

15. Pick up the right combination from the list to describe Evans in the light of what happens:

(a) agile, alert, altruistic.
(b) belligerent, bilious, blatant.
(c) cantankerous, calculating, cautious.
(d) deft, dramatic, dexterous.

Ans. (d) deft, dramatic, dexterous.

16. "You thinking of going for a swim, sir?" Which intriguing object made Jackson ask this question?

(a) A piece of swim suit.
(b) A tube of sunscreen cream.
(c) A bottle of anti-tan lotion.
(d) A semi-inflated rubber ring.

Ans. (d) A semi-inflated rubber ring.

17. "How am I supposed to concentrate on my exam... with someone breathing down my neck?" Who is being accused of breathing down Evan's neck?

(a) Governor
(b) Stephens
(c) McLeery
(d) Jackson

Ans. (b) Stephens

18. And within two minutes the Governor was wondering whether that could be a hoax. Select the suitable option which has made the Governor suspect a hoax.

(a) A false alarm from the prison.
(b) A phone call from the Secretory of Examination.
(c) A call from The Magistrates' Court.
(d) Evans asking the Governor for a blanket.

Ans. (c) A call from The Magistrates' Court.

19. On his every minute observation through peep hole, Stephen noticed Evans had covered himself with the regulation blanket. What was the first thought that flashed across the officer's mind?

(a) That Evans might be shivering with cold.
(b) That Evans may spring a surprise attack on McLeery.
(c) That Evans was trying to cheat in the exam.
(d) That Evans wanted to have a cosy sleep under the blanket.

Ans. (b) That Evans may spring a surprise attack on McLeery.

20. Good-for-a-giggle, gullible governor,- What is this sort of expression classified as in English language?

(a) Extended epithet
(b) Alliteration
(c) Transferred epithet
(d) Assonance

Ans. (b) Alliteration

21. What does Superintendent Carter say about the condition of 'McLeery' when they left him?

(a) He was groggy (b) He was dizzy (c) He was blabbering (d) He looked wan

Ans. (a) He was groggy

22. When the Governor was told that the ambulance could not find the injured person, the truth seemed to hit him with an almost physical impact somewhere __________.

(a) at the back of his mind (c) in the back of his mind

(b) right in the middle of forehead (d) in the back of his neck

Ans. (d) in the back of his neck

23. It had not been Evans, impersonating _______, who had walked out; it had been Evans, impersonating _______, who had stayed in. Fill in the blanks with the most appropriate pairs.

(a) McLeery, himself (b) himself, McLeery (c) McLeery, Mcleery (d) None of these

Ans. (c) McLeery, McLeery

24. _______ and then stood frozen to the spot, like a man who has just caught a glimpse of the Gorgon. Identify the literary devices used here.

(i) Hyperbole (ii) Personification (iii) Simile (iv) Metaphor

(a) (i) and (ii) (b) (ii) and (iii) (c) (iii) and (iv) (d) (i) and (iii)

Ans. (d) (i) and (iii)

25. "He sat up at last, and managed to smile ruefully." Select the word that best expresses the meaning of the underlined word.

(a) Magnanimously (b) Regretfully (c) Repentantly (d) Guiltily

Ans. (b) Regretfully

26. Name the chemical that was used to prevent clotting of the blood:

(a) Sodium nitrate (b) Tricitrate sodium (c) Trisodium nitrate (d) Trisodium citrate

Ans. (d) Trisodium citrate

27. And if you take an Ordnance Survey Map for Oxfordshire, you find that the six-figure reference _________ lands you bang in the middle of Chipping Norton."What is the six figure mentioned in the map?

(a) 303/271 (b) 313/271 (c) 313/241 (d) 333/241

Ans. (b) 313/271

28. Phew! That really had been a close call. What would have been a close call for Evans?

(a) Jackson asking about the semi inflated ring. (c) Stephens peeping through the key hole.

(b) Jackson asking him to take off his hat. (d) Governor calling the duty officer on phone.

Ans. (b) Jackson asking him to take off his hat.

29. The really important thing was for the phone to ring just before the exam finished. What was the purpose of this?

(a) To get everyone out of the way for a couple of minutes.

(b) To distract the attention of Jackson.

(c) To warn McLeery to be vigilant.

(d) To help McLeery to impersonate as Evans.

Ans. (a) To get everyone out of the way for a couple of minutes

30. So, you see, sir, that correction slip killed two little birds with a single stone, didn't it? What were the two little birds?

(a) The name of the road and time examination started.

(b) The name of the hotel, and the exact time the exam started.

(c) The name of the examiner and the duration of exam.

(d) The name of the street where the hotel was situated.

Ans. (b) The name of the hotel, and the exact time the exam started.

31. Find out the pair of given words that have a close connection

(a) Stephen and the silent officer at hotel.

(b) Rev McLeery and the van driver.

(c) The fake McLeery and the man at the wheel of the prison van.

(d) The invigilator and the silent officer.

Ans. (c) The fake McLeery and the man at the wheel of the prison van.

34. Evans is called 'Bit of card' in the initial part of the story. Select the best option to explain the meaning:

(a) a smart fellow
(b) a cheat
(c) a goofy and stupid fellow
(d) an intelligent fellow

Ans. (c) a goofy and stupid fellow

35. "Would have cost him a packet if he'd been outside." Select the suitable option from the given statements that denotes what would have cost a packet.

(a) O-level exam
(b) Individual tuition
(c) Material to study
(d) Conduct of examination

Ans. (b) Individual tuition

38. Based on your reading of the text identify from the given list the meaning of incommunicado.

(a) In communication with others.
(b) Restricting interaction with others.
(c) Prohibiting any form of contact with others.
(d) Keeping quiet.

Ans. (c) Prohibiting any form of contact with others.

39. "Evans the Break" as the prison officers called him. ________ he'd escaped from prison. Fill in the gap.

(a) twice
(b) once
(c) innumerable times
(d) thrice

Ans. (d) thrice

40. <u>A cat in hell's chance of</u> getting through. In the light of the context, what does the underlined phrase mean?

(a) A fat chance to get through.
(b) Hardly any possibility to clear the exam.
(c) A strong lucky streak.
(d) A cat has nine lives; so does Evans.

Ans. (b) Hardly any possibility to clear the exam.

42. Jackson and Evans had already become <u>warm enemies.</u> Two opposing words are forcibly collided in the underlined expression. What figure of speech is used in this expression?

(a) Portmanteau
(b) Metaphor
(c) Oxymoron
(d) Dramatic irony

Ans. (c) Oxymoron

43. 'When he's finished scraping that ugly mug of his.' This means:

(a) shaving his head.
(b) tonsuring.
(c) shaving his beard.
(d) washing his face.

Ans. (c) shaving his beard.

44. The way Evans persuades Jackson to allow him to wear the hat shows him as a:

(a) keen observer.
(b) a mind reader.
(c) a crafty old man.
(d) a confidence trickster.

Ans. (b) a mind reader.

45. "Just this once, then, Shirley Temple." Why is Evans called by this name?

(a) Because of his handsome features.
(b) Because of his feminine manners.
(c) Because of his penchant for dressing.
(d) Because of his long, wavy hair.

Ans. (d) Because of his long, wavy hair.

46. As Rev McLeery proceeded towards the prison, his over coat protected him from:

(a) freezing wind.
(b) torrential rain.
(c) steady drizzle.
(d) hail storm.

Ans. (c) steady drizzle.

47. "Nobody in his senses would take any chance with you." What is implied by this remark?

(a) That Evans was a consummate liar.
(b) That Evans can outwit anyone in language tests.
(c) That Evans is an expert in jail breaking.
(d) That Evans is a cut throat.

Ans. (c) That Evans is an expert in jail breaking.

48. Which was the worst feature of Evans detested by Jackson?

(a) His dirty nails.
(b) His smouldering eyes.
(c) His long tresses.
(d) His unkempt beard.

Ans. (c) His long tresses.

49. I'll be watching you like a hawk. Select the right figure of speech used here.

(a) Metaphor
(b) Simile
(c) Personification
(d) Antithesis

Ans. (b) Simile

50. 'And McLeery, his feet clanging up the iron stairs,' Name the right literary device used in the given sentence.

(a) Onomatopoeia (b) Alliteration (c) Assonance (d) Personification

Ans. (a) Onomatopoeia

51. Stephens took the key from its ring, and the cell lock sprang back with a thudded, metallic twang. Select the words that represent Onomatopoeia.

(i) Sprang back (ii) Thudded (iii) Metallic twang (iv) Ring

(a) (i) and (iv) (b) (iii) and (ii) (c) (i) and (ii) (d) (ii) and (iii)

Ans. (d) (ii) and (iii)

53. 'What if, quite unwittingly, the innocent McLeery had brought in something himself?' On a hind sight, this was exactly what happens in the play. How can this be explained in literary nomenclature?

(a) Repetition
(b) Backward glance
(c) Transferred epithet
(d) Retrospective irony

Ans. (d) Retrospective irony

54. McLeery patiently held out his arms at shoulder level. Why was this exercise done?

(a) For offering suitcase for scrutiny.
(b) For frisking his person.
(c) For blessing the examinee.
(d) For praying to Jesus.

Ans. (b) For frisking his person.

55. Name the author of the lesson.

(a) William Blake
(b) Sir Johnson
(c) H.L. Hegde
(d) Norman Colin Dexter

Ans. (d) Norman Colin Dexter

57. What kind of a person was Evans?

(a) Congenital Kleptomaniac
(b) Philanthropist
(c) Claustrophobic
(d) Misanthrope

Ans. (a) Congenital Kleptomaniac

59. Why did Evans drape a blanket around his shoulder?

(a) To conceal his efforts of changing dress to look like McLeery.
(b) Because he was feeling cold.
(c) To hide himself from the police.
(d) All of the above

Ans. (a) To conceal his efforts of changing dress to look like McLeery.

60. What two purposes did the correction slip serve?

(a) To give correct name of hotel of Evans and exact date and time of exam to Evans.
(b) To help Evan escape.
(c) To inform Evan Gang his plan of escape.
(d) All of the above

Ans. (a) To give correct name of hotel of Evans and exact date and time of exam to Evans.

62. What is Normal Colin Dexter known for?

(a) His writings
(b) His poems
(c) His plays
(d) His Inspector Morse series of novels

Ans. (d) His Inspector Morse series of novels

65. Why was the Governor not ready to take risk?

(a) To bring a good name.
(b) To stop Evan from taking exam.
(c) To avoid any bad name.
(d) None of these

Ans. (c) To avoid any bad name.

66. Who checked the cell thoroughly?

(a) The Police
(b) The Governor
(c) Jackson and Stephens
(d) Stephens

Ans. (c) Jackson and Stephens

67. Why did Evans request not to take off his hat?

(a) He was feeling cold.
(b) To give a smart look.
(c) He loved to wear.
(d) Evans considered it lucky for himself.

Ans. (d) Evans considered it lucky for himself.

68. Why couldn't Stephens identify Evans' trick?

(a) Because he was not trained.
(b) Because he was a new recruit.
(c) Because he was not experienced.
(d) Because he was ignorant.

Ans. (b) Because he was a new recruit.

69. How could Evans' plan of escape become a success?

(a) He was witty.
(b) He kept his hat on his head.
(c) He was cunning.
(d) He was shrewd.

Ans. (a) He was witty.

73. How did Evan outwit the Governor?

(a) By taking exam
(b) By putting his hat
(c) By keeping a letter
(d) By escaping again

Ans. (d) By escaping again

74. How was the Governor able to locate Evans?

(a) By putting together 6 figures.
(b) By decoding.
(c) With the help of Ordance survey map of Oxfordshire.
(d) All of the above

Ans. (d) All of the above

75. Where was Evan located?

(a) In the middle east.
(b) In Japan.
(c) In the middle of Chipping Norton.
(d) In the middle of Northern Ireland.

Ans. (c) In the middle of Chipping Norton.

76. From where did they find the name of the hotel where Evan was staying?

(a) From the police
(b) From the people
(c) Secret agent
(d) From the correction slip

Ans. (d) From the correction slip

85. How can we say that Evan could not get through the O-Level German examination?

(a) He is unable to understand even simple expression like Gutten Gluck.
(b) He was unable to study as much as he should have.
(c) He was very nervous.
(d) he was mentally ill.

Ans. (a) He is unable to understand even simple expression like Gutten Gluck

87. What precautions did the authorities take to conduct the examination smoothly?

(a) The Governor personally supervised security
(b) Evans' cell was checked thoroughly
(c) All belongings were taken away from Evan, the invigilator was frisked and a police officer was posted to keep a vigil
(d) All of the above

Ans. (d) All of the above

88. Why was the invigilator frisked?

(a) To ensure that he had no objectionable material with him.
(b) To check his true identity.
(c) To check if he was a real man.
(d) To ensure that he was not planning another escape.

Ans. (a) To ensure that he had no objectionable material with him.

89. What should be the Governor's plan to bring Evans back to prison from the hotel?

(a) He should have sent him by air.
(b) He should have sent him with more people.
(c) He himself should have travelled along.
(d) He should have heard him once.

Ans. (c) He himself should have travelled along.

90. What is Norman Colin Dexter known for?

(a) For his writings.
(b) For his poems.
(c) For his plays.
(d) For his Inspector Morse series of novels.

Ans. (d) For his Inspector Morse series of novels.

❑❑

www.ingramcontent.com/pod-product-compliance
Lightning Source LLC
Chambersburg PA
CBHW060113120726
48003CB00009B/2625
9789392563133